Ecclesial Movements
and
Communities

Ecclesial Movements
and
Communities
Origins, Significance, and Issues

Brendan Leahy

New City Press
Hyde Park, New York

Published in the United States by New City Press
202 Comforter Blvd., Hyde Park, NY 12538
www.newcitypress.com
© 2011 Brendan Leahy

Cover design by Durva Correia

Library of Congress Cataloging-in-Publication Data

Leahy, Breandan, 1960-
  Ecclesial movements and communities : origins, significance, and issues / Brendan Leahy.
    p. cm.
  Includes bibliographical references.
  ISBN 978-1-56548-396-5 (pbk. : alk. paper)
  1. Catholic Church—Societies, etc. 2. Christian communities—Catholic Church. I. Title.
  BX808.L43 2011
  267'.18209045—dc23   2011029494

Printed in the United States of America

Contents

Part 3
Considerations and Perspectives

1

Listening to What the Spirit
is Saying to the Churches

A Global Moment

Towards the end of his life, the renowned theologian, Karl
Rahner, reflecting on the future of the Church, observed that the elements of a fraternal, spiritual fellowship, that is, a communally-lived
spirituality, would emerge. He envisaged the renewed Church of the
future as one "built from below by basic communities as a result of
free initiative and association." He hoped that every effort would be
made "not to hold up, but to promote this development."[1]

Since the middle of the twentieth century there have been so many
new laboratory-like community experiences in the Church that it is
now possible to speak of these communities as an expression of
what "the Spirit is saying to the churches" (see Rev 2:7). It is a
"global moment."[2] Basic ecclesial communities have emerged in
South America, while the so-called "small Christian communities"
are coming to life within dioceses and parishes in Africa, and
in Europe. After a period when enthusiastic commitment to a
communitarian vision of the post Vatican II Church often ran out of
steam, there has been a resurgence of pastoral initiatives focused on
"small communities."[3]

This phenomenon is not confined to the Catholic Church.
Konrad Raiser, former secretary-general of the World Council of
Churches, has commented on the rise of new communities across
the churches. He calls them "communities of hope":

---

1. Karl Rahner, *The Shape of the Church to Come* (New York: Seabury, 1974), 108.
2. Joseph G. Healey and Jeanne Hinton (eds.), *Small Christian Communities Today:
   Capturing the New Moment* (Maryknoll, NY: Orbis, 2006).
3. See M. de C. Azevedo, *Basic Ecclesial Communities in Brazil: The Challenge of a
   New Way of Being Church* (Washington: Georgetown University, 1987); Richard R.
   Gaillardetz, *Ecclesiology for a Global Church: A People Called and Sent* (New York:
   Orbis, 2008), 85–132; Christian Hennecke (ed.), *Kleine christliche Gemeinschaften
   verstehen: Ein Weg, Kirche mit Menschen zu sein* (Würzburg: Echter, 2009).

Such communities are emerging in many parts of the world. They have become a source of renewal in church and society because they are held together by the one hope which transcends all human hopes and projects. They are free to forge close alliances with groups in civil society struggling to rebuild viable human communities in situations of fragmentation and disintegration. Often they have become the crystallizing point for efforts to build a new culture of solidarity and sharing, of dialogue and reconciliation.[4]

Raiser calls attention to an important aspect. The widespread appearance of new forms of community experience on the Church landscape is happening precisely at a time when the human race has entered a new stage of its history, a time of rapid and profound cultural changes. The Church of Christ is being called to engage with today's developments, contributing in new ways to building up a civilization of love. It is being guided by the Spirit to help people not only hear but, as it were, see and encounter the Risen Christ living among those gathered in his name (see Mt 18:20).

The words of the prophet Isaiah (43:19) come to mind: "I am about to do a new thing; now it springs forth, do you not perceive it?" A German pastoral theologian, Christian Hennecke has written that just as the explorers Moses sent ahead brought back news of the Promised Land, so today too, there are "explorers" who can give news of the new thing God is preparing. Attention must be paid to these "explorers." It is easy to overlook or ignore them, even though they bear a message for the whole Church.[5] The rise of new communities is a sign of our times which must be heeded in order to perceive what the Spirit is saying to the churches. They too can be among the explorers giving news of the new thing God is preparing.

---

4. Konrad Raiser, *To Be the Church: Challenges and Hopes for a New Millennium* (Geneva: WCC, 1997), 85.
5. Christian Hennecke, *Kirche, die über den Jordan geht* (Münster: Aschendorff, 2006).

New Ecclesial Movements and Communities

This book examines the rise of the "new ecclesial movements and communities."[6] Not only are they spiritual resources for the Church, but they are an expression of the Church on the move.[7] In its Directory of International Associations of the Lay Faithful, The Pontifical Council for the Laity provides concise descriptions for 122 new movements such as the Catholic Charismatic Renewal, Communion and Liberation, the Cursillo, Emmanuel, Focolare, Foyer de Charité, L'Arche, Legion of Mary, the Neocatechumenal Way, Regnum Christi, Sant'Egidio, Schoenstatt and Teams of Our Lady.

While the main and best-known movements were born in Europe, they have spread throughout the world. Many of them, to a greater or lesser extent, are found from North America to Australia, from Brazil to Sweden, from Ireland to Nigeria. Of course, many other movements have been born outside Europe, such as the Couples for Christ Movement, which began in Manila, Philippines; the Holy Trinity Community (Komunitas Tritunggal Mahakudus) founded in Malang, Indonesia; the Secular Missionary Carmel (Carmelo Misionero Seglar) established in Colombia; the Shalom Catholic Community created in Brazil; and the Christian Life Movement founded in Peru. The Madonna House Apostolate was formed in the United States.

Specific mention must be made of thousands of ecclesial communities within Charismatic Renewal that, as we shall see again later in the book, began in the United States and then spread worldwide. Many of the key communities belong to the Catholic Fraternity of Covenant Communities. Research has indicated that some 100 million people have been touched by the grace of charismatic renewal.

Undoubtedly, the movements demonstrate a great variety in terms of self-understanding and spirituality, external structures and procedures, training or formation methods, goals and fields of work. Yet the overall fact of their presence calls for theological and pastoral consideration. As has been pointed out on several occasions, the newness of the movements has yet to be understood adequately in

---

6. See Pope John Paul II's Homily on the Occasion of the Meeting with the Ecclesial Movements and the New Communities on May 30, 1998, published in Pontifical Council for the Laity, *Movements in the Church* (Vatican City, 1999), 219–224.

7. See Pope John Paul II's homily at the First International Meeting of the Movements, September 27, 1981, where he speaks of the Church as a movement, the Church in movement, *Insegnamenti di Giovanni Paolo II*, 4, 2 (1981): 305.

terms of the positive impact they can have in serving the Kingdom
of God at work in today's history.[8]

There have been contrasting views on the significance of ecclesial
movements. Some see them as a providential gift of the Holy Spirit to the
Church, a way of responding effectively to contemporary challenges.[9]
Others, who feel that the movements can arouse suspicion, regard them as
a dangerous infection, overthrowing territorial Catholicism and causing
a Tridentine form of pastoral care to collapse. For such observers, the
movements seem like a providential army that the Roman center will
use against the reform of the Church.[10] Yet others consider them to be
parallel churches, or unusual cults.[11]

In truth, it is still too close to the emergence of new ecclesial
movements in the twentieth century to be able to evaluate them
thoroughly.[12] Time is needed to get to know, appreciate and
distinguish the distinctive features of each one as well as explore
the theological horizons against which to appraise them. This being
said, the upcoming fiftieth anniversary of the great Pentecostal
event of the Second Vatican Council (1962–1965) offers a golden
opportunity to take a look at the presence of new ecclesial movements
and communities in the life of the Church in the light of the Council,
revisit how they emerged, examine what has been taught about them,
explore theological avenues that clarify their relevance and tease out
some specific aspects that arise.

There is a further reason why it is timely to explore the topic of
ecclesial movements. They are now passing through a period of
transition from a more effervescent foundational moment in contact

---

8. See Pope John Paul II's comments made in the context of launching the preparations for
the Jubilee Year 2000 in *L'Osservatore Romano* (Italian edition), May 27–28, 1996, n. 7.

9. In his *The Future Church: How Ten Trends are Revolutionizing the Catholic Church*
(New York: Doubleday, 2009), journalist and Vatican observer John Allen comments:
> In isolation, the movements tell the story of their membership, which is a rela-
> tively small piece of the larger Catholic pie.... Seen as part of expanding lay roles
> in the Church, the movements can be understood as incubators and laboratories
> for new approaches to the lay vocation in its broadest sense, which means that
> they carry implications for virtually every member of the Church, whether they
> belong to a formal group or not. (425)

10. Alberto Melloni "Introduction," *Concilium* 2003/3, 7–19, at 7.

11. For example, see Gordon Urquhart, *The Pope's Armada: Unlocking the Secrets of Mys-
terious and Powerful New Sects in the Church* (New York: Prometheus Press, 1999).

12. See Michael Walsh's comment to this effect in "That new-time religion," in *The
Tablet* (April 19, 1997), 503–504 at 504.

with the founder or original inspiring source, to a subsequent phase of creative fidelity to the original charismatic outpouring. Founders of movements who have died in the past twenty years include Pierre Goursat, co-founder of the Emmanuel Community (1991); Henri Caffarel, founder of Teams of Our Lady (1996); Msgr. Luigi Giussani, founder of Communion and Liberation (2005); Fr. Oreste Benzi, founder of the Comunità Papa Giovanni XXIII Association (2007); Eduardo Bonnin, founder of Cursillos (2008); and Chiara Lubich, founder of the Focolare (2008). Movements are moving into the ordinary rhythm and mission of the Church. This era of transition prompts a deeper recognition, among the movements themselves and in the Church as a whole, of the meaning and contribution ecclesial movements and communities are called to make to the Church and humanity.

Another reason for studying the movements, though not a specific focus of this work, is that some of them manifest spiritual and mystical dimensions worth exploring in the context of theological method, insight and interdisciplinary exchange.[13]

This Book

While acknowledging and occasionally referring to communities and movements in other churches, this book will focus primarily on movements within the Catholic Church, particularly against horizons that emerged from or were suggested by the teachings of the Second Vatican Council.

Ecclesial Movements is divided into three sections. After this introduction and a chapter that defines the nature of ecclesial movements, the first part offers a brief overview of their rise and spread. This section touches on the growing attention afforded them in

---

13. See Chiara Lubich et al, *An Introduction to the Abba School: Conversations from the Focolare's Interdisciplinary Study Center* (New York: New City Press, 2002). On the issue of mysticism and theology today see David Tracy, *Analogical Imagination* (New York: Crossroad, 1989), 360. See also, Karl Rahner, "The Theology of Mysticism," in K. Lehmann and L. Raffelt (eds.), *The Practice of Faith: a Handbook of Contemporary Spirituality* (New York: Crossroad, 1986), 70–77; and Rowan Williams, *Teresa of Avila* (London: Geoffrey Chapman, 1991), chapter 5. Among theologians influenced by the Charismatic Renewal, Peter Hocken names Bishop Alber de Monleon, O.P., Francis Sullivan and Bob Faricy. Among biblical scholars he names George Montague and Francis Martin. See Peter Hocken, "The Holy Spirit and the Word," in *Ecumenical Trends* 39 (2010/11): 169–175.

magisterial teaching and theological reflection, especially in Italy and Germany. The second section presents five theological keys to assist reflection on the phenomenon of movements. The third section explores some specific issues regarding the movements.

While reference will be made to the literature written about movements in recent years,[14] the specific nature, aim and methods of each individual community merits detailed attention. Occasionally, *Ecclesial Movements* offers a sketch of the origin or goal of a particular movement, but the treatment of each community is brief. For more specific information on each movement, its current projects and contact details, readers should visit the individual movements' websites. This book offers a more global treatment of the phenomenon itself rather than a detailed examination of any one movement or community.[15]

Movements and Communities in Our Faith Journey

When speaking about their encounter with the community, members often say it wasn't so much that they met an association or group but rather a Person who changed their lives. For the first time or in a new form, they had an encounter with Jesus Christ. Indeed, in many ways, the expression "baptism in the Spirit" is accurate. For those already baptized, Christianity suddenly came

---

14. As well as the excellent books produced by the Pontifical Council for the Laity in its *Laity Today* series, especially *Movements in the Church* (Vatican City, 1999), see J. P. Cordes, *Charisms and New Evangelization* (Maynooth: St. Paul Publications, 1992); Hans Urs von Balthasar, "Lay Movements in the Church," in *The Laity and the Life of the Counsels: The Church's Mission in the World* (San Francisco: Ignatius Press, 2003), 252–282; Michael A. Hayes, *New Religious Movements in the Catholic Church* (New York and London: Burns & Oates, 2005); Tony Hanna, *New Ecclesial Movements* (New York: Alba, 2006); Vincent Gragnani, "The Surprising Growth of Contemporary Lay Movements," in *America* 195 (4) (August 14–21, 2006): 17–20; Lawrence Cunningham, "New Ecclesial Movements," *Commonweal* 133 (19) (November 3, 2006): 29; Peter Hocken, *Church Forward: Reflections on the Renewal of the Church* (Stoke on Trent: Alive, 2007); Thomas P. Rausch, "New Ecclesial Movements: The Twelfth Cardinal Bernardin Conference," *Chicago Studies* 47 (2008): 358–365; Julian Porteous, *A New Wine and Fresh Skins: Ecclesial Movements in the Church* (Ballan, VIC: Modotti Press, 2010).

15. See the above-mentioned Directory of International Associations of the Faithful. See also the short booklets produced on several movements by the Catholic Truth Society. Readers will also note that I do not deal in detail here with Opus Dei because, though it has much in common with movements, its official status is that of a personal prelature. Likewise, the communities of Taizé and Bose see themselves more as semi-monastic communities than movements.

alive for them in a new way. A new window onto the gospel message opened up for them.

The history of the Church is full of such windows opening up. Complementary to the hierarchical-sacramental side of the Christian life, there have been many movements and communities of renewal such as the Benedictines, the Franciscans, the Carmelites and the Vincentians. If readers were to reflect on their own life story, they could recognize how, in their journey following Jesus Christ, they have been influenced, directly or indirectly, by religious orders or associations.

In my own case, I recognize with gratitude how communities born from charisms have been present in my life, some directly, others marginally, but each speaking a word that made a difference for me. I offer this book in grateful recognition of their influence.

By way of conclusion, I'd like to refer to a sentiment expressed by Bernard of Clairvaux (1090–1153) that hits the right note on which to set out. Writing about his religious order and how it related to other movements or orders in his time he commented:

> I admire them all. I belong to one of them by observance, but to all of them by charity. We all need one another: the spiritual good which I do not own and possess, I receive from others.... In this exile, the Church is still on pilgrimage and is, in a certain sense, plural: she is a single plurality and a plural unity. All our diversities, which make manifest the richness of God's gifts, will continue to exist in the one house of the Father, which has many rooms. Now there is a division of graces; then there will be distinctions of glory. Unity, both here and there, consists in one and the same charity.[16]

---

16. See Bernard of Clairvaux, *Apologia to William of Saint Thierry* 4.8, cited in John Paul II, Apostolic Exhortation, *Vita consecrata*, n. 52.

2

Defining "Ecclesial Movements"

Defining "ecclesial movement" or "community" is challenging because these realities are, by their nature, on the move; they are dynamic; they don't easily fit into neat categories. While the "movement" is used as an umbrella term, some groups prefer "community" or "association." Others feel uncomfortable with any term that seems to restrict the new experience they are living. Clearly, each movement or community has its own distinctive story. The charismatic energies behind the groups flow in different directions. Nevertheless, in order to reflect and provide a general overview, this book will use the term "movement."

The Term "Movement"

Alberto Melloni points out that "movement" was used in European political language in 1684 to indicate collective social agitation. A Jesuit, Louis Doucin, used it in the title of his work, *Histoire des mouvements arrivez dans l'Eglise au sujet d'Origène et de sa doctrine,* which appeared in Paris in 1700. Subsequently, the term was employed in relation to the development of philosophical ideas and literary tastes.[1]

In nineteenth-century England, the prominent "Oxford movement" focused on spiritual and theological reform that from 1833 onwards was embodied in Tracts published in the *Times.* Aspiring to be a current of renewal, it encouraged many like-minded Church men and women, particularly scholars under the leadership of John Henry Newman (1801–1890).

The philosopher and founder of sociology, August Comte (1798–1857), introduced the term to express his theories of social dynamics. Soon others were using the term, such as in referring for example to the "labor movement."

Towards the end of the nineteenth century, in Italy the all-embracing term "Catholic Movement" covered a variety of budding initiatives that gathered the Catholic world there in support of Christian democracy

---

1. Alberto Melloni, "Introduction," *Concilium* (2003/3), 7–19, at 9.

and social projects. In the first half of the twentieth century the phrase "Catholic Action Movement" came into widespread use not only in Italy but throughout the Catholic Church worldwide. In a more general sense this period saw "movement" used more and more to designate the many biblical and liturgical, patristic and ecumenical currents of renewal spreading throughout the Church.

"Ecclesial" Movements

What does it mean, then, when the word "ecclesial" is added to "movement"? At the World Congress of Ecclesial Movements and New Communities, sponsored by the Pontifical Council for the Laity in Rome from May 27 to 29, 1998 the then Cardinal Ratzinger provided a concise description that captures the essential features of ecclesial movements. Referring to the Franciscan movement of the thirteenth century as probably providing "the clearest instance of what a movement is," he affirmed:

> [M]ovements generally derive their origin from a charismatic leader and take shape in concrete communities, inspired by the life of their founder; they attempt to live the Gospel anew, in its totality, and recognize the Church without hesitation as the ground of their life without which they could not exist.[2]

According to this definition, movements are linked to "charisms" that are communicative in the sense that others are attracted by what the charismatic leader is doing and promoting, saying and writing. This, in turn, leads to a spiritual affinity between persons which develops into friendships based on the gospel. Eventually, movements are examined and officially recognized by authorities in the Church first at the local diocesan level and then by the competent office in Rome. In the light of their approval by the Church, they can offer themselves as forms or reflections of the one Church.[3]

---

2. Cardinal Joseph Ratzinger, "The Ecclesial Movements: A Theological Reflection on Their Place in the Church," in Pontifical Council for the Laity, *Movements in the Church* (Vatican City, 1999), 23–51, at 46–47. This article was also reproduced as "The Theological Locus of Ecclesial Movements" in *Communio* 25 (Fall 1998): 480–504.

3. On the link between members of movements and their founders, see Sister M. Elizabet (Virginia Parodi), *El vínculo con el Fundador. ¿Por qué? ¿Para qué?* (Narazet, San Martin, Argentina: Schoenstatt, 2011).

In that same talk Ratzinger went on to distinguish between these charismatic movements, and what he calls "currents," that is, waves of renewal — for instance in liturgy or devotion to Mary. He also notes the distinction between movements and "actions," such as petitions or campaigns to collect signatures in order to press for a change in some teaching or practice of the Church.

The term "ecclesial movement" is general enough to cover a wealth of forms produced by the life-giving creativity of the Spirit. Moving on from that first snapshot provided by Cardinal Ratzinger, it is possible to expand the definition by introducing other elements common among ecclesial movements. In his message to the 1998 World Congress of Movements, John Paul II underlined the dimensions of a common faith journey, communion, as well as the missionary witness associated with new communities that come to life around a charism:

> The originality of the particular charism that gives life to a movement neither claims, nor could claim, to add anything to the richness of the *depositum fidei* [deposit of the faith]....
> Nevertheless, it represents a powerful support, a moving and convincing reminder to live the Christian experience to the full, with intelligence and creativity.... In this light, the charisms recognized by the Church are ways of deepening one's knowledge of Christ and giving oneself more generously to him, while at the same time rooting oneself ever more deeply in communion with the entire Christian people.[4]

"Ecclesial" is used in reference to movements because it indicates one of the principal original features associated with the communities that have arisen in recent decades. While these movements are made up mostly of lay people, they also include bishops, priests and religious. In so doing, they reflect the whole Church. Accordingly, in affirming that "the Church herself is a movement" John Paul II implied the movements are expressions of the Church in movement.[5]

So it is not quite accurate to refer to many of the new movements and communities in the Church as "lay movements." As Charles Whitehead, one of the leaders of Charismatic Renewal puts it:

---

4. See Message of John Paul II to the World Congress of Ecclesial Movements, Rome, May 27–29, 1998, in Pontifical Council for the Laity, *Movements in the Church*, 15–19, at 18.

5. See his homily at the First International Meeting of the Movements, September 27, 1981.

They are for the whole Church.... The movements and new communities are truly the Church, in the sense of the community of the baptized which we find in the New Testament and in *Lumen Gentium*, and therefore the description "ecclesial movements" is more appropriate than "lay movements."[6]

No definition would be complete without underscoring the dynamic element of each movement's commitment to finding itself outside itself in the order of love — that is, in missionary outreach. In his message to the Second World Congress of the Ecclesial Movements and New Communities (Rocca di Papa, May 31 to June 2, 2006), Benedict XVI gave expression to this missionary desire that animates them:

> Bring Christ's light to all the social and cultural milieu in which you live. Missionary zeal is proof of a radical experience of ever-renewed fidelity to one's charism that surpasses any kind of weary or selfish withdrawal.... The extraordinary fusion between love of God and love of neighbor makes life beautiful and causes the desert in which we often find ourselves living to blossom anew. Where love is expressed as a passion for the life and destiny of others, where love shines forth in affection and in work and becomes a force for the construction of a more just social order, there the civilization is built.... Become builders of a better world according to the order of love in which the beauty of human life is expressed.[7]

Ecclesial Movements exhibit a variety of initiatives in the social field. The Community of Sant'Egidio is well known for its peace initiatives in places such as Mozambique, Algeria and the Balkans. The Focolare Movement has launched a project entitled "Economy of Communion," promoting a new economic model in the light of the gospel. It is also involved in many non-governmental social projects around the world.[8] The Teams of Our Lady work to build

---

6. Charles Whitehead, "The Role of the Ecclesial Movements and New Communities in the Life of the Church," in Michael Hayes, *New Religious Movements in the Catholic Church* (London and New York: Burns & Oates, 2005), 15–29 at 15.

7. This message is printed in Pontifical Council for the Laity, *The Beauty of Being a Christian: Movements in the Church* (Vatican City, 2007), 5–8, at 7.

8. See Amelia J. Uelmen, "*Caritas in Veritate* and Chiara Lubich: Human Development from the Vantage Point of Unity," in *Theological Studies* 71 (2010): 40–42.

up healthy marriages. The Communion and Liberation movement organizes many cultural events such as its large annual meeting in Rimini, Italy.

In L'Arche communities, people with and without disabilities who share their lives together, giving witness to the reality that persons with disabilities possess inherent qualities of welcome and wonderment, spirituality and friendship. These communities came to life in 1964 through the initiative of Jean Vanier, son of the Governor General of Canada:

> L'Arche was born in a quite unexpected and unplanned way. When I left the British Royal Navy in 1950 to "follow Jesus," I went to France, where I lived in a community of students of various nationalities and where I met the Dominican Father Thomas Phillippe, a holy man. A deep bond was created between us and he became my spiritual father. Then, when he became chaplain of a centre for thirty men with mental disabilities, he invited me to go to meet his "new friends." I was very touched by that visit, by the suffering and longing for human relationships of those men. And that prompted me to visit other institutions for the mentally impaired. That was in the 1960s.... Later, encouraged by Father Phillippe and helped by friends, I bought a little house in a small town a hundred kilometers from Paris, where I was able to provide a home for Raphaël and Phillippe, two men from a harsh and violent institution. So we began to live together: it was I who did the cooking.... Apart from the suffering, I also began to discover the gifts of handicapped persons and the call they make to us. Gradually I discovered what L'Arche is.[9]

There are now over 130 such communities in 30 countries worldwide. The "Faith and Light" communities that Jean Vanier co-founded in 1971 now number over 1,400 around the world. Through this international movement, people with developmental disabilities, their family and friends meet regularly to discuss hopes and difficulties and to pray together.

---

9. See Pontifical Council, *The Beauty*, 121–124.

Elements of Ecclesial Movements

Movements can be categorized in a number of ways. For instance, in his recent work, *A New Wine and Fresh Skins*,[10] Australian bishop Julian Porteous offers the following categories as a guide to the different characteristics of movements: a) movements that developed before the Second Vatican Council;[11] b) new movements that emerged after the Council;[12] c) communities founded by clerics, priests or religious;[13] d) communities founded by lay people;[14] e) movements that have taken the form of religious life.[15] He also sees the two other defining features of the movements as a) apostolic activity and b) countries and cultures of origin.

The German canon lawyer Christoph Hegge proposes five features that need to be kept in mind in defining ecclesial movements.[16]

1. A unique charism of a founder who is at the center and whose personal vocation attracts others to an experience of conversion to the gospel. Encounter with the charism leads to a radical renewal of one's baptism and a desire to live a collective spirituality.

2. The group that comes to life through the charism is composed of all categories of the faithful, young and old, single and married, religious, priest and bishop, reflecting the essentially communional image of the Church focusing particularly, though not exclusively, on one aspect of mission and journeying in the presence of Jesus, the Risen Christ among them.[17] Often this leads to a form of communion of goods. So an ecclesial movement also represents an image of an "incarnate" experience of Church showing its socio-cultural relevance.

10. See Julian Porteous, *A New Wine and Fresh Skins*, 9–50.
11. The Legion of Mary and the Schoenstatt Movement.
12. Charismatic Renewal, the Word of God Community, the Emmanuel Community, the Holy Trinity Community (Indonesia).
13. Opus Dei, Legion of Christ and its lay association, Regnum Christi, Communion and Liberation and Kkottongnae (founded in Korea).
14. The Focolare Movement, the Neocatechumenal Way, the Community of Sant'Egidio.
15. The Jerusalem Community, the Beatitudes Community.
16. See Christoph Hegge, *Rezeption und Charisma: Der theologische und rechtliche Beitrag Kirchlicher Bewegungen zur Rezeption des Zweiten Vatikanischen Konzils* (Würzburg: Echter, 1999), 223–232.
17. See H. Heinz, "Neuere geistliche Gemeinschaften — ein Anruf an unsere Zeit" in F. Wulf et al (eds.), *Nachfolge als Zeichen. Kommentarbeiträge zum Beschlu der gemeinsamen Synode der Bistümer in der Bundesrepublik Deutschland über die Orden und andere geistliche Gemeinschaften* (Würzburg, 1978), 150–163.

3. While all members are linked through the charism and its spirituality, the institutional structure of movements is elastic and flexible enough to allow for a variety of ways of belonging to the community. As the canonist J. Beyer comments, being united in one spirit, one structure and the same goal, unity of thought and action is their strength.[18] Here a distinction can be made between ecclesial movements and older religious families that often are divided into religious orders, regular third orders, secular third orders, and lay congregations, all of which find their roots in a common founder but have developed autonomously and differently.

4. The experience of a structural communion among people of all vocations brought about by a shared charism opens up a renewed understanding of the Church's pastoral, apostolic and evangelizing mission. The movements possess "a true and real spiritual pedagogy in their contents and method, and a particular form of expressing the communitarian sense of the Church, rendering it present in environments and situations needing witness and evangelization."[19]

5. Ecclesial movements and communities manifest the universality or catholicity of the faith. This is so, not so much in terms of internationality — though that is very much the case — but rather in the sense of the "universal relevancy of the message of Christ."[20] By way of their everyday life and activity, members of movements find themselves in dialogue with people in all kinds of social and cultural situations. They share their discovery with them. Not only that, but many movements engage in ecumenical dialogue and interreligious dialogue. In other words, they want to contribute to building the human family in today's world when the Church views itself as "sign and instrument of unity with God and humankind."[21]

---

18. "Le laïcat et les laics dans l'Eglise," *Gregorianum* 68 (1987): 157–185, at 180. See also J. Beyer, "Istituti secolari e movimenti ecclesiali," in *Aggiornamenti sociali* 34 (1983): 181–200, at 200.

19. J. Castellano Cervera, "I movimenti ecclesiali: Una presenza carismatica della Chiesa di oggi," in *Rivista di Vita Spirituale* 4–5 (1987): 495–518, at 507.

20. See P. J. Cordes, *Charisms*, 115.

21. G. Ghirlanda, "I movimenti nella comunione ecclesiale e la loro giusta autonomia," in Pontifical Council for the Laity, *Christifideles Laici: spunti per uno studio* (Vatican City, 1989–1990), 41–63, at 48.

Personal Witness Definitions

These definitions cannot give the full picture of what movements really are. For that, it is necessary to listen to the personal witness of people who have encountered them.

Michael Mulvey, Bishop of the Diocese of Corpus Christi in the United States, writes of his encounter with the Focolare Movement. Initially he was struck by the message of living the gospel in daily life and the spirit of brotherhood and communion among priests he met. Then, two years after his ordination in 1976, at a time when he was searching for a spirituality, a young woman visiting the parish where he was an associate pastor spoke to him of her spiritual experience in the Movement. The sense of joy she radiated impressed him deeply. He recalls their conversation as if it were a moment of annunciation: "Here is your way to follow." Spurred by this meeting, he began to explore the spirituality itself, but even more he began to live the gospel concretely. "I began to experience a new sense of life within me. I found that the gospel was not just a beautiful theory to talk about, to exegete, to pray over, but it was words that give life. It seemed that word by word, sentence by sentence, parable by parable, the gospel came to life within me. In finding that life, I knew that it was something that I wanted to share with others.... I will always remain grateful to Chiara Lubich for her 'yes' to God's call in founding the Movement."[22]

In the late 1960s, with other young students, Andrea Riccardi became involved in setting up the Community of Sant'Egidio in Rome. He narrates his experience in terms of discovering the stream of charisms that flows through the two millennia of church life: "Until then, I had known the Church only as a structural organization. I felt there had to be more, and I found it in the charisms of past centuries. Here I discovered the true richness of the Church."[23]

Frances Hopkins, former director of Cursillo for the Archdiocese of Liverpool, describes how in 1986, married with four children and working part-time for British Telecom, she took part in a Cursillo weekend. She was an active member of her parish, involved in various groups and RCIA. She expected Cursillo to be a quiet retreat but it turned out to be a decisive moment of encounter with Jesus

22. See his account in the "My life and the Focolare" section in *Living City* 49 (2010/3): 5.
23. "Rediscovering the Charisms," in *New City* 30 (2000/320), 4–5, at 4.

in her life: "I can remember to this day the growing understanding that Christ was with us, in others, in me, and that our natural and spiritual life were so well interwoven. It seemed to me that this was the way to live in the future."[24]

Benedict XVI's personal testimony of his encounter with movements during a difficult period when he was a professor of theology in Germany provides a suitable conclusion.

> For me personally it was a wonderful experience when, in the early 1970s, I came into closer contact with movements such as the *Neocatechumenal Way*, *Communion and Liberation*, and the *Focolare Movement* and so experienced the energy and enthusiasm with which they lived their faith and the joy of their faith which impelled them to share with others the gift they had received. That was the period in which Karl Rahner and others were speaking of a winter in the Church; and, indeed, it did seem that, after the great flowering of the Council, spring had been reclaimed by frost, and the new dynamism had succumbed to exhaustion.... Rahner's remarks about a winter in the Church were perfectly understandable; they expressed an experience we all shared. But then something suddenly happened which no one had planned. The Holy Spirit had, so to say, once again made his voice heard. The faith was reawakened, especially in young people, who eagerly embraced it without ifs and buts, without subterfuges and reservations, and experienced it in its totality as a precious, life-giving gift.[25]

---

24. "An Encounter with Christ," in *New City* 30 (2000/330), 4–5 at 5.
25. Cardinal Joseph Ratzinger, "The Ecclesial Movements," 24.

Part 1

The Emergence of Ecclesial Movements

Following the preliminary remarks in Chapters 1 and 2, this first part of the book will trace the history of the emergence of the movements. Undoubtedly, the Second Vatican Council was a key event along the journey but many developments before the Council were important in paving the way for their recognition. The post-conciliar period is particularly significant for clarifying the place of the movements and providing criteria for evaluating their authenticity.

This section, which covers 100 years or so of history, offers a necessarily relatively brief treatment. Nevertheless, tracing the emergence of movements is stimulating not least because it means noting the interplay of circumstances and key personalities, doctrinal developments and needs of the Church, all of which, from a faith perspective, form a history guided by the Holy Spirit.

3

Arising in the Century of the Church

In the 1920s, two prominent theologians — the Catholic Romano Guardini and the Evangelical Lutheran Otto Dibelius — spoke of the twentieth century as an era when the Church would re-awaken in people.[1] The movements express the realization of that prophecy. Perhaps it was necessary to wait until the twentieth century, the century of the re-awakening of the Church in souls, "to see such a blossoming and variety of autonomous lay movements in the Church, some of which may indeed take their orientation from great charisms of the past but most of which have emerged from new, independent inspirations of the Holy Spirit."[2] This chapter reviews the beginnings of the emergence of ecclesial movements, covering the period up to the Second Vatican Council.[3]

Remote Preparation in the Nineteenth Century

It is important to note that in the twentieth century ecclesial movements did not appear on the ecclesial horizon totally out of the blue. The previous century witnessed many socio-political developments that challenged the Church's self-understanding of identity and mission. The resulting theological and ecclesiological renewal laid the foundation for the arrival of ecclesial movements.

The nineteenth century renewal revolved around a rediscovery of the "mystery" dimension of the Church, a marked contrast with what had gone before. Although generalizations can be suspect, it is nevertheless commonly accepted that the primary model of

---

1. Romano Guardini, *Von dem Sinn der Kirche,* 5th ed. (Mainz: Matthias Grünewald Verlag, 1990), 19, and Otto Dibelius, *Das Jahrhundert der Kirche* (Berlin: Furche Verlag, 1926).
2. See Hans Urs von Balthasar, "Lay Movements in the Church," in *The Laity and the Life of the Counsels: The Church's Mission in the World* (San Francisco: Ignatius Press, 2003), 252–282, at 255.
3. For further information on the history of the emergence of movements, see Rosemary Goldie, *From a Roman Window* (Melbourne: HarperCollins, 1998): 120–133; Fidel Fernández Gonzáles, "Charisms and Movements in the History of the Church," in Pontifical Council for the Laity, *The Ecclesial Movements in the Pastoral Concern of the Bishops* (Vatican City, 2000): 71–103. See also Fidel Fernández, *I Movimenti: Dalla Chiesa degli apostoli a oggi* (Milan: RCS Libri, 2000).

Church, predominant from the Council of Trent (1545–1563) to the twentieth century, emphasized its hierarchical, sacramental and institutional elements. Several socio-religious factors that need not be explored at this point account for this emphasis. It is important to note, however, that the turning point in Western culture which accompanied the French Revolution also left a deep mark on the Church. Sensing the need to focus once again on the living, organic side of the Church, people began to seek ways of understanding it "internally." Robert Bellarmine (1542–1621) had portrayed the Church as a "perfect society," that had the instruments and structures needed to communicate salvation. But now a realization grew that something more was needed. Re-reading the Church Fathers opened up a discovery of the deeper "mystery" side of the Church.

For instance, the German theologian Johann Adam Möhler (1796–1838), influenced by the great Reformed theologian Friedrich Schleiermacher (1768–1834), writes in his first book, *Unity in the Church*: "The Church exists through a life directly and continually moved by the divine Spirit, and is maintained and continued by the loving mutual exchange of believers."[4] He directs his focus on the interior life that the Spirit generates in the members through their participation together in community life. The Church, he says, is defined first by its "soul," not by its "body."

His later work, *Symbolism*, reflects his more mature thought. In time, he portrays the Church as a test case in which divine grace and human freedom meet. He came to believe he could better relate and distinguish both the divine and human elements in the Church by employing a Christological rather than a pneumatological model. Focusing on the formula from the Council of Chalcedon (451) of the one Person, Jesus Christ, Son of God in two natures, he writes, "Thus, the visible Church, from the point of view here taken, is the Son of God himself, everlastingly manifesting himself among men in a human form, perpetually renovated, and eternally young — the permanent incarnation of the same, as in Holy Writ, even the faithful

---

4. Johann Adam Möhler, *Unity in the Church or The Principle of Catholicism Presented in the Spirit of the Church Fathers of the First Three Centuries*, ed. and trans. Peter C. Erb (Washington, D.C.: The Catholic University of America Press, 1996), 93. See also Michael J. Himes, "The Development of Ecclesiology: Modernity to the Twentieth Century," in Peter Phan (ed.), *The Gift of the Church* (Collegeville, MN: Liturgical Press, 2000), 45–68, especially 54–59.

are called 'the body of Christ.' "[5] While stressing the visibility of the Church, he insists on the continuous presence of the incarnate Christ in history. The Church is not merely structure. It is Christ extended over time.

Theologian Michael Himes remarks,

> [T]he development of [Möhler's] ecclesiology in interaction with his Christology and theological anthropology gradually affected the way in which subsequent theologians understood the Church. After him, the Church was no longer the bearer of the mystery of faith but was itself an aspect of that mystery. Ecclesiology grew from being primarily concerned with questions of institutional polity to treating of the Church's inner nature and external mission as a dimension of the economy of salvation.[6]

Möhler's thought also influenced the Roman school of theology.

Accompanying this river of theological renewal throughout the nineteenth century were many new forms of consecrated life, such as the new female religious orders. Encouraged by Leo XIII (1878–1903), during the nineteenth century were founded many social and welfare organizations and associations, such as the St. Vincent de Paul Conferences established by Frédéric Ozanam (1813–1853) and the German social work association set up by Adolph Kolping (1813–1865).

Developments in the Early Twentieth Century

At the beginning of the twentieth century, one that would be marked by two world wars and great historical changes, a new awareness began to grow among lay faithful of their ecclesial vocation, that is, their participation in the mission of the Church as the Body of Christ. In 1917 the Catholic Church's Code of Canon Law gathered its various legal texts into a single document. The third part of book II of this revised Code, "The Laity," provided for associations of the faithful. It recognized three kinds of associations that corresponded to the goals of pursuing spiritual perfection, fostering works of piety or charity, and promoting worship: secular

---

5. Johann Adam Möhler, *Symbolism: Exposition of the Doctrinal Differences between Catholics and Protestants as Evidenced by Their Symbolical Writings*, trans. James Burton Robertson (New York: Crossroad, 1997), 259.

6. Himes, "The Development of Ecclesiology," 59.

third orders, which promote Christian perfection according to the spirituality of the parent order to which they were associated; confraternities concerned with promoting worship and piety, such as the confraternities of the Sacred Heart, the Blessed Sacrament, the Brown Scapular, the Rosary, and other similar groups; and pious unions, whose purpose was works of charity or piety.

After the 1917 Code's promulgation, many ecclesiastical associations were erected.[7] Catholic Action grew. Secular institutes began to emerge. And a theology of the laity also began to come to life.

"Catholic Action" included a multitude of apostolic initiatives undertaken by lay people. In the beginning it referred to works organized and governed by pastors and bishops, but carried out by the laity. From Poland to Belgium, from France to Brazil, from Argentina to Bavaria, it took different forms.[8] Under Pius XI (1922–1939), Catholic Action focused on laity *participating* in the hierarchy's apostolate. Under Pius XII (1939–1958), in view of the numerous forms of lay apostolate, the concept of Catholic Action expanded to include all activities of lay people themselves who were inspired by faith and who worked in varying gradations of *collaborative* dependency on the hierarchy.[9]

In his memoirs, the former bishop of Sault Ste. Marie, Ontario (Canada), Alex Carter (1909–2002) narrates an episode that reveals the growing recognition of the need to rediscover the role of laity and the lay dimension of the Church.[10] As a young student in Rome, shortly before Pius XI died, Carter attended a papal audience that included a group of Canadian students. He recalls hearing a concise, powerful, and "very prophetic" address, in which the pope described the Church, the mystical body of Christ, as having become somewhat monstrous, with an enormous head but a shrunken body. Pius

---

7. On the rise of lay associations, see Maureen Dolan, *Partnership in Lay Spirituality: Religious and Laity Find New Ways* (Dublin: Columba, 2007), 60–75.

8. Ireland, for instance, did not have a Catholic Action movement as such. In ways the Legion of Mary was the expression of Catholic Action. See Maurice Curtis, *The Splendid Cause: The Catholic Action Movement in Ireland in the 20th Century* (Dublin: Greenmount Publications, 2008).

9. See Jeremiah Newman, *What is Catholic Action?* (Dublin: M. H. Gill and Son, Ltd., 1958). See also Christopher O'Donnell, "Apostolate" in *Ecclesia* (Collegeville, MN: Liturgical Press, 1996), 18–19. See also Hubert Jedin, *History of the Church,* Vol. 10: *The Church in the Modern Age* (London: Burns & Oates, 1981), 307–310.

10. Alex Carter, *A Canadian Bishop's Memoirs* (North Bay, Ont.: Tomiko Publications, 1994), 50–51.

urged the students to ask lay people to become, with them, witnesses of Christ, bringing Christ back into the workplaces and into the marketplaces.

In 1943, Pius XII's *Mystici corporis* highlighted the organic nature of the Church. This important encyclical paved the way for the ecclesiology of Vatican II. In it, the pope developed the Pauline notion of the Church as the Body of Christ with Christ the head and the Church a mystical body. He writes:

> The true meaning of the word "mystical," therefore, reminds us that the Church ... does not consist merely of social and juridical elements nor rest solely on such grounds.... That which raises the Christian society to a level utterly surpassing any order of nature is the Spirit of our Redeemer, the source of all graces, gifts, and miraculous powers, perennially and intimately pervading the Church and acting on her.[11]

Secular institutes offered a more specific form of consecration for men and women who lived out the evangelical counsels in the world, though without public vows. Striving for Christian perfection without the direct cooperation (or indeed, as Jedin notes, under the skeptical observation) of official ecclesiastical offices was a new development in the life of the Church.[12] Pius XII recognized the phenomenon of secular institutes, and in 1947 dedicated his letter *Provida Mater Ecclesia* to them.[13]

The work of Yves Congar (1904–1995) on the laity, *Jalons pur une théologie du laïcat* (1953), marked another significant step in recognizing ecclesial movements.[14] Taking up themes found in John Calvin as well as John Henry Newman, Congar outlined how lay people share in the Church's priestly, kingly and prophetic functions, which are rooted in Jesus Christ's preaching of the Kingdom of God. He also

---

11. Pius XII, Encyclical Letter on the Church as the Body of Christ, *Mystici corporis* (June 19, 1943), *AAS* 222–233.

12. Jedin, *The Church in the Modern Age*, 326.

13. AAS 39 (1947): 114–124. See also the *motu proprio* a year later, *Primo feliciter*, AAS 40 (1948): 283–286, and the Instruction *Cum sanctissimis*, AAS 40 (1948): 293–297. See Hans Urs von Balthasar's commentary, *Der Laie und der Ordenstand* (Freiburg, 1949); Jedin, *History of the Church*, 326–331. See also Christopher O'Donnell, "Secular Institutes," in *Ecclesia*, 421–424.

14. See Yves Congar, *Lay People in the Church: A Study for a Theology of Laity*. Trans. Donald Attwater (London: Bloomsbury, 1957). See also Gabriel Flynn, *Yves Congar's Vision of the Church in a World of Unbelief* (Burlington, VT: Ashgate, 2004).

wrote on the renewal of Christian society through groups "directed to a common leading of Christian life."[15] Attentive to the voice of the Spirit, he commented that the emergence of these new groups must "mean something." He added, "essentially, it answers to a need to rediscover the Church and, in a sense, to re-enter and renew her from below."

Congar observed how "many of our contemporaries find that for them the Church's machinery, sometimes the very institution, is a barrier obscuring her deep and living mystery which they can find, or find again, only from below, through living Church cells wherein the mystery is lived directly and with great simplicity." Indeed, "a need is felt to seek, beneath the ready-made administrative machinery, the living reality of basic communities, the aspect in which the Church herself is, at the same time as an objective institution or hierarchical mediation, a community to whose life all its members contribute and which is patterned by give-and-take and a pooling of resources." Recognizing the difficulties that some might raise regarding freedom of association, Congar affirms: "The faithful have full freedom, within the bounds of the Church's communion, to associate themselves with this or that theological tradition, with any 'spirituality,' to engage in any work of intellectual or cultural creation, to initiate enterprises ..."

During the period following World War II up to Vatican II, the theology of the People of God emerged strongly. Based on a rich biblical notion, it undergirded a new sacramental understanding of the Church, emphasizing the common priesthood of all the baptized.[16] The revival of biblical and patristic studies at this time also generated a new look at the notion of catholicity,[17] the Church's unity in diversity, and the image of the Church as communion. Further developments included, in October 1951, the First World Congress for the Lay Apostolate, in Rome. Forty delegates from sixteen countries met to discuss the possibility of forming a world federation. A Second Congress for the Lay Apostolate was held in 1957.[18]

---

15. For the following see Congar, *Lay People*, especially 324–329.
16. On the Church as People of God, see Yves Congar, "The Church: People of God," in *Concilium* 1 (1965): 7–19.
17. Henri de Lubac, *Catholicism: Christ and the Common Destiny of Man*, trans. L. Sheppard and E. Englund (San Francisco: Ignatius Press, 1988 [first published in 1938]).
18. See Kevin Walsh, "Lay Apostolate Congress at Rome," in *The Furrow*, 8 (1957): 730–735.

New Associations of Lay Faithful

A number of new associations came to life during the first half of the twentieth century. Gradually, it became clear that they functioned primarily as spiritual networks with three distinguishing characteristics:

a) They had a strong sense of originating in a charism of foundation in which others associated with the founder participated freely and flexibly. For instance, Frank Duff (1889–1980) founded the Legion of Mary in Dublin during a period of great poverty, just at the time of Irish independence. Believing in the call of all the baptized to holiness, his movement promoted spiritual development and advancing the kingdom of Christ through Mary.[19]

During World War II, the Focolare Movement came to life in Italy around Chiara Lubich (1920–2008). Discovering the gospel as a code of life that could be lived from the perspective of unity and fraternity, she and her followers sought to bring Jesus' art of loving into all aspects of their lives, thereby renewing relationships at all levels around them and so contributing to the realization of Jesus' last will and testament: "may they all be one" (Jn 17:21).[20]

The Cursillo Movement also began in the context of World War II around Eduardo Bonnin (1917–2008). At a time when religion was being more and more marginalized in Spain, the Young Men's Catholic Action began to plan a large-scale pilgrimage in 1948 to Compostela. In preparation they provided training courses for the pilgrim leaders. On the island of Mallorca, after their courses these leaders met regularly to pray, study, and develop their understanding of what it really meant to be a Christian. Working with their parish priest they developed "little courses" ("Cursillos de Christianidad"). Because they experienced a measure of success, they decided to formalize them. Bonnin presided over the first "official" Cursillo in January 1949. This was followed by "short courses" of study and

---

19. Leon O' Broinn, *Frank Duff: A Biography* (Dublin: Gill & MacMillan, 1982), and Legion of Mary, *The New Evangelisation: Priests and Laity — The Great Challenge of the New Millennium* (Dublin: Legion of Mary, 2008).

20. See Jim Gallagher, *Chiara Lubich: A Woman's Work: The Story of the Focolare Movement and Its Founder* (New York: New City Press, 1997); Chiara Lubich, *Essential Writings: Spirituality, Dialogue, Culture.* Michele Vandeleene, editor (New York and London: New City Press, 2007), and Pontifical Council, *The Beauty,* 91–98.

spiritual preparation aimed at bringing young people back to the faith. Small communities soon developed and spread throughout Spain and beyond. They met regularly for prayer and support in the task of evangelization, whether in the workplace, factory, office, sports club, local neighborhood or parish.[21]

In America, the Madonna House apostolate's "little mandate" of love developed around Catherine de Hueck Doherty (1896–1985). Having lived through various personal traumas, Catherine's strong social concern and spiritual intuitions of the Christian East gave life to a community of lay men and women as well as priests who all sought to live the revolution of love based on the life of a Christian family: the life of Nazareth.[22]

b) These new associations were made up of people of all vocations and walks of life — lay, celibate and married, priests, religious, young and old — with a wide variety of forms of commitment, something quite new before Vatican II. At that time the classic "states of life" were normally lived as distinct and almost separate units — priests, religious and lay. Each state of life was like a self-contained arrangement; moreover, each included further distinctions of rank and position. The movements were moving in a different direction.

In the aftermath of World War II, a young Jesuit, Riccardo Lombardi (1908–1979), became convinced that the time had come for terms like "brotherhood" and "sisterhood" to take their place beside "equality" and "freedom." He began to preach this message, primarily in Italy, and it soon spread. Others, including lay people, priests, and bishops gradually began to follow him. On February 10, 1952, Pius XII officially approved the group that developed around Lombardi as "The Movement for a Better World."

c) A third feature that distinguished the pre-conciliar era was an interest among new groups in renewing ecclesial life itself as well as bearing witness and spreading the gospel. At a time when the Church, especially in Europe, was seeing the rise of systematic or

---

21. See Dominic Wiseman, "A Weekend for Christ," in *The Tablet* (12 April 1997), 466–467, and Dominic Wiseman and Chris Bryden, *Cursillos in Christianity* (London: CTS, 2001).

22. Lorene Hanley Duquin, *They Called Her the Baroness: The Life of Catherine de Hueck Doherty* (New York: Alba House, 1995). On lay movements in the United States before Vatican II see Gary MacEoin, "Lay Movements in the United States before Vatican II," in *America* (August 10, 1991): 61–65.

practical atheism, these new movements were providing fresh energy. In France, traditionally considered the Church's elder daughter, Jean Godin's 1943 book *France, pays de mission?* ("France – A nation of mission?") caused quite a stir. An unprecedented institutional self-examination and renewal began there, and spread throughout Europe. The theological work of *ressourcement* (returning to the original sources of the Scriptures, the Church Fathers, the dynamism of the early life of the Church) came into its own. Writers such as Henri de Lubac (1896–1991), Jean Daniélou (1905–1974), Hans Urs von Balthasar (1905–1988), Yves Congar (1904–1995), Marie-Dominique Chenu (1895–1990), and Louis Bouyer (1913–2004) provided an impetus for religious revitalization. The "something new" that ecclesial movements and communities were offering clearly spoke to this situation.

In the early 1950s, realizing the need to rebuild the Christian presence in the student world, Father Luigi Giussani (1922–2005), a professor at the Theological Faculty near Milan, decided to give up his academic post and dedicate himself to teaching religion in schools. The small group of students that soon gathered around him led to the establishment of the Student Youth Movement. The Archbishop of Milan at that time, Giovanni Battista Montini, who became Pope Paul VI, encouraged this new movement. Soon it involved undergraduates and adults.[23]

During this period of growth the movements were subjected to study and scrutiny.[24] Time was needed to clarify their place in the Church, and the Second Vatican Council played an important part in bringing about that clarification.

---

23. Luigi Giussani, *The Work of the Movement: The Fraternity of Communion and Liberation* (Milan: Coop. Editoriale Nuovo Mondo, 2005).
24. See Bernhard Callebaut, *Tradition, Charisme et Prophétie dans Le Mouvement International Des Focolari (1943–1965): Analyse Sociologique* (Bruyères-le-Châtel: Nuovelle Cité, 2010).

4

Setting Important Parameters:
The Movements and Vatican II

In his work on the Second Vatican Council, John W. O'Malley remarks that "the best — indeed, the indispensable — approach to understanding Roman Catholicism today is through Vatican II."[1] The Council, a true event of the Spirit, continues to guide the Catholic Church's journey. It provides a magisterial and theological compass, as well as serving as the "essential and fundamental Magna Charta" of the Church today.[2] Though the Council did not deal specifically with ecclesial movements, conciliar doctrine became crucial to recognizing their place in the Church. The Council's "hermeneutic of reform," as Benedict XVI puts it, provided a multi-faceted framework for reading and receiving the new ecclesial communities.

Research needs to be done on how the existence of movements impacted the Council. Nevertheless, the canonist Gianfranco Ghirlanda has remarked that they were moving in directions being pointed out by the Spirit, and so the Council assembly, as an event of the same Spirit, "could not but make its own these directions."[3] Indeed, lay men and women such as Frank Duff, the Irish founder of the Legion of Mary, James Norris, the American activist known for his work with refugees, and the Australian theologian Rosemary Goldie, a member of the Permanent Committee for International Congresses of the Lay Apostolate, were invited as auditors to the Council.

The Dominican theologian Yves Congar played an active role in formulating the conciliar texts. He explains, "Something happened at the Council and the dominant values in our way of looking at

---

1. John O'Malley, *What Happened at Vatican II* (Cambridge, MA: Harvard University Press, 2008), 2. See also Matthew Lamb and Matthew Levering, *Vatican II: Renewal within Tradition* (Oxford: Oxford University Press, 2008).

2. See John Paul II, Apostolic Letter at the Beginning of the New Millennium, *Novo millennio ineunte* (January 6, 2001), n. 57, and Benedict XVI's dialogue with the clergy of the diocese of Belluno-Feltre, Treviso, July 24, 2007.

3. See his introduction to the Italian translation of Christoph Hegge's work on the reception of Vatican II and movements cited in a previous chapter, *Il Vaticano II e i Movimenti Ecclesiali: una recezione carismatica* (Rome: Città Nuova, 2001), 9.

the Church were changed by the Council."[4] In order to place the Church in a better position in the world so as to communicate God in modern times, the Council undertook a thorough review of its identity and mission. Its theological, canonical, and pastoral perspectives became relevant in understanding ecclesial movements; just so, the movements themselves became important in interpreting the Council.[5]

Mystery-Communion-Mission

The Council endorsed the notion of associations of the faithful: "The most holy council earnestly recommends these associations, which surely answer the needs of the apostolate of the Church among many peoples and countries.... Among these associations, moreover, international associations or groups of Catholics must be specially appreciated at the present time."[6] But of greater significance for ecclesial movements was its proposal that the Church be renewed through the rediscovery of the three themes that run through Council documents: mystery, communion and mission.[7] The Council proposed a vision of the Church as icon of the Trinity.[8]

The Church is Mystery. The Council underscored the "mystery" dimension of the Church. It affirmed that, in a way analogous to its founder and Lord Jesus Christ, the Church is a human-divine reality. Since it is founded and rooted in the plan of God who revealed himself eschatologically in history through Jesus Christ, then what should emerge most is the divine plan of salvation, not the figure of a Church made up of detached structures, ministries and powers:

---

4. See Yves Congar, "Moving Towards a Pilgrim Church," in Alberic Stacpoole, *Vatican II by Those Who Were There* (London: Geoffrey Chapman, 1986), 129–152, at 129.

5. On the history of Vatican II see Jedin, *The Church in the Modern Age*, 299–335.

6. The Decree on the Apostolate of the Laity, *Apostolicam actuositatem*, 20–21.

7. For an overview of the ecclesiology of missionary communion that runs through the documents of the Second Vatican Council, bringing out the pneumatological, communal and sacramental dimensions of the Church, see John J. Markey, *Creating Communion: The Theology of the Constitutions of the Church* (New York: New City Press, 2003).

8. On the recent developments on ecclesiology from a Trinitarian perspective, see Anne Hunt, "The Trinity and the Church: Explorations in Ecclesiology from a Trinitarian Perspective," in *Irish Theological Quarterly* 70 (2005): 215–236.

[T]he society structured with hierarchical organs and the Mystical
Body of Christ, are not to be considered as two realities, nor are
the visible assembly and the spiritual community, nor the earthly
Church and the Church enriched with heavenly things; rather
they form one complex reality which coalesces from a divine
and a human element. For this reason, by no weak analogy, it is
compared to the mystery of the incarnate Word. As the assumed
nature inseparably united to Him, serves the divine Word as a
living organ of salvation, so, in a similar way, does the visible
social structure of the Church serve the Spirit of Christ, who
vivifies it, in the building up of the body (see *Eph.* 4:16).[9]

The notions of the Church as a perfect society and institution that
prevailed after the Council of Trent (1545–1563) were re-presented
within the dimensions of mystery typical of the New Testament and
of the Church Fathers. In its origin and deepest identity, the Church
is mystery. It is the icon of the Trinity, coming to life in the free,
loving and wise plan of the Triune God who wants all to share in his
life.[10] Born from God and from humanity, the People of God journeys within history in relation to and towards God. Called together
by the gospel of salvation, the Church is the Mystical Body of Christ
shaped by the grace of the Holy Spirit poured out at Pentecost, the
Spirit who brings about the conversion of hearts and our adoption as
children of God (see Gal 4:6).

In short, therefore, the Church is a pilgrim people of men and
women within history, linked together not merely through bonds of
family, race, custom, or human goals, but as "a people made one
with the unity of the Father, the Son and the Holy Spirit."[11] This
focus on the divine-human reality of the Church constitutes the heart
of the spiritual renewal promoted by the Council.[12]

The Church is Communion. From the key conciliar notion of
Church as Mystery emerges another — Church as Communion.
Indeed, it has been declared authoritatively that the ecclesiology

---

9. The Dogmatic Constitution on the Church, *Lumen gentium*, 8.
10. See The Dogmatic Constitution on Divine Revelation, *Dei verbum*, 8.
11. S. Cipriano, *De orat. dom.* 23: PL 4, 553, cited in *Lumen gentium*, 4.
12. Hermann Josef Pottmeyer, "Neue Sammlung und Sendung: die Chance eines Endes?"
    in Essen Diocese's series of "Dokumente," *Umbau als Neuorientierung und Aufbruch
    wahrnehmen* (Essen: Zentralabteilung Kommunikation, 2007), 3–30.

of communion is *the* key ecclesiological idea of Vatican II.[13] The opening statement of the constitution on the Church affirms the communitarian sense of the Church gathered around the Crucified and Risen Christ:

> Christ is the light of the nations.... Since the Church is in Christ like a sacrament or as a sign and instrument both of a very closely knit union with God and of the unity of the whole human race, it desires now to unfold more fully to the faithful of the Church and to the whole world its own inner nature and universal mission.[14]

The Council's notion of vertical and horizontal communion includes several strands.

Equal dignity of all the baptized. The notion of the Church as communion recalls the equal dignity of all the baptized and the new commandment of love that is to be the law that regulates its life.[15] The People of God, formed as an icon of the Trinity and sharing in the very relationship of love between the Father and the Son in the unity of the Spirit, is called to live communion, striving towards full unity of mind and heart (see Jn 17:20–21).

The mutual communion among the members of the People of God, a gift of the Spirit, comes from communion with Christ, head of his body, the Church, and through him from communion with the Father. In other words, all the baptized share in the same dignity in that they are "re-clothed" with the one Christ as sons and daughters in the Son (see Gal 3: 27–28). Accordingly, the Church is a family of the children of God in which all are brothers and sisters with one Father and one Teacher (see Mt 23:8–12).

Distinction and relationship among the vocations. The notion of communion highlights the distinction and relationship among

---

13. See "The Final Report" of the 1985 Extraordinary Synod of Bishops in *Origins* 15 (December 19, 1985): 444–50. See also Walter Kasper, *Theology and Church* (London: SCM, 1989), 148–165. Neil Ormerod has argued that communion ecclesiologies stress harmony and integration but at the expense of taking historical disruptive change seriously. He proposes the ecclesiology of communion needs to be balanced by the emphasis on mission of the Church as defining its identity. See "The Structure of a Systematic Ecclesiology," in *Theological Studies* 63 (2002): 3–30. This link of communion and mission is implicit in Vatican II and was brought out more explicitly in John Paul II's encyclical *Christifideles laici* and other documents. See also Dennis Doyle, *Communion Ecclesiology* (New York: Orbis Books, 2000).

14. *Lumen gentium*, 1.

15. Ibid., 9.

vocations in the Church. The unity of the Church does not eliminate diversity of the members and functions. Unity requires diversity: "Now there are varieties of gifts, but the same Spirit; and there are varieties of services, but the same Lord; and there are varieties of activities, but it is the same God who activates all of them in everyone. To each is given the manifestation of the Spirit for the common good" (1 Cor 12:4–7). Twenty years after the Council, in his apostolic exhortation on the Laity, *Christifideles laici*, John Paul II summarized the Council's teaching in this regard. He describes the Council's vision of the unity, distinction, and mutual relations in the Church-communion among the three fundamental states of life of the People of God: laity, ordained ministry and religious life. They are different yet complementary, in a dynamic relationship to one another.[16]

The Church is Mission. The third major theme that characterizes the purpose of the Church is mission. The Council's deep yearning for the evangelization of the contemporary world, though not made as explicit as it might have been, culminates in the missionary decree *Ad gentes*. In it the Council defines evangelization as "that activity through which, in obedience to Christ's command and moved by the grace and love of the Holy Spirit, the Church makes itself fully present to all persons and peoples in order to lead them to the faith, freedom and peace of Christ by example of its life and teaching, and also by the sacraments and other means of grace."[17]

Ad gentes does not present mission as propaganda or organizational strategic planning. Precisely as a new People of God (born in the "mystery" revealed in Jesus Christ) and as a sacrament and sign of communion, the Church is transparent to Jesus Christ, and as such is the "sure seed of unity, hope and salvation for the whole human race."[18] The Church realizes that the deepest of bonds link it with humankind and its history.[19] In its teaching on mission, the Council underlines the universality and dialogical nature of the Church's outreach.

Universal sharing in the mission of Jesus Christ. Taking up the theology of the triple office of prophet, king and priest that Pius XII

16. John Paul II's Post-Synodal Apostolic Exhortation on the Vocation and Mission of the Lay Faithful (December 30, 1988), *Christifideles laici*, 55.
17. The Decree on the Missionary Activity of the Church, *Ad gentes*, 5.
18. *Lumen gentium*, 9.
19. The Pastoral Constitution on the Church in the Modern World, *Gaudium et spes*, 1.

had applied to Christ, the Council teaches that because the whole people of God is united to Jesus Christ through faith and baptism, in the Holy Spirit it shares — albeit in different ways — in the priestly, prophetic and royal mission of Christ (see 1 Pet 1:9–10). [20] It realizes its triple ministry of offering its life to God (priestly ministry), of listening to and proclaiming the word of salvation (prophetic ministry) and of service to humankind (royal ministry) above all by bearing witness to the newness of life received from God, the dignity and freedom of the children of God, and the law of mutual love given by Christ (see Jn 13:34).

Sent out to the whole world. In the power of the Holy Spirit, the risen Christ, who lives in the midst of his disciples to the end of time, sends the Church out to share the gift it has received (see Mt 18:20; 28:19–20). So "this way the Church both prays and labors in order that the entire world may become the People of God, the Body of the Lord and the Temple of the Holy Spirit."[21] Its debt of love to Christ and to all of humanity pushes the Church to reach out in mission. Moreover, the Church is the prolongation and continuation of the missions of the Son and the Holy Spirit: "As the Father has sent me, so I am sending you" (Jn 20: 21).

Parameters for Ecclesial Movements

These three broad themes opened up important parameters for understanding ecclesial movements. Some of them can be mentioned here briefly.

First, the Council widens the notion of lay apostolate by rooting it in the baptismal identity and mission of every Christian.[22] All the baptized, lay and ordained, are brothers and sisters in the one common project of building up the family of humankind for which Jesus gave his life. The laity are not the Church's proletariat, but active, vibrant members living out their baptism. Through their baptism,

---

20. See *Lumen gentium*, 10–12, 25–27, 34–36. See also the Decree concerning the Pastoral Office of Bishops, *Christus dominus*, 12–16, and the Decree on the Ministry and Life of Priests, *Presbyterorum ordinis*.

21. *Lumen gentium*, 17.

22. See Jesús Castellano Cervera, "Baptism, Source of Vocation and Mission," in Pontifical Council for the Laity, *Rediscovering Baptism* (Vatican City, 1998), 38–61. Cardinal Suenens of Malines, who had developed a particular interest in the role of the Legion of Mary, founded in Ireland, was especially prominent in promoting Vatican II's renewed awareness of the sacrament of baptism as foundational to lay apostolate.

every time they bear witness to him in word and action in their family and work place, they share in the prophetic-teaching mission of Jesus. Every time they pray for the needs of others in the world, every time they unite their sufferings and fatigue with Jesus, they share in his mission of sanctification. Every time they build up the community around them, locally or broadly in national and international politics and economics, they share in Jesus' pastoral or kingly priesthood.

Second, by underlining the universal call to holiness the Council opens the way for greater communion among all the baptized — lay, religious or ordained. It calls them to live out together their essential baptismal vocation to holiness, recognizing their equal dignity as Christians in a communion that extends beyond the visible confines of the Church.[23] *Lumen gentium*, 10, states famously: "Though they differ from one another in essence and not only in degree, the common priesthood of the faithful and the ministerial or hierarchical priesthood are nonetheless interrelated: each of them in its own special way is a participation in the one priesthood of Christ." This text clarifies that there is but one priesthood — Christ's — with two distinct forms of participation, the universal and the ministerial. Both are interrelated in communion.

Third, in presenting a dynamic sense of revelation and God's continuing dialogue with the Church, the Council underlines the Holy Spirit's role in the ever-deeper penetration of the gospel along the Church's journey, through charisms and spiritual experience.[24] The Dogmatic Constitution on Divine Revelation, *Dei verbum* brings this out in its description of how the Church transmits its life and message dynamically from one generation to another. It speaks of the "sense of the faith" in which all the faithful share.

Dei verbum states:

> There is a growth in the understanding of the realities and the words which have been handed down. This happens through the

---

23. See the Decree on the Apostolate of the Laity, *Apostolicam actuositatem*, 4, 15, 81–22; *Christus dominus,* 17, 29, 30; *Ad gentes* 15, 38, 39, 41; the Decree on the Adaptation and Renewal of Religious Life, *Perfectae caritatis,* 22; the Declaration on Christian Education, *Gravissimum educationis*, E 8; *Gaudium et spes*, 68, 75, 90; the Declaration on Religious Freedom, *Dignitatis humanae,* 2, 6, *Presbyterorumo ordinis*, 8–9. See also L. Gerosa, "Le 'charisme originaire': Pour un justification théologique du droit des associations dans l'Église" *NRT* 112 (1990): 234–235.

24. *Dei verbum*, 8.

contemplation and study made by believers, who treasure these things in their hearts (see Lk 2:19, 51) through a penetrating understanding of the spiritual realities which they experience, and through the preaching of those who have received through episcopal succession the sure gift of truth. For as the centuries succeed one another, the Church constantly moves forward toward the fullness of divine truth until the words of God reach their complete fulfillment in her.

It is significant that this text mentions not only a greater understanding of revelation but a process of advancing towards the fullness of divine truth. Charisms and spiritual movements play an important role along this journey.[25]

Fourth, the Church's rediscovery of its charismatic dimension has paved the way for understanding the place of movements in the Church. John O'Malley points out that the notion of "charism" was part of the Council's new lexicon, indeed one of the "interiority-words" that marked it.[26] "Charism" was clearly something new. The ecclesiologist, Francis A. Sullivan, recalls how in 1963 the American bishops attending the Council asked him to give a presentation on the question of charisms. Although he had been teaching the course on the Church at the Gregorian University for about six years, it was the first time he had ever prepared a lecture on the charisms of the faithful. He comments, "I am quite sure that I was not the only Catholic ecclesiologist of that period of whom the same would have been true."[27] When he consulted the standard encyclopedias of Catholic theology, he was astonished that the prestigious *Dictionnaire de Théologie Catholique* contained no article on the charisms.

In other dictionaries, however, Sullivan found two different notions. One considered charisms as rare and extraordinary gifts of grace (such as miraculous phenomena associated with the lives of saints or mystics); the other defined them as useful gifts that equip all the baptized for various kinds of service in the body of Christ. The lively debate during the second session of the Council concerning

---

25. See the International Theological Commission, "On the Interpretation of Dogmas," in *Origins* 20 (1990/1): 12.

26. John W. O'Malley, *What Happened at Vatican II*, 50.

27. Francis A. Sullivan, *Charisms and Charismatic Renewal* (Dublin: Gill and Macmillan, 1982).

the Church's rediscovery of its charismatic dimension reflects both of these perspectives. One side contended the charismatic principle had basically ceased once the initial foundation of the Church was over (sometimes called the "dispensationalist" viewpoint), while the other underlined how charisms belong to the very nature of the Church and as such will always be found in it.[28]

Lumen gentium, n.12, contains the main text on the place of charisms.[29] It states that the Holy Spirit sanctifies and leads the People of God not only through sacraments and ordained ministries but also through charisms, be they be extraordinary or ordinary.

> It is not only through the sacraments and the ministries of the Church that the Holy Spirit sanctifies and leads the people of God and enriches it with virtues, but, "allotting his gifts to everyone according as He wills," He distributes special graces among the faithful of every rank. By these gifts He makes them fit and ready to undertake the various tasks and offices which contribute toward the renewal and building up of the Church, according to the words of the Apostle: "The manifestation of the Spirit is given to everyone for profit." These charisms, whether they be the more outstanding or the more simple and widely diffused, are to be received with thanksgiving and consolation for they are perfectly suited to and useful for the needs of the Church. Extraordinary gifts are not to be sought after, nor are the fruits of apostolic labor to be presumptuously expected from their use; but judgment as to their genuinity and proper use belongs to those who are appointed leaders in the Church, to whose special competence it belongs, not indeed to extinguish the Spirit, but to test all things and hold fast to that which is good.

This passage, among others, became a key text for interpreting the interplay among the Church's charismatic and institutional dimen-

---

28. Cardinal Suenens' address on October 22, 1963 on this theme was particularly significant. His view that charisms belong to the very nature of the Church reflected theological writings of the 1950s. The text of this address is to be found as "The Charismatic Dimension of the Church," in Yves Congar et al (eds.), *Council Speeches at Vatican II* (London, 1964), 18–21. See also P. Mullins, "The Theology of Charisms: Vatican II and the New Catechism," *Milltown Studies* 33 (1994): 123–164.

29. See also *Lumen gentium* 4 and 7; *Presbyterorum ordinis* 9; *Actuositatem apostolicam* 3; *Ad gentes* 28. The subsequent treatment of charism in the Code of Canon Law was limited to the Introduction to the Code.

sions and the movements viewed as an expression of the charismatic gifts. This topic will be revisited in the section that reviews the 1998 meeting of the movements with John Paul II.

In recent decades the theme of charism has been linked with ministry.[30] Richard Gaillardetz points out that "few if any at the Council could have anticipated the flourishing of lay ministries that would occur in the decades after the Council." The rediscovery of charism, a pneumatological theme, "provided a helpful theological framework for interpreting that later postconciliar development."[31]

As well as underlining each baptized individual's charism, the Second Vatican Council also applied the Pauline expressions on charism to apostolic communities, their founders and spiritualities. In doing so, the foundation that the Council laid would support further theological reflection on the phenomenon of movements and communities that after the Council were emerging more clearly into the daylight.[32] In other words, the term "charism" came to be used not only in Paul's individual-centered meaning (as in 1 Cor 12:7–10: "to one is given ... to another ... to another ...") but also in a communitarian sense of sharing in a common spirituality or religious family. This became important for later developments in understanding ecclesial movements and communities.

30. See Carolyn Osiek, "Relation of Charism to Rights and Duties in the New Testament Church," in *The Jurist* 41 (1981): 495–313. See also Zeni Fox, *New Ecclesial Ministry: Lay Professionals Serving the Church* (Chicago: Sheed & Ward, 2002), 311–313.
31. Richard Gaillardetz, *Ecclesiology for a Global Church: A People Called and Sent* (New York: Orbis Books, 2008), 137.
32. See Rom 12: 5–8 and 1 Cor 12:4, cited in *Perfectae caritatis*, October 28, 1965, n. 8.

5

Encouraging, Clarifying, Providing Criteria: From the Second Vatican Council to the 1987 Synod on the Laity

The Second Vatican Council set the stage for movements to be recognized, indeed to multiply. In the new atmosphere that followed the Council, lay and ordained Catholics alike felt an increasing need to form free and spontaneous groups in which they could deepen their Christian life together and exercise effective Christian witness.[1] Movements that had caused perplexity during the 1950s were approved. Many others came to life.

In 1970 Louis Bouyer commented that the movements were part of a single broad sweep of renewal in the Church, stretching from monasticism onwards. He considered them to be "pilot" communities that could help guide the faithful towards the ultimate encounter with Christ at the Parousia. Indeed, he drew inspiration from John Wesley's dynamic notion of the Church (and the "Awakening" movements). In the Wesleyan tradition, such groups in the Church were understood as attempts at developing a more intense faith, hope and charity, by which Christians provided each other with mutual and permanent support.[2]

The Neocatechumenal Way is an example of a new movement (although its members prefer the expression "Way") that came to life after the Council. Francisco Kiko Argüello, a young painter from a middle-class Spanish Catholic family, had become disillusioned with his professional success and also had lost his faith. He began to question the meaning of his life. On one occasion he went into his room and began to cry out to God, "If you exist, help me. I don't know who you are. Help me!" This experience of prayer opened up a profound experience that prompted him to abandon his comfortable life and live among the poor in Palomeras Altas, a Madrid shantytown. He brought with him only a guitar, a crucifix and a Bible. He offered his neighbors catechesis, celebrated the

---

1. See Jacques Maritain's description of this need in *Carnet de Notes* (Paris: DDB, 1965), 235ff.
2. Louis Bouyer, *The Church of God* (Quincy, IL: Franciscan Herald Press, 1982), 456–461. (Original French edition published as *L'Eglise de Dieu* [Paris: Cerf, 1970]).

Word of God with them and then joined them for the Eucharist in small groups.

In Palomeras Altas he met Carmen Hernández, a teacher in a religious missionary institute who had been living a similar life. Soon both Kiko and Carmen began to bring their program to a number of parishes in Madrid, where people would be led by stages to the kerygma, or news of salvation. Word, liturgy and community became the three pillars of what they called the *Way*, with catechesis its principal work. The fundamental idea of their "Way" is that adults' infant baptism is like a dormant seed that must be revived.

The Neocatechumenal Way developed rapidly. In 1974, when Pope Paul VI met with the Neocatechumenal communities for the first time, he greeted them, "Here are the fruits of the Council! And this is something that consoles us enormously. You accomplish after baptism what the early Church once did before it: before or after is secondary. The fact is that you aim at the authenticity, at the fullness, at the coherence, at the sincerity of Christian life. And this is a great merit that consoles us enormously."[3]

Another movement that emerged in the late 1960s and early 1970s is the Community of Sant'Egidio. It started out among the alumni of a well-to-do school in Rome. Imbued with the desire to change the world typical of the social revolution in the air at that time, they headed out of town on their motorbikes to befriend poor families, the lonely and the elderly; to run schools for children; to build houses and feed the hungry. Every day they met in churches to read the gospel and to pray. Their central meeting-place was a square in the Trastevere area of Rome called Sant'Egidio, from which the community takes its name. Soon the Community of Sant'Egidio spread in Italy, then further afield. Its three pillars are prayer, communicating the gospel and friendship with the poor.

The Communion and Liberation movement emerged before the Council, but its first "fraternity groups" were set up in the latter half of the 1970s. Using a method based on communion, university graduates wished to strengthen their membership in the Church as adults, and to act on the responsibilities that this entails. Soon the

---

3. See report of the Neocatechumenal Way's plans to mark the 40th anniversary of its presence in Rome, "Neo-catechumenate Marks 40 Years in Rome" [http://www.ze-nit.org/article–24720?l=english, accessed August 12, 2010].

Fraternity of Communion and Liberation spread from Italy to other countries; this diffusion led to the establishment of Communion and Liberation.[4] The essence of the Communion and Liberation charism is the proclamation that God became Man. The movement affirms that this man, Jesus of Nazareth, who died and rose again, is a present event. The visible sign of this event is communion, that is to say, the unity of a people led by a living person, the bishop of Rome. Only in God made man, and hence within the life of the Church, can men and women become more truly who they are and humanity more truly human.

Encouraging, Directing, Instructing — Pope Paul VI and Movements

The popes that followed the Council provided strong support for the movements. The first of the post-conciliar popes, the saintly Paul VI (1963–1978), assumed the unenviable task of steering the Bark of the Church in turbulent times. In 1970, summarizing the aim of the Council, he wrote, "It wanted to create an atmosphere of collective and mutual pastoral (outreach). It wanted to strengthen the working bonds of love that unite us all in Christ. It wanted to give to the Church in its modern structures — enthusiasm, solidarity, the liveliness of the early Christian community. If we were to use advertising language we could say the Council wanted to be 'operation heart.' "[5]

It was this "operation heart" that the new communities and movements seemed to encapsulate. Pope Paul VI encouraged this:

> Newness seems the characteristic promise of the Council: spiritual re-awakening, aggiornamento, easy and happy ecumenism, a new expression of Christianity according to the needs of our times, the reform of the law and laws of the Church.... A vision of newness, youthfulness, courage, happiness, peace — this is what the Council proposed to the Church.... Let's desire, yes, and let's work to give the post-Conciliar Church a new face! Above all an interior renewal.[6]

---

4. In 1975 the theologian Hans Urs von Balthasar dedicated his work, *In Gottes Einsatz Leben* (Einsiedeln, 1971) to the Communion and Liberation movement (English translation: *Engagement with God* [London, 1975]).

5. Weekly Wednesday Audience, July 8, 1970. See *Insegnamenti* VIII (1970): 701.

6. Weekly Wednesday Audience, August 4, 1971. See *Insegnamenti* IX (1971): 666–670.

As the new life of movements began to manifest itself, Pope Paul VI encouraged recognition of the contribution of new movements and communities to the Church through numerous meetings and addresses, and by approving their statutes.[7] Chiara Lubich, founder of the Focolare Movement, said that Paul VI had provided her movement with a "precious legacy of encouragement, direction and instruction" that would always remain alive.[8] In 1973 he assigned to the Pontifical Council for Laity the official Vatican responsibility for ecclesial movements.

The Charismatic Dimension Rediscovered — Pope John Paul II and Movements

Pope John Paul II (1978–2005) offered unprecedented support in promoting the role of movements in the life of the Church. Continuing Pope Paul VI's positive approach, he acknowledged these new communities as providential fruits of the action of the Holy Spirit and bearers of renewal for the Church's apostolic life and mission. For him they were clearly linked with the Second Vatican Council and the "new Pentecost" that Pope John XXIII so desired. From the beginning of his pontificate he made a point of meeting with movements.

> I followed their work attentively, accompanying them with prayer and constant encouragement. From the beginning of my Pontificate, I have given special importance to the progress of ecclesial movements, and I have had the opportunity to appreciate the results of their widespread and growing presence during my pastoral visits to parishes and my apostolic journeys. I have noticed with pleasure their willingness to devote their energies to the service of the See of Peter and the local Churches. I have been able to point to them as something new that is still waiting to be properly accepted and appreciated.[9]

The movements and communities frequently experienced John Paul II's warm and encouraging support, most evident at the milestone 1998 Pentecost meeting of movements at St. Peter's Square. In numerous

---

7. Barbara Zadra, *I movimenti ecclesiali e i loro statuti* (Rome: PUG, 1997).

8. See her remark in her interview with Franca Zambonini, *Chiara Lubich: A Life for Unity* (New York: New City Press, 1992), 129. A collection of Pope Paul VI's addresses to members of the Focolare Movement was published in Italian, *Paolo VI al Movimento dei Focolari* (Rome: Città Nuova, 1978).

9. Message to the World Congress of Ecclesial Movements, May 27–29, 1998, *op.cit.*, 16.

other audiences and meetings, letters, visits and lunches, he cultivated vibrant relationships with the founders, leaders and members of the new movements. To give but one example, during a lunchtime conversation Chiara Lubich proposed that after her, the president of the movement would be a woman, even though the Focolare includes bishops, priests and men religious. The pope warmly supported this idea; eventually it was codified in the Movement's statutes.

Ian Ker notes, "Pope John Paul, following ... the early lead given by Pope Paul VI, [was] firmly in the tradition of the popes who, at critical times in the Church's life, have discerned dramatic new ways in which the Spirit has raised up new charismatic movements for the renewal and the propagation of the Christian faith."[10]

John Paul II's theology was shaped by the Second Vatican Council.[11] This perhaps explains his appreciation of movements as an expression of the charismatic principle. It is also evident, however, that he understood the charismatic principle in the light of his own deeply personal awareness of the role of the Spirit in the life of the Church and humanity. For instance, in his encyclical on the Holy Spirit, *Dominum et vivificantem*, he reiterated the Second Vatican Council's affirmation that the Church "is in Christ like a sacrament or as a sign or instrument both of a very closely knit union with God and of the unity of the whole human race."[12]

John Paul II develops this notion in reference to the event of Christ with its supreme gift of the Spirit: "As a sacrament, the Church is a development from the Paschal Mystery of Christ's 'departure,' living by his ever new 'coming' by the power of the Holy Spirit, within the same mission of the Paraclete — Spirit of truth. Precisely this is the essential mystery of the Church, as the Council professes."[13] In other words, born at the foot of the Cross and made manifest at Pentecost, the Church is an event, brought about by the Holy Spirit, of the continuous and ever new coming of the crucified and risen

---

10. Ian Ker, "The Radicalism of the Papacy: John Paul II and the New Ecclesial Movements," in William Oddie, *John Paul the Great: Makers of the Post-Conciliar Church* (London: CTS, 2003), 49–68, at 68.

11. See Brendan Leahy, "John Paul II and Hans Urs von Balthasar," in Gerald O'Collins and Michael Hayes (eds.), *The Legacy of John Paul II* (London: Continuum, 2008).

12. *Lumen gentium*, 1. See further on this section Piero Coda, "The Ecclesial Movements, Gift of the Spirit," in *Movements in the Church*, 78–80.

13. The Encyclical Letter on the Holy Spirit in the Life of the Church and the World, *Dominum et vivificantem* (May 18, 1986), 63.

Jesus Christ into the hearts of the disciples and in the midst of them united in his name (Mt 18:20).

Accordingly, John Paul II also affirms that "while it is an historical fact that the Church came forth from the Upper Room on the day of Pentecost," in a certain sense "one can say that she has never left it. Spiritually, the event of Pentecost does not belong only to the past: the Church is always in the Upper Room that she bears in her heart."[14] In this sense, he understood the Church to be in an ever new situation of Pentecost. And he saw that, based on charismatic gifts and working with the hierarchy, the new movements "form part of those gifts of the Holy Spirit with which the Church, Spouse of Christ, is adorned."[15] This is precisely the point that he develops further in his message to the 1998 World Congress of Ecclesial Movements, in which he describes the Church's charismatic dimension as "co-essential."

Discerning the Movements with Criteria of Ecclesiality

The Council generated an extensive body of theological literature on the topic of charism. Well-known authors such as Karl Rahner, Hans Urs von Balthasar and Avery Dulles reflected on the theme, which exploded into life through the charismatic renewal, and was reinforced through the theology of ministry.

The International Catholic Charismatic Renewal emerged two years after the close of Vatican II.[16] The Pentecostal Movement began in 1900, with Charles Fox Parham and his Bethel Bible School students in Topeka, Kansas. In 1967 Catholic lay faculty members at Duquesne University, Pittsburgh contacted neo-Pentecostal Protestants to learn how to receive the "baptism in the Spirit." They then shared this religious experience with a group of Catholic students at a retreat. This new outpouring of the Spirit soon led to the formation of various prayer groups. From there what became a movement of prayer and religious experience spread to Notre Dame and other universities as well as to parishes, convents and monasteries throughout the United

---

14. Ibid., 66.
15. See for instance his address to a gathering of movements in *Insegnamenti di Giovanni Paolo II*, 10, 1 (1987): 477–478.
16. See M. Robeck, *Azusa Street. Mission and Revival. The Birth of the Global Pentecostal Movement* (Nashville, TN: Thomas Nelson, 2006). See also P. Hocken, "Charismatic movement" and "Pentecostals" in Nicholas Lossky et al. (eds.), *Dictionary of the Ecumenical Movement* (Geneva: WCC, 2002):164–167 and 900–902 respectively.

States and Canada, then worldwide. At Pentecost, during the Holy Year of 1975, 10,000 came to Rome from all parts of the world for the International Congress of the Charismatic Renewal. Many of the charismatic renewal groups became covenant communities. The experience of a Charismatic Renewal prayer group, for instance, led Pierre Goursat (1914–1991) and Martine Laffitte-Catta to found the Emmanuel Community, in Paris.

By 1982 Francis Sullivan was able to write that "the words 'charism' and 'charismatic' are in such common use among Catholics today that it is hard to realize that they were so unfamiliar to most of us less than twenty years ago."[17] This focus on charism, generated by the Charismatic Renewal as well as by the Second Vatican Council's emphasis on the notion of charism, undergirded the newly developing theology of ministries in the Church. In 1985, for example, Avery Dulles commented, "In grappling with the interplay of the institutional and the charismatic ... we shall be dealing with one of the most crucial problem-areas in ecclesiology."[18]

From the 1960s onward the Charismatic Renewal continued to grow. As early as 1976 Cardinal Leon Josef Suenens interpreted Charismatic Renewal as a movement of the Spirit offered to the entire Church and destined to rejuvenate every part of the Church's life. By the early 2000s, more than 120 million Catholics worldwide had become linked to the Catholic Charismatic Renewal. Charles White-head, a leader of Charismatic Renewal, explains the phenomenon:

> The Catholic Charismatic Renewal is not a single unified worldwide movement as others are. It does not have a founder or a group of founders as other movements do, and it has no formal courses of initiation or membership lists. It's a highly diverse collection of individuals, groups, ministries and activities, often quite independent of one another, in different stages of development and with differing emphases. One of the characteristics of the Charismatic Renewal is the enormous variety of expressions and ministries, all inspired by the Holy Spirit and carried out in his power, which have a home under

---

17. Francis A. Sullivan, *Charisms and Charismatic Renewal: A Biblical and Theological Study* (Dublin: Gill and Macmillan, 1982), 9.
18. Avery Dulles, *A Church to Believe In: Discipleship and the Dynamics of Freedom* (New York: Crossroad, 1985), 21.

its umbrella. Whilst we major on relationships and networks rather than on structures, we nevertheless all share the same fundamental experience of the empowering presence of the Holy Spirit, and we all have the same general goals. Our patterns of informal relationships are to be found at local, national, and international levels, and are characterized by free association, dialogue, and collaboration.[19]

By the 1980s, many other new ecclesial movements were becoming increasingly evident in different forums of church life. Sometimes they were represented on diocesan and pastoral structures. They contributed to the manifestations of the universal church such as the World Youth Days. Indeed, in many ways, the World Youth Days developed out of the large-scale gatherings that some of the movements held for young people. Increasingly, it became clear that ecclesial movements deserved more articulate theological and pastoral consideration. The birth and spread of the movements had certainly brought unexpected newness, but this innovation struck some as disruptive, giving rise to questions, uneasiness and tensions. Such growth and change generated inevitable frictions, in which different sides were at fault in different ways.[20]

Whitehead pinpoints some of the issues: "Members of movements and communities often made mistakes in their attitudes to other parishioners, in their behavior and in their unrealistic expectations of parish life. We have often given an impression of being elitist, looking upon others as in some way sub-Christians."[21] The new movements raised difficult questions: Was there not a risk of setting up parallel pastoral entities within a diocese or parish? Was it appropriate for members of religious orders and diocesan priests to be involved in movements? How can the Church preserve and promote the individual movements in a true Catholic spirit? How is each movement connected with the Church as a whole and also with other movements? How can the Church maintain its unity when there is spontaneously irrupting multiplicity?

A first international meeting of movements was held in Rome from September 23 to 27, 1981, and a second near Rome, in Rocca di

---

19. Charles Whitehead, *What is the Nature of the Catholic Charismatic Renewal?* (Locust Grove, VA: Chariscentre, 2003), 3.
20. See Ratzinger, "The Ecclesial Movements," 24–25.
21. Whitehead, "Ecclesial Movements," 28.

Papa, from February 28 to March 4, 1987.[22] More and more literature began to be published on the theological rationale of ecclesial movements, including both positive and negative pastoral assessments.[23] This period of tension, with prejudices and reservations being expressed, tested the movements' fidelity and verified their charisms. Against this background of positive and negative appraisal, a lively discussion concerning movements took place during the 1987 Synod of Bishops on the Laity.[24] This particular synod was remarkable in that it offered lay leaders of movements an opportunity to address the gathered bishops.

In *Christifideles laici*, the document that the Synod produced, quoting both Vatican II and Canon Law, Pope John Paul II embraced the enthusiasm as well as the reservations expressed.[25] Beginning the Apostolic Exhortation, he notes how "the Holy Spirit continues

---

22. See M. Camisasca e M. Vitali (eds.), *I movimenti nella chiesa degli anni '80. Atti del primo convegno internazionale* (Milan, 1982) and "I Movimenti nella chiesa oggi" in *La Civiltà Cattolica* 132, 1981/3, pp. 417–28. On the second meeting in Rocca di Papa on February 28 – March 4, 1987, see *I movimenti nella chiesa. Atti del secondo colloquio internazionale, "Vocazione e missione dei laici nella Chiesa oggi"* (Milan, 1987).

23. See A. Favale (ed.), *Movimenti ecclesiali contemporanei: Dimensioni storiche, teologico-spirituali ed apostoliche* (Rome, 1982); Cervera Castellano, "Tratti caratteristici dei movimenti ecclesiali contemporanei," *Rivista di vita spirituale* 39 (1985): 560–573; J. Müller and O Krienbühl (eds.), *Orte lebendigen Glaubens. Neue geistliche Gemeinschaften in der katholischen Kirche* (Freiburg/Schweiz, 1987); C. Garcia and Cervera J. Castellano, *Corrientes y movimientos actuales de espiritualidad* (Madrid, 1987); F. Valentin and A. Schmitt (eds.), *Lebendige Kirche. Neue geistliche Bewegungen* (Mainz, 1988); Piero Coda, "I movimenti ecclesiali: Una lettura ecclesiologica," *Lateranum* 57 (1991): 55–70; Generalsekretariat des Zentralkomitees der deutschen Katholiken, *Miteinander auf em Weg. Einladung zum Dialog zwischen Gemeinden, Verbänden und geistlichen Gemeinschaften und Bewegungen, Berichte und Dokumente* (Bonn, 1995); Piero Coda, "I Movimenti ecclesiali e la Chiesa in Italia," *Communio* (1996, n. 149): 64–73; Manuel Bru, *Testigos del Espíritu. Los nuevos Líderes católicos. Movimientos y comunidades* (Madrid, 1998); Piero Coda, "I movimenti ecclesiali, dono dello Spirito: Una riflessione teologica," *Nuova Umanità* 20 (1998): 351–374; J. P. Cordes, *Segni di speranza: Movimenti e nuove realtà nella vita della chiesa alla vigilia del Giubileo* (Rome, 1998); Fidel Gonzáles Fernándes, *I movimenti. Dalla Chiesa degli apostoli ad oggi* (Milan: RCS Libri, 2000); Peter Wolf (ed.), *Lebensaufbrüche: Geistliche Bewegungen in Deutschland* (Vallendar, 2000); Cervera J. Castellano, *Carismi per il terzo millennio: Movimenti ecclesiali e le nuove comunità* (Rome, 2001); C. Hegge (ed.), *Kirche bricht auf. Die Dynamik der Neuen Geistlichen Gemeinschaften* (Münster, 2005).

24. See K. Lehmann, "I nuovi movimenti ecclesiali: motivazioni e finalità," in *Il Regno Documenti* 32 (1987): 27–31; B. Secondin, *Segni di profezia nella Chiesa. Comunità gruppi movimenti* (Milan, 1987). See also Robert Moynihan, "At Synod, a Split on Lay Movements?" *National Catholic Register* 63 (October 25, 1987): 1.

25. *Christifideles laici* (December 30, 1988).

to renew the youth of the Church" and how "he has inspired new aspirations towards holiness and the participation of so many lay faithful. This is witnessed, among other ways, in ... the flourishing of groups, associations and spiritual movements" (n. 2). Later in the same document he comments:

> In some ways lay associations have always been present throughout the Church's history as various confraternities, third orders and sodalities testify even today. However, in modern times such lay groups have received a special stimulus, resulting in the birth and spread of a multiplicity of group forms: associations, groups, communities, movements. We can speak of a *new era of group endeavors* of the lay faithful. (N. 29)

In affirming that lay people in the Church are free to form such groups, the pope is clear that such freedom is not granted to them by higher authorities as such. It is not, as he puts it, a "concession" by authority, but actually flows from the sacrament of baptism, which calls the lay faithful to participate actively in the Church's communion and mission. The pope also points out the "profound convergence among movements when viewed from the perspective of their common purpose, that is, the responsible participation of all of them in the Church's mission of carrying forth the Gospel of Christ, the source of hope for humanity and the renewal of society."[26] Therefore, the charisms manifested in such movements were to be received in gratitude as a gift for the Church.

Furthermore, he asserts, "Beyond this, the profound reason that justifies and demands the lay faithful's forming of lay groups comes from a theology based on ecclesiology, as the Second Vatican Council clearly acknowledged in referring to the group apostolate as a 'sign of communion and of unity of the Church of Christ' " (n. 29). However, although the Second Vatican Council's ecclesiology of communion clearly expresses the "right" to form lay associations, the Pope affirms the need to formulate "criteria" for discerning the authenticity of the forms which such groups take in the Church. After all, the Church is a "sign and instrument of unity."

The pope, therefore, proposes "criteria for ecclesiality" to discern the authenticity of the forms that such groups take in the Church's

---

26. *Christifideles laici*, 29.

communion.[27] *First*, the community or movement should be an instrument leading people to holiness in the Church. *Second*, each movement should be a forum where the Catholic faith as the Church interprets it is professed responsibly. *Third*, each community should be in a strong and authentic communion with the pope and with the local bishop in the local church. They should be willing to work together with others. *Fourth*, movements should take as their own the Church's missionary goals of evangelization, sanctification of humankind and the Christian formation of people's conscience in order to spread the Gospel into all walks of life. *Fifth*, the movements should exhibit a *commitment to being present in human society* so as to bring about more just and loving conditions. The movements demonstrate their success in meeting these criteria by the fruits they show in their organizational life and in their works.

These criteria have proven important in evaluating new communities and movements. In *Vita consecrata,* the post-synodal Apostolic Exhortation on the Consecrated Life and its Mission in the Church and in the World (March 25, 1996, n. 62), John Paul II repeats that while there is reason to rejoice at the Holy Spirit's action in bringing new communities to life, there is also a need for discernment regarding these charisms.

Cardinal L. J. Suenens

This discussion would not be complete without referring to a major figure in the story of Vatican II and charisms, before, during and after the Council. Through his encouragement and his writings, Cardinal Suenens (1904–1996) contributed much to a new understanding of movements and communities. During the Council, Cardinal Suenens took the lead in promoting the idea that charisms were not limited to the first few centuries of the Church. In doing so, he advanced a theme that Pope John XXIII had spoken of in his opening address at the Second Vatican Council — the new Pentecost in the Church.[28] Suenens saw that charisms were not a mere "peripheral or accidental phenomenon in the life of the Church," but belonging to the very nature of the Church and so "of vital importance for

---

27. Ibid., 30.
28. See his pastoral and theological study of the Charismatic Renewal Movement, in Cardinal Leon Joseph Suenens, *A New Pentecost?* (London: Darton, Longman & Todd, 1975).

the building up of the mystical body."[29] He contended that Church always contains charisms, both the ordinary and the extraordinary. Accordingly, he proposed that they receive greater emphasis in the Council's treatment of the Church as the People of God.

Before the Council, Cardinal Suenens had been in close contact with the Legion of Mary and afterward with the Focolare Movement, but in the late 1960s he became very involved in the Charismatic Renewal Movement. He met with the Catholic leadership of the new movement in the United States — Ralph Martin, Steve Clark, Kevin Ranaghan, Father Jim Ferry — as well as in Europe. He discussed the importance of the Catholic Charismatic Renewal with the pope and the curia. From 1974 to 1986, as a guide to the Renewal, he composed six "Malines Documents," that offered precious insight into its possibilities and its needs. He wrote many works on charismatic renewal, including *Charismatic Renewal and Social Action*, with his long-time Brazilian friend, Dom Helder Camara; and *Renewal and the Powers of Darkness* (1982), with a foreword by Cardinal Joseph Ratzinger.[30]

---

29. See Leon Joseph Cardinal Suenens, "The Charismatic Dimension of the Church" in Y. Congar, H. Küng, D. O'Hanlon (eds.), *Council Speeches of Vatican II* (London/ New York, 1964), 18–21.
30. See *A New Pentecost?* (London: Darton, Longman & Todd, 1975); *Charismatic Renewal and Social Action* (London: Dartman and Todd, 1980); *Renewal and the Powers of Darkness* (London: Dartman and Todd, 1983).

6

A Significant Milestone — Pentecost 1998

John Paul II guided preparations for the 2000 Jubilee Millennium celebrations with keen interest. He saw the turn of the twentieth century as a time to live "a new Advent." From the beginning of his papacy, he set his gaze on the entrance of the Church into the third millennium.[1] In his 1994 apostolic letter, *Tertio millennio adveniente*, he proposed dedicating the three years preceding the Jubilee to the Trinity, focusing 1997 on Christ, 1998 on the Spirit and 1999 on the Father.

In his 1996 homily at the Vigil of Pentecost, John Paul II inaugurated preparations for the Jubilee Year. In that address, the pope once again spoke about the ecclesial movements, repeating something he first noted in 1984: "They are a sign of the freedom of forms in which the one Church is realized and they represent a sure novelty that still needs to be adequately understood in its positive efficacy for the Kingdom of God working today in history."[2]

Concerning Jubilee celebrations, he said that during 1998, the year dedicated to the Holy Spirit, he would be counting especially on the "common witness and collaboration of the movements."[3] This came to pass on May 31, 1998, when over 300,000 members of movements and ecclesial communities gathered in St. Peter's Square.

The 1998 Pentecost Meeting — A Decisive Turning Point

Cardinal Rylko, who later became president of the Pontifical Council for the Laity, described the iconic gathering of movements with the pope on Pentecost 1998 as a "decisive turning point for the life and mission of movements and communities."[4] Four founders of new movements offered their testimonies to the pope and to the packed St. Peter's Square: Chiara Lubich of the Focolare, Msgr. Luigi Giussani of Communion and Liberation,

---

1. See the opening paragraph of his first encyclical letter, *Redemptor hominis* (April 3, 1979).
2. *Insegnamenti*, VII 2 (1984), 696.
3. See his homily for the Pentecost Vigil on the occasion of the Inauguration of the Mission in the City of Rome, May 25, 1996.
4. Cardinal Stanislaw Rylko, "Preface" to Pontifical Council, *The Beauty*, xii.

Kiko Argüello of the Neocatechumenal Way and Jean Vanier of L'Arche. Speaking on behalf of Charismatic Renewal and all the movements present, Charles Whitehead expressed thanks to the pope for the gathering.

As the pope himself noted, this "truly unprecedented" event was the first time these movements and communities had gathered together with the pontiff. Although he himself had met with movements one by one, Pentecost 1998 allowed him to encounter them all together, and the movements to encounter each other. In his address,[5] he framed his reflection in terms of the Pentecost experience and the Second Vatican Council's rediscovery of the charismatic dimension in the Church:

> The institutional and charismatic aspects are co-essential as it were to the Church's constitution. They contribute, although differently, to the life, renewal and sanctification of God's People. It is from this providential rediscovery of the Church's charismatic dimension that, before and after the Council, a remarkable pattern of growth has been established for ecclesial movements and new communities.[6]

John Paul II also called attention to "a new stage" unfolding for the movements — ecclesial maturity. He invited them to bring forth the more "mature" fruits of communion and commitment that "the Church expects from you." He explained his own passionate commitment to the movements:

> In our world, often dominated by a secularized culture which encourages and promotes models of life without God, the faith of many is sorely tested, and is frequently stifled and dies. Thus we see an urgent need for powerful proclamation and solid, in-depth Christian formation. There is so much need today for mature Christian personalities, conscious of their baptismal identity, of their vocation and mission in the Church and in the world! There is great need for living Christian communities! And here are the movements and the new ecclesial communities: they are the response, given by the Holy Spirit,

---

5. For the text of the address on May 30, 1998 see Pontifical Council for the Laity, *Movements in the Church*, 219–224.
6. Ibid., 221.

to this critical challenge at the end of the millennium. You are this providential response.[7]

The pope listed what he had observed in the movements: how they had helped people rediscover their baptism, appreciate the gifts of the Spirit, gain a new trust in the sacrament of reconciliation and recognize the Eucharist as the source and summit of all Christian life. Their involvement in movements had helped families to become true "domestic churches." The movements also had fostered vocations to ministerial priesthood and religious life, and to the new forms of lay life inspired by the evangelical counsels.

Reminding those gathered at St. Peter's Square of the role that competent ecclesiastical authorities have in discernment, he concluded with a rousing mandate:

> Today, from this upper room in St. Peter's Square, a great prayer rises: Come, Holy Spirit, come and renew the face of the earth.... Come, Holy Spirit, and make ever more fruitful the charisms that you have bestowed on us.... Today from this square, Christ says to each of you: "Go into all the world and preach the gospel to the whole creation" (Mk 16:15). He is counting on every one of you, and so is the Church. "Lo," the Lord promises, "I am with you always to the close of the age" (Mt 28:20).[8]

The World Congress

During the three days preceding the Pentecost Vigil, 350 delegates from around the world, representing 54 movements and new communities as well as observers from other churches, met in Rome.[9] This world congress aimed to deepen theological reflection on the specific nature of ecclesial movements and to facilitate the exchange of experiences among the various representatives, together with some bishops and participants engaged in other forms of life and Christian witness. Cardinal Stafford, who at that time was president of the Council for the Laity, commented that it "surpassed expecta-

---

7. Ibid., 222.

8. Ibid., 224.

9. For the reactions of an ecumenical observer to the Congress, see Diane Cooksey Kessler, "Can We Make a Difference?" in *Ecumenical Trends* 27 (December 1998): 5–8.

tions," adding "there was something very special about the week."[10]
The movements' character emerged as "particular events" arising
from the Holy Spirit who, as the agent of the new evangelization,
inspires the actual forms of the Church's missionary activity.

In his message to the congress, John Paul II referred to the movements as one of "the most significant fruits of that springtime in the
Church which was foretold by the Second Vatican Council."[11] It was
encouraging, he said, to see how "this springtime is advancing and
revealing the freshness of the Christian experience based on personal encounter with Christ." He stressed again unity between the
institutional and the charismatic dimensions of the Church: "Both
are co-essential to the divine constitution of the Church founded by
Jesus, because they both help to make the mystery of Christ and his
saving work present in the world. Together they aim to renew, each
in its own way, the self-awareness of the Church, which in a certain
sense may be called a 'movement.' "

This affirmation of the "co-essential" nature of the charismatic
and institutional profiles of the Church is significant. The Church
cannot be limited only to its institutional-hierarchical dimension.
The movements, associations, and communities that grow from
charisms are also the work of the Spirit guiding the Church.

At the congress, Cardinal Joseph Ratzinger gave an address that
came to be considered a Magna Charta for any reflection on the
theological locus of the movements.[12] One comment in particular
left a strong impression on the gathered delegates: "Not everything
should be fitted into the straightjacket of a single uniform organization; what is needed is less organization and more spirit!"[13]

A Significant Church Event

A priest who took part, Silvano Cola, noted, "Perhaps it will
take years to realize the full import of Pentecost '98."[14] Certainly
the comments of many participants reflect their appreciation of the

---

10. See his Foreword to *Movements in the Church*, 5.
11. The text of his Message is in *Movements in the Church*, 18–19.
12. See "The Ecclesial Movements: A Theological Reflection on Their Place in the Church,"
    in Pontifical Council for the Laity, *Movements in the Church*, 23–51.
13. *Movements in the Church*, 50.
14. For the following comments see Silvano Cola's article, "Pentecost '98," in *Being One*
    8 (1999), 4–6.

magnitude and significance of the event. Oreste Pesari, executive director of the International Catholic Charismatic Renewal, commented: "I believe that the first gift we received was that of feeling at home, feeling we are fully Church. Not that we were not so before, but now there is a new awareness of this in us and in others."

He and many others felt that God had bestowed a gift that participants could bring to the whole Church. "Over and above how things will work out concretely," Pesari evaluated, "this Pentecost meeting has been a new outpouring of the Holy Spirit, a new joy, a new life. I believe that the Church of the third millennium has really begun." According to the chaplain of the European Cursillo Movement, "This event has been a confirmation for us of our belonging to the Church. It has prompted us further to go and evangelize the world around us. It was great getting to know the other movements. Now we will work even more in communion with the other realities of the Church. The power of mission lies in communion."

Luigi Giussani, founder and leader of the Communion and Liberation movement, wrote to his community,

> The encounter with John Paul II was for me the greatest day of our history. It was the "cry" that God gave us as witnesses of unity, of unity of the whole Church. At least that is how I felt it: we are one. I said this also to Chiara Lubich and to Kiko Argüello, who were beside me in St. Peter's Square: How can you not but cry out our unity in such occasions? Our responsibility is for unity, right to valuing also even the smallest good thing there is in the other.[15]

The event made a deep impression not only on the movements' leaders, but also on others who attended.[16] One woman who had been struggling with belief said, "My faith has been revived because the pope bore witness to his faith with his life. I will bring home with me an awareness that I can still believe." A bus driver who had brought participants from Germany, a Lutheran, commented, "I have accompanied many pilgrimages to Rome before, but this has been different because I experienced communion, freedom and joy." One young person reflected, "I found hope again in St. Peter's

---

15. See Liugi Giussani, "Lettera alla fraternità," in *Tracce*, June 1998, 9 (translation mine).
16. The following comments are contained in Silvano Cola's article "Pentecost '98."

Square. The Church will go ahead despite everything." Another remarked: "While I was in the Square that day, I felt a new certainty of the presence of the Holy Spirit. He is working, albeit in different ways, in various movements. You could sense the real communion in Jesus Christ among the members of the various movements. The phrase of St. Paul's came to mind: 'One is the Spirit who works all in everyone.' I came away with a certainty that the Lord is working with his Spirit in the midst of the world and that his Church is growing strongly and qualitatively in faith. This event can surely be considered a source of great hope for the future of humanity."

One woman recollected the day vividly: "I could see the beauty of each movement and I was able to rejoice in the wide variety of movements. It was a special moment for me. I felt I belonged to a Church that is one, and at that moment I felt this one Church was receiving me into her bosom. Part of the Vigil ceremony was the witness offered by some of the movements' founders to the many and varied charisms they had received from the hands of God. Their gentle, loving and strong words showed how charisms have been incarnated in the heart of humanity. Those gathered before the pope that day could visualize the countenance of the post-Conciliar Church — a people on a journey who, in obedience to her pastors, come to the immense Upper Room of St. Peter's Square in order to listen to 'that voice' and regain strength for the journey. The pope was happy. 'I count on you,' he said. These words penetrated everyone's heart. It was as if the Scripture reading about Pentecost was becoming incarnate. It was happening also for us."

Growing in Communion

John Paul II's invitation that the movements grow in a more mature communion found willing listeners. The leaders, representatives, and members of the various movements began to explore how they could strengthen even more their relationships of communion with one another. Bishops too nurtured an increased pastoral attention towards the movements. In the following year approximately 200 congresses of movements met locally all over the world. They indicated their willingness to strengthen their communion with one another and in missionary collaboration with their local churches.

In a special follow-up conference organized by the Focolare Movement, the Community of Sant'Egidio and Charismatic Renewal, the founders and leaders of 41 ecclesial movements and new communities met in Speyer, Germany, on June 7–8, 1999.[17] John Paul II sent a letter of encouragement with Bishop Rylko, who at the time was secretary of the Pontifical Council for the Laity.

Also in 1999, a hundred representatives of the world's bishops along with some of the movements' founders gathered for a study seminar to reflect on this "phase two" in the history of the new communities.[18] They reflected on the movements' missionary drive as well as their close link to the Petrine ministry, considering how they could contribute to their local pastoral apostolate and action. In other words, how could the movements bear as much fruit as possible in the local churches?

A conversation with Cardinal Ratzinger raised several interesting topics. Cardinal Simonis from Holland wondered, for instance, where exactly the movements fitted into the Vatican's Curial structures. Would they require a separate Vatican department or congregation? Would the Church need to add a new classification — movements — to the usual three "classes" of priests, religious and laity? Replying to these questions, Cardinal Ratzinger commented that the tripartite division of priests, religious and laity is fundamental in the Church now, and in the future. He continued, "It seems to me, however, that after Vatican II, there has been great communication between the three states, in the sense that new ways of linking, new forms of co-operation between the different vocations are being found."[19] Concerning the place of movements in the Curia, Ratzinger admitted certain issues did need to be clarified. For example, is it appropriate that the Pontifical Council for the Laity that is responsible for the movements, should also take responsibility for families of consecrated life and fraternities of priests, even though other congregations normally deal with consecrated life and clergy? He concluded, "The question will have to be determined one day.... I think that organization must follow life. It is better therefore to see how life evolves, without rushing to tackle the organizational

---

17. See Chiara Lubich, "Für eine Kiche der Zukunft: Der Dialog unter Neuen Geistlichen Gemeinschaften seit Pfingsten 1998," in Christoph Hegge, *Kirche bricht auf: Die Dynamik der Neuen Geistlichen Gemeinschaften* (Münster: Aschendorff Verlag, 2005), 94–112.

18. Pontifical Council for the Laity, *The Ecclesial Movements in the Pastoral Concern of the Bishops* (Vatican City, 2000).

19. See *Pastoral Concern of the Bishops*, 228–231, at 229.

questions."[20] He added that the intercommunication among the three states of life within the movements may indeed provide a stimulus for closer collaboration among the offices of the Roman Curia.

Concerning the positive incorporation of movements into the parish and into the particular Church, Ratzinger commented, "It is not possible simply to give a recipe" for making this happen. While recognizing that each bishop, as head of the Church in his own diocese is the final arbiter, he also acknowledged that "some rules are necessary but then a great deal depends on the persons involved. That is my experience. If the persons — the parish priest, the groups and also the bishops — are amenable, solutions will be found."[21] Bishops must consider the gifts that these movements bring to the Church, but also must "help the movements to find the right road ... with the responsibility for peaceful harmony within the Church." The bishops also have the responsibility to help priests open themselves to such movements and guide them as well as the faithful in their dioceses to an awareness of the astonishing variety of ways that the Holy Spirit has opened up. Discerning the proper relationship between the movements and the local church requires "spiritual and human understanding that is able to combine guidance, gratitude, openness and a willingness to learn."

The tone of Cardinal Ratzinger's observations was encouraging, practical and full of wisdom. He advocated attitudes and values that would find an authoritative confirmation in a significant letter that John Paul II issued in early 2001, *Novo millennio ineunte* ("At the Beginning of the New Millennium"), which the concluding chapter will treat in more depth. The next chapter, then, will discuss how this encouraging approach continued after Cardinal Ratzinger became Pope Benedict XVI.

---

20. Ibid., 230.
21. Ibid., 232.

7

Pope Benedict XVI and Movements

Just one month after his election as pope, Benedict XVI called for another large gathering of ecclesial movements, signaling his intention to continue his predecessors' encouragement of them. And on June 3, 2006, that gathering took place. This chapter's reflection on Benedict XVI's view of movements needs to begin, however, by acknowledging the "hermeneutic of reform" that emerged during the Second Vatican Council, as it is the lens through which Pope Benedict views in the movements the work of the Risen Christ in the power of the Spirit.

Addressing the Roman Curia on December 21, 2005, the pope spoke of this hermeneutic as one "of renewal in the continuity of the one subject-Church which the Lord has given to us ... a subject which increases in time and develops, yet always remaining the same, the one subject of the journeying People of God." For Benedict, the ecclesial movements and communities express a key notion from the Second Vatican Council's document on divine revelation, *Dei verbum* — the People of God's continuous renewal within the continuity of the great Tradition of the Church.

The Pope's Prior Contact with Movements

We have already noted that Pope Benedict speaks to and of movements from his own first-hand experience. As early as the 1960s, when he was a professor at Tübingen, he met with some movements, including the Neocatechumenal Way. His own studies of the Church Fathers convinced him that baptism had become an almost forgotten sacrament. In the Neocatechumenal Way, however, he discovered young people, struck by the discovery of the gospel, participating in a new post-baptismal catechumenate. Journeying together in the adventure of faith, they had re-appropriated their baptism as individuals, and as a community.

Towards the end of the 1960s, in an era marked by Marxist revolutionary spirit, theologians such as Henri De Lubac, Hans Urs von Balthasar, Marie-Joseph Le Guillou and Louis Bouyer, together with Cardinal Ratzinger, had been planning a new theological and cultural review. In Italy Ratzinger met people who had truly understood the Christian revolution — Msgr. Luigi Giussani and the Communion and Liberation movement. This contact led to the establishment and publication of the international Catholic review, *Communio.* While bishop of Regensburg, through his contact with the Paderborn professor Heribert Mühlen, Ratzinger met the Charismatic Renewal. He noticed how the young Christian members of this movement were energized by the power of the Spirit.

At the time that he met these movements, he had been feeling a growing disillusionment with a theology that, with the increasing bureaucratization of the Church in Germany, was losing its enthusiasm for the faith. Ratzinger saw how the movements were expressions of the Council teachings, bearing fruit in ways that other more organized or programmed initiatives were not. While Archbishop of Munich, he wrote to a colleague from his student days: "I have heard that you have become involved in the Focolare Movement. That makes me happy. I believe the Movement is one of the most positive aspects of the Church in recent times and a real hope for renewal is being born from it."[1]

As prefect of the Congregation for the Doctrine of the Faith, Joseph Cardinal Ratzinger was in a privileged position to evaluate the movements' impact. In a 1985 interview he affirmed:

> Every council, in order really to yield fruit, must be followed by a wave of holiness.... What is hopeful ... is the rise of new movements which nobody had planned and which nobody has called into being, but which have sprung spontaneously from the inner vitality of the faith itself. What is manifested in them ... is something like a pentecost season in the Church.... I find it marvelous that the Spirit is once more stronger than our programs and brings himself into play in an altogether different way than we had imagined.... Our task — the task of the office holders in the Church and of theologians — is to keep the door open to them, to prepare room for them.[2]

Some years later, in another published interview he discussed various difficulties that had arisen regarding the movements. He

---

1. See Silvano Cola, "La sinfonia della vita ecclesiale: Benedetto XVI e i Movimenti Ecclesiali," *Gen's* 25 (2005), 110–113 at 110.
2. See Vittorio Messori's interview with Cardinal Ratzinger, *The Ratzinger Report* (London: Fowler Wrights Books, 1985), 43–44.

advised against getting fixated on such problems: "One can always raise objections to individual movements ... but whatever else you may say, we can observe innovative things emerging there. In these movements, Christianity is presented as an experience of newness and is suddenly felt by people — who often come from very far outside — as a chance to live in this century."[3]

In the Preface to the 2000 edition of his classic *Introduction to Christianity*, Cardinal Ratzinger spoke of the new movements where "faith becomes a form of lived experience, the joy of setting out on a journey and of participating in the mystery of the leaven that permeates the whole mass from within and renews it."[4]

Before becoming pope, at the May 1998 World Congress of Movements, Ratzinger made his most significant statement concerning the theological place of movements in the Church. This address will be discussed in the next section of this book.

Approaching the Movements with a Great Deal of Love

Given his long-standing relations with movements, the support and encouragement he gave them after becoming pope comes as no surprise. In a May 30, 2005 address to the Italian Episcopal Conference, he spoke of the movements' contribution in terms of mission:

> You have also shed light on the need for parishes to assume a more missionary attitude in their daily pastoral work so as to be open to a more intense collaboration with all the living forces available to the Church today. It is very important in this regard to strengthen the communion between the parish structures and the various "charismatic" groups that have sprung up in recent decades and are widespread in Italy, so that the mission can reach out to all the milieus of life.[5]

At the World Youth Day in Cologne (summer 2005), he pointed out the relevancy of movements for young people. Having recommended to the young people gathered there the *Compendium of the Catechism of the Catholic Church*, he noted, "Obviously books alone are not enough. Form communities based on faith! In recent

---

3. See Peter Seewald's interview with Cardinal Ratzinger, *Salt of the Earth: The Church at the End of the Millennium* (San Francisco: Ignatius Press, 1997), 127.

4. *Introduction to Christianity* (San Francisco: Ignatius Press, 2004), 19.

5. Address to the 54th Assembly of the Italian Bishops' Conference, Verona, May 30, 2005.

decades, movements and communities have come to birth in which
the power of the Gospel is keenly felt. Seek communion in faith,
like fellow travelers." He also indicated that "the spontaneity of new
communities is important, but it is also important to preserve communion with the Pope and with the Bishops. It is they who guarantee
that we are ... living as God's great family, founded by the Lord
through the Twelve Apostles."[6]

A few months later, he encouraged German bishops to "approach
movements with a great deal of love":

> After the Council, the Holy Spirit endowed us with the gifts of
> the "movements" ... places of faith where young people and
> adults try out a model of life in faith as an opportunity for life
> today. I therefore ask you to approach movements with a great
> deal of love. Here and there, they must be corrected or inte-
> grated within the structures of the parish or diocese. Yet, we
> must respect the specific character of their charism and rejoice
> in the birth of communitarian forms of faith in which the Word
> of God becomes life.[7]

At the June 3, 2006 meeting of the movements in St. Peter's Square
— just a month after he had become pope — Benedict XVI described
the vocation of ecclesial movements as "schools of freedom":

> The Ecclesial Movements want to and must be schools of
> freedom, of this true freedom. Let us learn in them this true
> freedom.... We want the true, great freedom, the freedom of
> heirs, the freedom of children of God. In this world, so full of
> fictitious forms of freedom that destroy the environment and
> the human being, let us learn true freedom by the power of the
> Holy Spirit; to build the school of freedom; to show others by
> our lives that we are free and how beautiful it is to be truly free
> with the true freedom of God's children. The Holy Spirit, in
> giving life and freedom, also gives unity. These are three gifts
> that are inseparable from one another.[8]

---

6. Homily at the Mass in Marienfeld (Cologne), Sunday, August 21, 2005.
7. Address to the Bishops of the German Bishops' Conference on their *ad limina* visit
   in the Consistory Hall, November 18, 2006.
8. Homily at the Prayer Vigil on the Solemnity of Pentecost on the occasion of the meeting with the ecclesial movements and communities, St. Peter's Square, June 3, 2006.

Pope Benedict does not discount the difficulties. In a 1997 interview with Peter Seewald, he acknowledges the tensions that can arise. For instance, in 1997 John Paul II had encouraged the initiators of the Neocatechumenal Way to examine their thirty-year experience of the *Way*, and to formalize it with a written statute. In July 2002 the Neocatechumenal statutes were approved by the Holy See, even though certain issues regarding the celebration of the Eucharist at their meetings remained to be clarified. Benedict facilitated the resolution of this problem by overseeing a letter dated December 1, 2006 and signed by Cardinal Francis Arinze, prefect of the Congregation for Divine Worship. Addressed to the initiators and directors of the Neocatechumenal Way, Kiko Argüello, Carmen Hernández and Father Mario Pezzi, it established guidelines that the *Way* must follow in the celebration of Mass. The letter states that the catechumenate communities must follow "the liturgical books approved by the Church, without adding or omitting anything." At the same time, however, it accepts several adaptations that the Neocatechumenal Way has introduced in the celebration of Mass as part of its liturgical-catechetical itinerary.

Benedict sees how ecclesial movements are important for all members of the Church, including bishops. On February 8, 2007, in order to underline the new maturity of communion among movements, the pope met with bishops close to two movements — the Focolare and the Community of Sant'Egidio. He repeated his conviction that "that the multiplicity and the unity of the charisms and ministries are inseparable in the life of the Church." He continued, "this unity and multiplicity which comprises the People of God in some way also makes itself manifest today, with many bishops being gathered here with the Pope, near to two different Ecclesial Movements, characterized by a strong missionary dimension." He emphasized for bishops the value of involvement in movements: "The communion between bishops and Movements, therefore, provides a valid impulse for a renewed commitment by the Church in announcing and witnessing to the Gospel of hope and charity in every corner of the world."[9]

---

9. See his address to Bishop Friends of the Focolare Movement and Bishop Friends of the Community of Sant'Egidio, February 7, 2007.

In the Post-Synodal Exhortation *Pastores gregis*, Benedict XVI clarifies how "the relationships of exchange between bishops ... goes well beyond their institutional meetings" (n. 59), noting that "it is what occurs also in conventions such as yours, where not only collegiality is experienced, but an episcopal fraternity." This fraternity "draws from the sharing of the ideals promoted by the movements a stimulus to render more intense the communion of hearts, to make stronger the reciprocal support and a more active commitment to show the Church as a place of prayer and charity, a home of mercy and peace."

In an October 18, 2010 letter to seminarians, Benedict XVI describes the movements as "a magnificent thing. You know how much I esteem them and love them as a gift of the Holy Spirit to the Church." In doing so he underlines the importance of mutual acceptance and understanding among the movements in the unity of Christ's Body.

Holiness and the Radicality of the Gospel

Benedict XVI, in a manner reminiscent of his predecessor John Paul II, remains convinced that the movements are a vital source of life within the Church not yet fully discovered. He views them also as movements of holiness. In his May 13, 2010 address to Bishops at the Shrine of Our Lady in Fatima, he recalled the words of John Paul II: "The Church needs above all great currents, movements and witnesses of holiness" because "it is from holiness that is born every authentic renewal of the Church ... [and] a renewed form of presence in the heart of human existence and of the culture of nations."[10] He continued,

> One could say, "the Church has need of these great currents, movements and witnesses of holiness ... but there are none!" In this regard, I confess to you the pleasant surprise that I had in making contact with the movements and the new ecclesial communities. Watching them, I had the joy and the grace to see how, at a moment of weariness in the Church, at a time when we were hearing about "the winter of the Church," the Holy Spirit

---

10. See Pope John Paul II, Address for the XX Anniversary of the Promulgation of the Conciliar Decree, *Apostolicam actuositatem*, November 18, 1985.

was creating a new springtime, awakening in young people and adults alike the joy of being Christian, of living in the Church, which is the living Body of Christ. Thanks to their charisms, the radicality of the Gospel, the objective contents of the faith, the living flow of her tradition, are all being communicated in a persuasive way and welcomed as a personal experience, as adherence in freedom to the present event of Christ.[11]

Five months later, in Palermo, he recounted the story of the recently beatified Chiara Luce Badano, who had been a member of a movement. Noting the important role of Chiara Badano's family as a "miniature church," the pope also pointed out that each miniature church is inserted into the "great Church," that is, into the family of God that Christ came to form. Ecclesial movements and associations are expressions of that great Church. They serve not themselves, but Christ and the Church. They produce fruits of holiness.[12]

11. Fatima, May 13, 2010.
12. See his address to young people and families of Sicily, Palermo, October 3, 2010.

Part 2

Reading the Phenomenon

This section provides keys to reading the phenomenon of ecclesial movements. Although previous chapters have touched on some of this material, it is worthwhile presenting more directly a number of the avenues that theological reflection has pursued regarding movements.

To begin, considering how the movements serve to transmit the Second Vatican Council will lead secondly to an exploration of movements in terms of the polarity between institution and charism suggested by the council's rediscovery of the charismatic principle. Next is the exploration of a perspective that Cardinal Ratzinger advanced in 1998, that movements express apostolic succession in the transmission of the Christ event. Fourth, is a review of the relationship between movements and evangelization. Finally, by way of synthesis, movements are examined in the light of the Church's Marian principle.

Although the keys proposed here are separated for the purposes of exposition and exploration, they all are inter-related. These mutually related viewpoints provide different angles from which to look at the topic of movements.

8

Reception of the Second Vatican Council

The Second Vatican Council concluded in 1965, but the reception of that Pentecostal event is far from complete. In broad terms, reception means the lively, ongoing, Spirit-led process of the Church's "taking over" or appropriating as a whole the vision and implications in doctrine and practice of the council.[1] The reception of Vatican II has been the subject of frequent discussion in recent years. Hermann Pottmeyer, for instance, comments:

> Just as the Council understood itself to be a Pentecostal event, its authentic reception can only be a renewal of the Church in the Holy Spirit. Here the task confronting a hermeneutic of the Council goes far beyond an objective interpretation of the texts. Something more is needed ... a recognition and distinction or discernment of spirits ... The religious and spiritual depth of many conciliar texts has thus far really not been adequately appreciated and received.[2]

Not that the Spirit leaves the letter of the council behind. It makes itself known from the direction given in the texts. Pottmeyer also notes, however, that

> above and beyond its technical meaning ... "reception" means the acceptance of the gifts of God that make his reign a reality. Rightly, then, does the Council urge pastors to discover and heed the charisms that the Spirit of God bestows on his Church. New forms of charismatic experience, of community structures, of lay participation, and of commitment to the poor and social justice, as well as developments in the separated

---

1. See William G. Rusch, *Ecumenical Reception: Its Challenge and Opportunity* (Grand Rapids, MI: Eerdmans, 2007). On the broader issue of reception see Yves Congar, "Reception as an Ecclesiological Reality," *Concilium* (1972), n. 77, 43-68; Ormond Rush, *The Eyes of Faith: The Sense of the Faithful and the Church's Reception of Revelation* (Washington, DC: The Catholic University of America Press, 2009).

2. Hermann J. Pottmeyer, "A New Phase in the Reception of Vatican II: Twenty Years of Interpretation of the Council," in Giuseppe Alberigo, Jean-Pierre Jossua and Joseph A. Komonchak (eds.), *The Reception of Vatican II.* Trans. Matthew J. O'Connell (Washington, DC: The Catholic University of America Press, 1987), 27–43, at 41.

churches, can be gifts of the Holy Spirit, and reception of them can be part of the reception of the Council.[3]

Various authors have affirmed that the movements seem to have been created precisely so that people can understand and experience the ecclesiology of Vatican II.[4] Two authors — Piero Coda, president of the Sophia University Institute and president of the Italian Theologians' Association, and Ian Ker of Oxford University — offer useful explanations of the function of the movements in the reception of the Second Vatican Council.

The Ecclesiology of Communion as a Modern Form of "Spiritual Exercises"

The new ecclesial movements and communities have made a significant impact in Italy. Piero Coda has long reflected on their import, pursuing many avenues in doing so.[5] In one of his approaches, he considers the meaning of movements in terms of the reception of the church's self-understanding of its mission in the contemporary world as put forward at the Second Vatican Council in light of the mystery of the triune God and the ecclesiology of missionary communion. In their emergence he discerns the Spirit at work, giving flesh and bone to the motifs of mystery, communion, and mission that permeate the council's vision.

Coda acknowledges that post-conciliar initiatives in local churches throughout the world have led many to encounter the letter and spirit of the council's ecclesiology. He notes that the Council of Trent (1545–1563) was followed by effective programmed implementation of its agenda. The council would not have passed into the life-stream of the sixteenth century Catholic Church and profoundly renewed it without exceptional pastors like St. Charles Borromeo. Alongside such great pastors, Coda notes, other charismatic realities and

3. Hermann J. Pottmeyer, "A New Phase," 42.
4. See J. Beyer, "I 'movimenti ecclesiali'," in *Vita consacrata* 23 (1987), 143–156, at 156. See also "Il movimento ecclesiale: questioni attutali," in *Vita consacrata* 26 (1990): 483–494 and "I movimenti nuovi nella Chiesa," in *Vita consacrata* 27 (1991): 61–77.
5. Piero Coda, "I movimenti ecclesiali: Una lettura ecclesiologica," in *Lateranum* 57 (1991): 55–70. See also his "The Ecclesial Movements, Gift of the Spirit," in Pontifical Council for the Laity, *Movements in the Church*, 77–104; "Movimenti ecclesiali e nuove comunità nella mission della Chiesa: collocazione teologica, prospettive pastorali e missionarie," in *Nuova Umanità* 31 (2009): 213–228.

communities that came to life at that time had a great influence in how the council was received. One such example would be Ignatius Loyola and the Jesuits.

In the same way, in the twenty-first century the whole People of God is being called to a faithful and creative reception of the teachings of Vatican II. Clearly, history will remember many distinguished pastors for their initiatives in this regard. The Spirit is certainly working through a renewed appreciation of charisms distributed among the lay faithful as they live out their baptismal priesthood. Coda notes, however, that there is nothing to stop the Holy Spirit, now, as then, from working in the Church not only through the widespread outpouring of charisms in baptism but also through special charisms in the form of new movements and communities.

The present age requires such an intervention. Coda, a Hegelian scholar, takes his cue for this conviction from contemporary cultural perspectives. He has identified the beginning of the twenty-first century as the end of modernity and the beginning of a clearly new but not yet well-defined epoch. Modernity has produced definite gains, especially its humanism centered on the subjectivity of the human being, an insight that has led the Church itself to a greater consciousness of the dignity, rights and freedom of the person. Nevertheless, as the era of modernity comes to a close civilization as a whole has realized that it needs something more. This affects the Church's own self-understanding and its communication of the reality of salvation.

The new planetary awareness of the human family, with its context of openness and reciprocal political, economic, cultural and spiritual respect, generates a new recognition that human differences of culture, tradition and religion need to be accepted, understood and managed. Coda reads Vatican II's ecclesiology against the horizon of this broad cultural agenda. Christian revelation suggests that "God and humanity, the I and the other, are not dialectical antagonists according to the dualistic logic of the servant/master (Hegel), but in Christ are accepted, revealed and redeemed in the space of the Trinitarian reciprocity: the reciprocity that subsists between Father, Son and Holy Spirit."[6]

---

6. Piero Coda, "The Ecclesial Movements," 92. See also John Paul II's Encyclical Letter, *Dives in misericordia*, n. 1, where he describes the linking of theocentrism and anthropocentrism as "one of the basic principles, perhaps the most important one, of the teaching of the last Council."

The Second Vatican Council's emphasis upon Trinitarian unity contributed to the Church's building up a culture of reciprocity that can mend civilization's tattered fabric of co-existence.[7] Word and sacrament generate, nourish, and guide the Church, which is serviced by ministry and charism. But the resultant communion is not just a sacramental and ontological fact. The community of disciples who constitute the Church are called in Christ to *live* a Trinitarian dynamic of communion among themselves and towards others in the spirit of the "new" commandment, the law of the people of God (see *Lumen gentium*, 9). This mystery-communion lived out among disciples is the sign and instrument for humanity of encounter with the Risen Christ. In the light of similar notions, Dietrich Bonhoeffer spoke of the Church as "the Christ who is present," Christ existing as community.[8]

According to Coda, the identity and mission of the gifts of the Spirit that animate the ecclesial movements should be read in this broad context of a new emerging culture of reciprocity. For all their limits, the movements' emergence is somehow a sign of the times, related to a new need that the experience of salvation be presented as a dynamic life of communion that begins to fulfill people already within history. In this sense, the movements give flesh to a missionary dynamic of communion, witness, proclamation and incarnation of the gospel in the pluralistic and multi-faceted context of the contemporary world. They express a "come and see" experience (see Jn 1:43–51) relevant to contemporary culture.

Coda suggests that a movement can offer an "event" that people experience in terms of reciprocal relationships among all the vocations of the baptized, who share equal baptismal dignity. This "event," itself a life-fulfilling experience of salvation, is an experience in miniature of the complementarity of the various vocations, ministries and charisms in the organically and hierarchically structured communion of the Church.

What Coda proposes, then, is that movements offer an experience of the *anthropological* dynamic inherent in the ecclesiology of communion. Communion means to be "one in Jesus Christ" (Gal 3:28), in that oneness "as I and the Father are one" (Jn 10:30). By being

---

7. See for instance *Lumen gentium*, 4; *Gaudium et spes*, 22 and 24.
8. See Brendan Leahy, " 'Christ Existing as Community': Dietrich Bonhoeffer's Notion of Church," in *Irish Theological Quarterly* 73 (2008): 32–59.

in communion in Christ Jesus, individuals become fully human in God's plan. Certainly, this is a grace that the Church transmits sacramentally. But "being in communion" is also something that Christians must learn, a journey upon which they need to embark in their everyday lives as they follow Jesus Christ and him crucified. Movements provide opportunities, as it were, for people to train or do exercises in a lifestyle of communion. The movements, then, are like modern communitarian forms of "spiritual exercises" in the dynamic of being-in-Christ.

In short, in the movements and new communities, faith assumes anthropological consistency and historical visibility. As such, within the limits of history not yet fully realized, the movements provide something of the experience described in the First Letter of St. John:

> We declare to you what was from the beginning, what we have heard, what we have seen with our eyes, what we have looked at and touched with our hands, concerning the word of life — this life was revealed, and we have seen it and testify to it … we declare to you what we have seen and heard so that you also may have fellowship with us; and truly our fellowship is with the Father and with his Son Jesus Christ. (1 Jn 1:1–3)

Unity before Distinction

Ian Ker, a respected Oxford scholar, has spent years researching the life and thought of John Henry Newman, leader within the Church of England of the famous nineteenth century Oxford movement. In Newman's thought, Ker finds a rich vein of insight and intuition that guides his reading of post Vatican II developments and the importance of movements in this context.[9]

His study of history showed Newman that councils are often moments of great trial for the Church — intrigue among those taking part in the council itself and the resistance that often rises up afterwards. Full understanding of such broad, deep events requires interpretation.

Newman pointed out that it took 300 years to digest and metabolize the Council of Trent; likewise the significance of Vatican I

---

9. Ian Ker, "New Movements and Communities," in *Louvain Studies* 27 (2002): 69–95. See also Ker, "Il dovere della pazienza: Newman e i Concili," in *L'Osservatore Romano* (Italian edition), November 26, 2010.

was not appreciated fully in its own day. The follow-up to a council requires far more than theologians working out the strength of a particular teaching, like lawyers parsing the acts of parliament. Rather, the voice of the whole Church has to be heard and Catholic attitudes and ideas have to assimilate and harmonize the teaching of the councils. Such a process demands patience, because the teaching of a council becomes more authentic gradually, as it emerges more clearly over the course of time. Ker believes the full significance of the Second Vatican Council will also emerge only over time.

Newman suggests that councils open up new directions not only by what they teach explicitly but also by what they do not say, emphasize, or state in a balanced manner. Vatican I, for instance, limited its teaching to the papacy. That council had planned to provide a teaching document on the broader notion of Church, but had to be suspended at the outbreak of the Franco-Prussian war and the capture of Rome by the Kingdom of Italy. The council, limited to only partial completion of its agenda, left much important work unfinished. That unfilled space, however, inaugurated a development in ecclesiology that almost a century later led to the Second Vatican Council's dogmatic constitution on the Church, *Lumen gentium*.

Ker explores how similar phenomena have followed Vatican II. It would be expected that as Church life unfolded in the wake of the council, or as new problems emerged, further developments would be required. In fact, that is what has happened. After Vatican II, the chapters in *Lumen gentium* on the hierarchy and laity gained particular attention. Because the abrupt conclusion to Vatican I had left undeveloped a statement concerning an overall vision of the Church, specifically the relation of bishops to the successor of Peter, and the status of the laity, Vatican II addressed these issues.

After Vatican II, however, in Ker's view, the significance of *Lumen gentium's* first chapter, "The Mystery of the Church" was not noticed. He believes that in the long run this chapter might be the most important text of the council. It provides the basis for a complete understanding of the Church as the People of God, a concept that initially after the council was "widely believed to be about the laity, whereas in actual fact it is about all the baptized, that is, all the members of the Church."[10] It was "of considerable

---

10. Ian Ker, "New Movements," 71.

importance for the revitalization of the Church"[11] that *Lumen gentium* did not begin by emphasizing the Church's hierarchical nature, as was normal prior to Vatican II, but by presenting its sacramental nature. The council did not speak of a division between clergy and laity, something quite different from the clericalized vision common before Vatican II. Instead, it highlighted "that the members of the Church are not first and foremost either clergy or laity but simply Christians who all initially receive the three sacraments of initiation, baptism, confirmation, and Eucharist."[12]

Pre-Vatican II clericalism unfortunately encouraged on the one hand anti-clericalism, and on the other undue deference to the clerical state and depreciation of the lay state. After the council, in Ker's view, there was a risk of the pendulum swinging toward a new kind of unilateral focus on the laity. The recovery at the council of the charismatic dimension "has tended to be sidelined because of a new preoccupation with the laity as opposed to the clergy."[13] Ker notes that the same deeply felt assumptions about the nature of the Church that existed prior to the council have persisted, although subtly. For many, the clerical/lay structural vision of the Church endures.

Ker considers the new movements and communities important because they represent an experience of the organic and unified community of the baptized as presented in the New Testament and *Lumen gentium*:

> This bringing together of all the baptized within one community and for a common mission is hugely significant. It is so unlike what Catholics have become accustomed to. For we might say that division rather than unity has been the practice, if not the theory. Catholics understand particular associations for particular groups of the laity.... They assume that priests too are grouped separately from other baptized Christians.[14]

Vatican II encouraged a new perspective, one that begins from the Church of all the baptized and then distinguishes how some serve the organic communion in particular ways. Ker finds the inclusivity of movements attractive. He notes that they "are not ageist, that is,

11. Ibid.
12. Ibid., 74.
13. Ibid., 76.
14. Ibid., 79.

they include the very elderly as well as children, which again sets them apart from other initiatives in collaborative ministry and committees for the bureaucracy of the institutional church."[15]

In *On Consulting the Lay Faithful in Matters of Doctrine*, Newman — as did other nineteenth century theologians — called attention to the organic communion among all the baptized, independent of any one person's particular status in the Church. He found this organic communion first described in the Church of the fourth century. For this reason Ker believes that Newman would have been particularly pleased to see how the first two chapters of *Lumen gentium* underline this communion. The Second Vatican Council also replaced the Thomistic expression *gratia gratis data* (grace freely given) with the term "charism," a transliteration of the New Testament Greek word "charisma." Although Newman did not use the term "charism," Ker considers the notion of special graces given to individuals for the benefit of the whole Church an important part of Newman's thought, both when he was Anglican and also as a Catholic. Newman saw in these graces the response of the Holy Spirit to the specific needs of the Church in a particular time, as exemplified in the contributions of Benedict and Dominic, Ignatius Loyola and Philip Neri. Without Ignatius of Loyola and the Society of Jesus, for example, it would be difficult to imagine how the reforms of the Council of Trent could have taken place. In Ker's view, Newman would have seen the ecclesial movements similarly in relationship to the reforms of Vatican II.

Evangelization

Ker observes that although Vatican II produced a decree on missionary activity, *Ad gentes*, it did not really develop the theme of evangelization. Just nine years after the council, Paul VI issued his call for evangelization, *Evangelii nuntiandi*. Ker considers the movements to be relevant in advancing this aspect, which was implicit in the council but developed afterwards. Piero Coda also considers the theme of evangelization as central in identifying the role and place of the movements in the Church. This topic will be developed further in Chapter 11.

---

15. Ibid., 78–79.

9

Institution – Charism

In its rediscovery of the charismatic principle in the Church, the Second Vatican Council established a parameter for reading and interpreting the place of the new ecclesial movements. In time, these movements came to be viewed as an expression of the Church's charismatic element, embedded in the very heart of its inner dynamic between institution and charism. On this basis, John Paul II spoke of them as an expression of the "co-essential" charismatic dimension of the Church:

> I have often had occasion to stress that there is no conflict or opposition in the Church between the institutional dimension and the charismatic dimension, of which the movements are a significant expression. Both are co-essential to the divine constitution of the Church founded by Jesus, because they both help to make the mystery of Christ and his saving work present in the world. Together they aim at renewing in their own ways the self-awareness of the Church, which in a certain sense can be called a "movement" herself, since she is the realization in time and space of the Father's sending of his Son in the power of the Holy Spirit.[1]

To explore more deeply this understanding of movements as an expression of the co-essential charismatic dimension of the Church, this chapter will trace briefly the history of the Church's own teaching and theological reflection on charisms, revisit the Second Vatican Council's teaching (with the assistance of Luigi Sartori and Albert Vanhoye) and then note some theological points made by two well-known twentieth century theologians, Karl Rahner and Avery Dulles.[2]

Charisms — A Historical Overview

The word "charism" is related to many Greek terms, including *charis* (grace) and *eucharistein* (to give thanks). The suffix, *-ma,* expresses the result of an action indicated by a verb. Broadly speaking,

---

1. John Paul II, Message to the World Congress, 19.
2. See also Giuseppe Rambaldi, "Carismi e laicato nella Chiesa. Teologia dei carismi, comunione e corresponsabilità dei laici nella Chiesa," in *Gregorianum* 68 (1987): 57–101.

in the New Testament the word signifies "gracious grace" or "gift," but its specific meaning depends upon the context where it appears.[3] Even though the New Testament recounts a great variety of God's gifts and uses the word charism in some significant texts, Albert Vanhoye points out that "these texts do not offer any clear teaching on what are today referred to as 'charisms.' ... It is not possible to demonstrate that the word charisma has technical sense in the New Testament."[4]

In the New Testament, Paul uses the word most frequently. He does so in reference to the gift of redemption and eternal life (Rom 5:15–16; 6:23) and to the gifts given to the people of Israel (Rom 11:29). Among charisms Paul also includes bodily healings (1 Cor 12:30) and the graces of the ministers of evangelization (1 Cor 12:8–10; 29–30; Rom 12:6–8), as well as the graces that establish a person in a way of life in the Church — virginity, marriage, pastoral ministry — conferred by the laying on of hands (1 Cor 7: 7; cf. 1 Tim 4: 14; 2 Tim 1:6).

Significantly, Paul uses the metaphor of the body and its members to show that the variety of gifts is not contrary to unity but necessary to it. It builds up the body of Christ. He lists charisms, placing that of the apostles first, those of the prophets second, and others after them (1 Cor 12:27–30). He notes how the Church in Corinth was abundantly favored with charisms (1 Cor 1:4–7; see 1 Cor 12:4–11). He mentions having heard of charisms in the Church of Rome, or having expected to find them there (Rom 12: 4–8). The letter to the Ephesians also contains a list (Eph 4:11–13). Paul is clear: charisms are given for the common good in Christ's body: "To each is given the manifestation of the Spirit for the common good" (1 Cor 12:7).

In the second century, Irenaeus uses the word "charism" for any gift of divine grace, including the Holy Spirit. In reaction to the exaggerated spiritualism of Montanism and Gnostics who rejected the incarnation, denigrated the flesh, and downplayed Church structures, Irenaeus reflects on the whole dynamic of the economy of salvation, underlining the link between the Holy Spirit and the Church. In that regard, he notes that the charisms of the Spirit are placed in the Church, who is kept ever young by the Spirit.

---

3. See Gerhard Kittel, *Theological Dictionary of the New Testament* (Grand Rapids, MI: Eerdmans, 1964), Vol. 9: 402–407.

4. See Albert Vanhoye, "The Biblical Question of 'Charisms' after Vatican II," in René Latourelle, *Vatican II: Assessment and Perspectives: Twenty-Five Years After* (1962–1987), Vol. 1 (Mahwah, NJ: Paulist Press, 1988), 439–468 at 464.

[The faith transmitted by the Church] by work of the Holy Spirit, like a precious deposit contained in a valuable vase, is ever rejuvenated and also rejuvenates the vase that contains it. To the Church, in fact, was entrusted the gift of God (see Jn 4:10) like a breath that is blown into the living being shaped from the soil of the ground (see Gen 2:7), so that all her members, by participating in it, are vivified by it; and in her has been deposited the communion with Christ, that is the Holy Spirit... In fact, "God has appointed, in the Church first apostles, second prophets, third teachers" (see 1 Cor 12:28) and imbued her with all the remaining operation of the Spirit (see 1 Cor 12:11).... For where the Church is, there too is the Spirit of God; and where the Spirit of God is, there too are the Church and every form of grace.[5]

With the rise of monasticism, the charismatic dimension emerges not simply as a dimension *of* the Church or in reference to bearers of charisms, but also in the more specific sense as a structure *in* the Church, a charismatic communitarian expression within the Church. In the fourth and fifth centuries, however, because of a wary attitude regarding charisms associated with extraordinary phenomena and exaggerations found in the heretical spiritualist Montanist movement, as well as because of the increasing numbers of Christians and the many Christological and Trinitarian theological issues that had to be resolved, theological reflection on charisms grows scant. If anything, a wariness of charisms enters in. Augustine hardly touched on the topic.[6] Over time a sense emerges, as expressed for instance by Pope Gregory the Great (590–604), that the charismatic outpouring was linked to the early beginnings or Golden Age of the apostolic era of the Church.

With the rise of the mendicant religious orders and the need to discern the authenticity of new experiences that were appearing in

---

5. *Adversus Haereses* 3:24.1, ed. A. Rousseau and L. Doutreleau, *Sources chrétiennes*, vol. 211 (Paris: Cerf, 1974): 472–475 as translated in P. Coda, "The Ecclesial Movements," 82. See further Brendan Leahy, " 'Hiding behind the Works': the Holy Spirit in the Trinitarian Rhythm of Human Fulfilment in the Theology of Irenaeus," in Vincent Twomey and Janet E. Rutherford, *The Holy Spirit in the Fathers of the Church: The Proceedings of the Seventh International Patristic Conference, Maynooth, 2008* (Dublin: Four Courts Press, 2010): 11–31.

6. E. D. O'Connor believes Augustine never used the term "charism." See "The New Theology of Charisms in the Church," in *The American Ecclesiastical Review* 161 (1969): 145–159 at 147.

the Medieval Age (for instance the case of St. Brigid of Sweden's private revelations), a new interest in charisms and their discernment grew up. In its theology, the Medieval Latin commentators and teachers did not use the word "charism," but rather "gratia" or grace. They distinguished between the gifts of the Holy Spirit necessary for salvation, i.e. the gifts that arise from sanctifying grace (*gratiae gratum faciens*, grace making gracious) and other gifts of the Spirit called gratuitous gifts (*gratiae gratis data*, grace freely given and conferred on a person or group for the salvation of others).[7] These latter correspond to what we today call "charisms."[8]

St. Thomas Aquinas (1225–1274) also distinguishes between sanctifying grace and gratuitous gifts (*gratiae gratis datae*). He notes the usefulness of the latter for spreading and confirming the faith. He places his treatment of them right in the heart of his treatise on morality, as if to underline their centrality in the life of the Church. Reflecting on the life of the Spirit in the lives of the faithful and in the Church,[9] Aquinas presents the Holy Spirit as the soul vivifying the body which is the Church, giving efficacy to all ministries and sacraments in the Church. He uses two key words to describe the work of the Spirit in human beings. By "inhabitation," the Spirit dwells within them and by "innovation" makes them new. Answering whether the Spirit can be sent to a person in whom the third divine Person is already indwelling, and if so, how this is to be understood, Aquinas answers: "There is an invisible sending also with respect to an advance in virtue or an increase of grace ... Such an invisible sending is especially to be seen in that kind of increase of grace whereby a person moves forward into some new act or some new state of grace."[10] (On this basis, in the 1980s Francis Sullivan concluded that "there is no reason why Catholics,

---

7. See *Summa Theologica*, I–II, q. 111, aa. 1–4. See also *Summa Theologica* I–II, q. 111 2–2 ae, qq. 171–174, 176–178; *Summa c. Gentiles* III: 154; *In Rom* 12, lect. 2 (976–982); *In 1 Cor* 12 and 14; *In Eph* 4, lect. 4 (210–212); *In Heb* 2, lect. 1 (99). The gifts of the Spirit (wisdom, knowledge, etc.) are also distinct from these graces.

8. See H. Schürmann's article on the spiritual gifts of grace where he recalls the great and radiant charisms of Benedict, Francis, Ignatius and others, noting the light and effects that came from them to the Church. See "I doni spirituali della grazia," in G. Baraúna, *La Chiesa del Vaticano II* (Florence: Vallecchi, 1965), 561–588, at 579.

9. See E. Stiegman, "Charism and Institution in Aquinas," in *Thomist* 38 (1974): 723–733. See also Jean-Pierre Torrell, *Saint Thomas Aquinas*. Vol 2: *Spiritual Master*. Trans. Robert Royal (Washington, DC: The Catholic University of America Press, 2003), 213–214.

10. *Summa Theologica* I, q. 43, a.6, ad 2.

who believe that they have already received the Holy Spirit in their sacramental initiation, should not look forward to a new 'sending' of the Spirit to them, which would move them from the 'state of grace' in which they already are into some 'new act' or 'new state of grace.' "[11])

After the Middle Ages, theological reflection on the topic of charisms was limited, in no small part because theology and spirituality had a certain parting of the ways. Increasingly, charismatic experiences such as those associated with the rise of the mendicant orders and those manifest in later founders such as Teresa of Avila and Ignatius of Loyola came to be viewed from a hagiographical and spiritual perspective. The theological impact of their religious experience and charism for ecclesiology received little consideration. Instead, these founders and their followers were understood as having been endowed with exceptional and miraculous gifts, typically given in extraordinary fashion only to mystics and saints. In addition, the polemics that arose in the centuries after the Reformation drove the ecclesiologies of the Reformation and Counter-Reformation to focus principally on institutional issues, leaving scant attention to charism.

In the nineteenth century, however, the German legal theorist R. Sohm (1841–1917) explored anew the notion of "charism."[12] Applying the concept of charismatic organization to the Church, he proposed that the early Church was purely a spiritual and charismatic body, governed by the word and charismatic leadership. Only subsequently did charism get transformed into office. Though his thesis met with controversy (his proposal that institutional aspects of the Church such as canon law should be rejected as an abandonment of the early ideal of Christianity was considered clearly too radical) it did highlight the active role of the Spirit in the Church.

In reaction to Sohm's thesis, the German theologian and church historian, Adolf von Harnack (1851–1930), contended that the early Church contained two types of ministry — the universal charismatic and the local administrative. He gave priority to the charismatic. Following von Harnack, Protestant liberalism tended to emphasize the charismatic, prophetical and purely personal community, whereas

---

11. Francis Sullivan, *Charism*, 71–72.
12. See Enrique Nardoni, "Charism in the Early Church since Rudolph Sohm: An Ecumenical Challenge," in *Theological Studies* 53 (1992): 646–662.

the Catholic neo-scholastic tradition underlined the institutional and hierarchical principle in the Church.

The sociologist and political economist Max Weber (1864–1920), also drawing upon Sohm's work, defined charism as "a certain quality of an individual personality by virtue of which he is set apart from ordinary men and treated as endowed with supernatural, superhuman, or at least specifically exceptional qualities."[13] Charismatic authority, he wrote, is distinct from traditional authority based on the past and from rational authority based on the need for administration. Charismatic authority is founded on the inspiration of a leader or exercised by a charismatic group or band. The charismatic leader or group transforms a given institutional setting by infusing into it charismatic vision and aura. In this light too, writing on the sociology of religion, Weber interprets religion as originating through a charismatic surge, usually most intense during the charismatic founder's lifetime. Afterward, institutionalization and bureaucratization set in.

At the same time in history, the language of charism was beginning to re-appear in Church documents. The First Vatican Council (1869–1870) mentions "charism" in an apologetic sense, linking it to the role of the hierarchy and the Roman pontiff's prerogative of infallibility. The reference in Vatican I was Christological: in instituting the Church, Jesus Christ promised to assist Peter and gave him the grace to do so.

Pius XII referred to charism in the encyclical *Mystici corporis* (1943) and again at the canonization of Pius X. On the one hand, he presents charism in terms of a miraculous gift that relates to the extraordinary phenomena associated with saints and mystics. On the other hand, however, he also broadens the notion of charism, underlining gifts given for the Church as a whole. In other words, charisms have an ecclesial role. Viewing the Church as an organic body, he speaks of charism as an element, indeed almost a principle of the structure of the Church and affirms: "One must not think, however, that this ordered or 'organic' structure of the body of the Church contains only hierarchical elements and with them is complete; or, as an opposite opinion holds, that it is composed only of those who enjoy

---

13. See *The Theory of Social and Economic Organization*. Translated by A. M. Henderson and Talcott Parsons (New York: Oxford University Press, 1947), 329. For Max Weber's thought on charism and institution see S. N. Eisenstadt's collection of selected papers in *Max Weber: On Charism and Institution Building* (Chicago and London: University of Chicago Press, 1968).

charismatic gifts —though members gifted with miraculous powers will never be lacking in the Church."[14] Pius XII seems to believe that charisms can be found also on the more general level of ecclesial life. Jesus Christ, he affirms, foresaw and ordered both the charismatic and institutional aspects, both equally informed by the Holy Spirit.

Pius XII clearly recognizes the creator Spirit always at work in the Church — not just in the early Church — and believes in the free action of the Spirit throughout its history, distributing gifts also outside the hierarchy. Nevertheless, Pius XII gives clear priority neither to the hierarchic nor to the charismatic. On the one hand he writes that it must be held uncompromisingly that "those who exercise sacred power in this Body are its chief members,"[15] but he also asserts that as the human body is inferior to the soul, "so the social structure of the Christian community, though it proclaims the wisdom of its divine Architect, still remains something inferior when compared to the spiritual gifts which give it beauty and life, and to the divine source whence they flow."[16]

In the 1950s another development, especially in Germany, focused attention on the theme of charism in its relation to Church; as a consequence, the theology of charism became a point of lively theological interest even before the Second Vatican Council. Scripture scholars began to reflect on the issue of charism and institution in the Church as reflected in the early Church. Many found particular inspiration in Ernst Käsemann, a Lutheran scripture scholar who argues that in contrast with the idea of institutionally-guaranteed offices in the Church, Paul maintained a doctrine of charisms. In Käsemann's view the New Testament contains a dialectic between charism and institution. The ecclesiology evident in Paul's letters emphasizes the Spirit and charisms, whereas the Deuteropauline letters, the pastoral letters, and Luke's writings focus on the authority of ministers typical of a "proto-catholicism." Influenced by Sohm and von Harnack, Käsemann maintains that the early Church made a clear distinction between "charismatic ministers" and "administrative ministers."[17]

Inspired by Käsemann, the Catholic theologian Hans Küng described the community at Corinth as a good example of a "charismatic

---

14. *Mystici corporis*, 17. AAS 35 (1943): 200; see 47, ibid., 215.
15. Ibid.
16. Ibid., 63.
17. See Ernst Käsemann, "Ministry and Communion in the New Testament," in *Essays on New Testament Themes* (SBT 41; London: SCM, 1964).

organization," the expression of the "Pauline constitution of the Church."[18] On this basis he then sought to describe the charismatic structure of the Church:

> The charismata are not primarily extraordinary but common; they are not of one kind, but manifold; they are not limited to a special group of persons, but truly universal in the Church. All this implies that they are not a thing of the past (possible and real only in the early Church), but eminently contemporary and actual; they do not hover on the periphery of the Church but are eminently central and essential to it. In this sense one should speak of a charismatic structure of the Church which embraces and goes beyond the structure of its government.[19]

Küng's ecclesiology, which underlines charism, offered new directions. In a sense he turned the then prevailing Catholic perspective upside-down by affirming the charismatic origin and dimension of the Church's hierarchical structure. While this approach helps in clarifying that there is no structural contradiction between charism and institution, Küng's thesis risks giving the impression, however, that institutional ministry in its present form is the result of a decline in true charismatic origins. In other words, Küng overly idealizes a charismatic springtime in the early Church.[20]

Vatican II

The documents of the Second Vatican Council make fifteen direct references to the notion of charism, not including the many other cognate terms or notions such as "gift," "graces," "operations," "virtues," "ministry," "vocation," "munera" (office). Accordingly, the Italian theologian Luigi Sartori contends that in the Council's documents a wealth of texts, around a hundred, could be said to refer to the theme of charisms.[21] As Chapter 4 mentioned, there was

---

18. See Hans Küng, "The Charismatic Structure of the Church," in *Concilium* 4 (1965): 23–33 and *The Church* (London: Search Press, 1968).
19. "The Charismatic Structure," 30–31.
20. A disciple of Küng's developed this thesis in a more radical manner. See G. Hasenhüttl, *Charisma: Ordnungsprinzip der Kirche* (Freiburg, 1969). L. Boff also took this up in *Igreja: Carisma e Poder* (Petropolis, 1981).
21. Sartori, "Carismi" in Giuseppe Barbaglio and Severino Dianich (eds.), *Nuovo Dizionario di Teologia* (Milan: Paoline, 1988), 79–98, at 91.

a controversial debate on this issue at the Council. Nevertheless, Vatican II teaches clearly that, as Rino Fisichella puts it, "the prophets and the prophetic charism can't be relegated hastily only to the period of the primitive Church; they are always a constituent part of the Church and always possess a permanent and irreplaceable significance for the Church."[22] The prominence that the Council gives to charisms is a theologically important fact. There is a clear distinction — but not an opposition — between institution and charism. The charisms are described as endowing people with a readiness and willingness to undertake activities helpful to the Church. Charisms are given to the "faithful of every order" — not just to laity or to ordained ministers but to both laity and ordained ministers.

Charisms within a Trinitarian Ecclesiology

As already noted, the Second Vatican Council presents a Christo-centric and Trinitarian vision of the Church. Created to mirror Christ who leads the faithful in the Spirit to the bosom of the Father, the Church is the realm of mutual being-for-one-another in a way that resembles the life of the Trinity. The Spirit is the principle of the Church's dynamic unity. The third divine person maintains the Church as a movement of eternal youthfulness awaiting the coming Christ: "The Spirit and the Bride say to the Lord Jesus: Come!" (Rev 22:17; LG 4).

Charisms, given by the Spirit, play an important role in this eschatological tension in the Church guided by the Spirit towards its fulfillment at the end of time.[23] They allow for the distinctiveness of diverse ways of building up the one body of Christ as it strives towards its fulfillment when God will be "all in all." The unity of the Church, in other words, is understood eschatologically as the recapitulation, gathering and appreciation of the multiform grace of God as it moves towards the full and perfect life that is full participation in the triune life of God.

The Council encourages attentiveness to the "most simple and common" charisms.[24] In so doing it underscores the variety of gifts as distinct aspects linked to the freedom of each baptized person.

---

22. See Rino Fisichella, "Prophecy," in René Latourelle and Rino Fisichella (eds.), *Dictionary of Fundamental Theology* (New York: Crossroad, 1994), 795.
23. Sartori, "Carismi," 93.
24. *Lumen gentium*, 12.

As Sartori puts it, "The Church has to be able to present itself to the world as a life that does not mortify, nor flatten from fear, nor surround with suspicion, nor level out the variety of gifts and values that the Spirit gives rise to within the Church, but rather it has to be able to promote it. In other words, the Church must present itself as the place of authentic freedom in charity."[25]

Apart from underlining the simple charisms given to all the baptized, Vanhoye notes another significant application of the notion of charism. The New Testament does not use the word "charism" as linked to apostolic communities, but the Council applies Pauline expressions that contain the term "charism" to contemporary apostolic communities, their founders and spiritualities. "(The New Testament) does not speak of the charisms of founders of religious orders or of the charisms of different religious institutions. It is the history of the Church that leads the Council to apply the words of Romans 12:5–8 and 1 Corinthians 12:4 to them. Reference to the New Testament remains the norm, not in the sense of an obstacle to development, but in that of dynamic inspiration accompanied by discernment."[26]

The concept of charism, in other words, was viewed in the Council not only in an individual sense (as in 1 Cor 12:7–10: "to one … to another …") but also in a communitarian sense, attaching to a community or institution and lasting over time. Tony Hanna writes of new ecclesial movements as "collective charisms," or founding charisms "to be constantly lived, conserved, deepened and developed in harmony with the Body of Christ which is in constant growth. Collective charisms … can be … open to new forms of presence and expression in different historical circumstances."[27]

Charism and Hierarchy

The Council affirms that different charisms should be welcomed "with gratitude and consolation" but also states that "judgment as to their genuineness and proper use belongs to those who are appointed leaders in the Church, to whose special competence it belongs, not in-

---

25. Ibid.
26. See Albert Vanhoye, "The Biblical Question of 'Charisms' after Vatican II," in René Latourelle, *Vatican II: Assessment and Perspectives*, 439–468 at 465. Rom 12:5–8 and 1 Cor 12:4 are cited *Perfectae caritatis*, October 28, 1965, n. 8.
27. See Tony Hanna, *Ecclesial Movements*, 187. See Apostolic Letter on the Renewal of Religious Life, *Evangelica testificatio* (June 29, 1971), 11–12.

deed to extinguish the Spirit, but to test all things and hold fast to that which is good (see 1 Thes 5:12 and 19–21)."[28] Interestingly, Sartori remarks that the Second Vatican Council was held in an atmosphere of optimistic recovery of trust in charisms. It wasn't particularly concerned about the issue of the criteria of discernment. It is simply stated in a generic sense that the judgment regarding the genuineness of charisms is up to the hierarchy. St. Paul's warning about the discernment of spirits is referred to but without giving precise norms.

Yet it is clear that Vatican II's ecclesiology promoted communion not confusion. As St. Paul states: "God is a God not of disorder but of peace" (1 Cor 14:33). Neither the New Testament nor Vatican II warrants a contrast between inspiration and institution, charism and structure, prophecy and authority. Paul himself, in addressing the community at Corinth, established that there is a variety of charisms but this variety is always in view of the common good; he also explained that God had established a hierarchy of positions and a multiplicity of gifts. To view charism and hierarchy in opposition is a departure from Pauline categories. Institutional and charismatic aspects within the Church can be distinguished, but they cannot be separated completely or viewed as countering one another. Albert Vanhoye states:

> The Church is the body of Christ and, as such, the temple of the Holy Spirit. The institutional dimension of the body "is joined and knit together by every ligament with which it is equipped" (Eph 4:16; cf. 2:20–21) and in the concrete condition of authentic communion "in the Spirit" (Eph 2:22). The Church thus is a charismatic-institutional structure, formed by means of the sacraments, in which institution and grace are closely united by virtue of the mystery of the incarnation.[29]

The Primacy of Love

Echoing Paul, the Council also points to a central theme that underlies any consideration of the relationship of charism and institution — charity. Love, in fact, is the prime principle of the whole life of the Church. It is at the heart of the sacramentality of the Church. A

---

28. *Lumen gentium*, 12. Cf., *Lumen gentium,* 7 and *Presbyterorum ordinis*, 9.
29. See "Charism" in René Latourelle and Rino Fisichella, *Dictionary of Fundamental Theology*, 103–108, at 106.

charism is authentic not only if it expresses charity but also if it contributes to making the general charism of the Church emerge, that is, its nature as *the* gift of love offered by Christ to humanity. Ultimately, true charisms serve to love, to build up the Church so that it may be for the world a sign and instrument of unity and salvation in Christ.[30]

Love becomes an art to be lived both by those entrusted with the task of investigating and judging the authenticity of charisms as well as by those endowed with new charisms to be communicated to the whole Church. With regard to those whose task it is to discern the authenticity of charisms, Alois Grillmeier acknowledges this task is "one of the most difficult arts in the guidance of men and Churches, and though final judgment rests with the holders of office, this does not dispense or exclude the faithful as a whole from being involved in the duty of investigation."[31] With regard to founders or communities and by extension, members of movements, Castellano Cervera describes what is required as a great love for the Church, "the passion to serve (the Church), the true sense of the Church, the 'feeling with the Church' and the feeling Church (*sentire Ecclesiam*)."[32]

In consoling fashion, when the Council declares that "the Spirit instructs and directs the Church with different hierarchical and charismatic gifts,"[33] it is also issuing a reminder that hierarchical gifts are also gifts of the Spirit. Through the action of the Spirit pastors are made "fit and ready to assume" their ecclesial responsibilities in a personal, spiritual fashion. This is a point Benedict XVI often underlines. Bishops, priests and deacons receive charism through sacramental ordination.

Ultimately, any reflection on the interaction of charism and institution in terms of love needs to draw on the model of all love — the triune God. The German theologian and bishop Klaus Hemmerle, writing expressly in reference to the new ecclesial movements, suggests exercising the dynamic of *perichoresis* (a lively, ever new, mutual dwelling in one another) in the mutual relationships of institutional office holders and charismatics in the Church:

---

30. Sartori, "Carismi," 94.

31. "The People of God," in *Commentary on the Documents of Vatican II,* ed. Herbert Vorgrimler, 5 vols. (London: Burns & Oates, 1967), 153–85, at 166.

32. J. Castellano Cervera, "I movimenti ecclesiali. Una presenza carismatica della Chiesa di oggi," in *Rivista di vita spirituale* 4–5 (1987); 495–518, at 509.

33. *Lumen gentium,* 4.

Since both institution and charism belong to the Church in a constitutional manner, the Church is thereby constitutionally placed in a tension between the institutional aspect that must integrate continually the charism and the charism must revive continually and unsettle the institutional aspect. It is therefore neither possible to contain the spiritual movements through a simple regulation nor break the historical continuity and ecclesial structures in the name of early Christianity. The great and dramatic task is called reciprocal *perichoresis*.[34]

Karl Rahner

The theological writings of Karl Rahner (1904–1984) were important in the reception of the Council's doctrine on charisms. Already in the 1940s he had written on charism and institution. Just before the Council he wrote on what he called "the dynamic element in the Church." Sartori concludes that while Rahner starts out with an understanding of charism more in the sense of extraordinary, miraculous gifts he ends up explaining it in terms of normal and personal gifts of the baptized.[35] Charisms may be extraordinary but they also become daily bread, normal and usual in the life of the Church. Though not referring directly to new ecclesial movements as such, Rahner's theology and commentary on charisms is important in interpreting their significance.

Taking as his starting point God's self-communication in the history of salvation that culminates in Jesus Christ, Rahner reflects on how the encounter between divine freedom and human freedom embraced within the Son of God incarnate, Jesus Christ, is communicated through the Church, the primordial sacrament of Christ in the world. He asks how in history God assures the victory of grace. The ordinary way is that of institution, the fixed, unchanging form, the element and principle of continuity and stability in the Church. Two clear expressions of this would be infallibility and the efficacy "*ex opere operato*" of the sacraments. Charism, on the other hand, represents the varying,

---

34. K. Hemmerle, "Im Austausch Gestalt gewinnen. Nach-Denkenswertes zur Bishofssynode 1987 über 'Die Berufung und Sendung der Laien in Kirche und Welt,'" in E. J. Kirkenbeil (eds.), *Miteinander Kirche sein. Idee und Praxis* (Munich, 1990), 11–18, at 15.
35. Sartori, "Carismi," 85.

changing and unexpected side of the Church's dynamic renewal
and movement.

In other words, as well as the institutional forms of mediating
the life of grace, there exist charisms that equip members of the
Church in the freedom of their human response to the Christ event
to carry out tasks within the life of the pilgrim community. Or
put another way still, there are charisms of office (since ordained
ministry is itself charism!) and also free spontaneous charisms that
correspond to each individual's immediate relationship to God.
Rahner contends that charism guarantees the institution in the
sense that human freedom is weak and defective but through God's
action in a charism a person is enabled to be faithful in freedom to
living under the institution.

The Holy Spirit is always active in the history of the Church,
leading to a constant, ongoing discovery of the newness of Jesus
Christ. Through charisms, the Church grows and develops in the
way she understands herself and the way she organizes herself. For
this reason, Rahner contends there is a need to open the structure
of the Church so that charisms, vis-à-vis the institutional side of
the Church, can work as renewing ferment.

In terms of the interaction of charism and institution, Rahner
observes that while the Church might be able to maneuver and administer institution, when it comes to charism it has to leave room for
God's ever new and original initiative regarding both the coming to
life of the charism itself and the way it is to be established in relation
to the institution:

> [T]the charismatic is essentially new and always surprising. To
> be sure it also stands in inner though hidden continuity with
> what came earlier in the Church and fits in with her spirit and
> with her institutional framework. Yet it is new and incalcu-
> lable, and it is not immediately evident at first sight that ev-
> erything is as it was in the enduring totality of the Church. For
> often it is only through what is new that it is realized that the
> range of the Church was greater from the outset than had pre-
> viously been supposed. And so the charismatic feature, when
> it is new, and one might say it is only charismatic if it is so,
> has something shocking about it. It can be mistaken for facile

enthusiasm, a hankering after change, attempted subversion, lack of feeling for tradition and for the well-tried experience of the past.[36]

Avery Dulles

The late Avery Cardinal Dulles has been acclaimed as "perhaps the most productive and respected American Catholic theologian of our time."[37] To borrow the title of one of his last McGinley Lectures, his theological writings reflect "the Ignatian charism at the dawn of the twenty-first century." Robert Imbelli comments that "in Dulles, the oft-lauded Catholic 'both/and' approach found an exemplary practitioner. He was steadfast in his fidelity to *Lumen gentium's* insistence that the church of Christ consists of two inseparable dimensions: the charismatic and the institutional. To speak of the 'institutional church' as though there were some other, purely spiritual church preserved in Platonic perfection would be fantasy."[38]

His 1992 book *The Craft of Theology: From Symbol to System* offers a summary of his ecclesial vision:

> As a great sacrament it [the Church] extends in space and time the physical body of the Lord. It is not a mere pointer to the absent Christ, but the symbolic manifestation of the present Christ. The members of Christ, insofar as they are remade in Christ's image by the power of the Holy Spirit, represent Christ to one another and to the world. He identifies himself with them. Especially is this true of the saints, those who allow themselves to be totally transformed in Christ. The Church, in its most basic reality, is a holy fellowship built up through the self-communication of the triune God.[39]

---

36. See Karl Rahner, *The Dynamic Element in the Church* (Freiburg: Herder; London: Burns & Oates, 1964), 83.
37. See Patrick W. Carey, "Cardinal Avery Dulles, S.J., Among the Theologians: A Memorial Reflection," in *Theological Studies* 71 (2010): 773–791. See also Robert Imbelli, "Model of the Church: Cardinal Avery Dulles, S.J.," in *Commonweal*, January 16, 2009.
38. Imbelli, "Model of the Church."
39. *The Craft of Theology: From Symbol to System* (New York: Crossroad, 2001), 35.

Though his *Models of the Church* contains surprisingly few references to charisms,[40] Dulles dedicates an important chapter of *A Church to Believe in: Discipleship and the Dynamics of Freedom*[41] to this theme. He clearly outlines his view that institutional elements of the Church exist because of and to serve the charismatic, and that the charismatic elements are not for individual aggrandizement but for communal growth and well-being.

Attempting to synthesize various magisterial and theological approaches to the issue of the interrelationship of institution and charism, Dulles reflects on the topic in terms of how the lordship of Christ, present in the power of the Spirit, is exercised over the Church.

The institutional and the charismatic are irreducibly distinct aspects of the Church in its pilgrim condition. Both aspects pertain to the wayfaring Church. The institutional element in the Church satisfies the public, regular, and officially approved teaching, sanctifying, and pastoral functions. The charismatic gifts are free graces imparted according to the good pleasure of the Holy Spirit, as well as spiritual gifts endowed upon people for their office, state of life and social responsibilities: "It is characteristic of the Holy Spirit to be a source of creativity, energy, enthusiasm and freedom."[42]

The dialectical tension between institution and charism must be understood in the framework of the Church as sacrament. The Church as a whole is a sign of Christ and his grace. The institutional elements externally signify what the Church represents and effects in the world. The charismatic aspect is no less essential than the institutional because different individuals appropriate the grace of Christ in various ways: "The Church ... would not be truly Church without both the institutional features, whereby it manifests its own abiding essence, and the charismatic features, whereby God efficaciously transforms the interiority of concrete persons."[43]

The Church never has been, and never can be, without institutional elements. The Church never has been, and never can be, without charismatic elements. A Church without charisms could only be a Church without

---

40. *Models of the Church : A Critical Assessment of the Church in All its Aspects.* Second Edition (Dublin: Gill and Macmillan, 1988).
41. *Models of the Church,* 19–40.
42. "Institution and Charism," 30.
43. Ibid., 31.

grace. Charisms and institutions seem to have grown concurrently, most strikingly in the period after Pentecost. The charismatic lives off the institutional. The institutional in the Church lives off the charismatic.

Ideally, the institutional and charismatic dimensions are in a mutually responsive, open relationship involving correction, gratitude and conciliation. Clashes can arise, however. Avery Dulles points out that in exceptional situations it may be necessary that charismatically gifted leaders take responsibility for resisting the official leadership. He recognizes, however, that the office-holders have the final word, since it is their function to discern the true and false charisms. But the charismatic dimension can indeed help offset the vocational hazards of the official side of the Church, maintaining the institution's flexibility. In doing so, however, charismatic figures must be mindful that "criticism ... can have no place in the Church unless it proceeds from faith, from love, and from the recognition of the rights of office, and unless it aims to build up the body of Christ in unity."[44] Dulles concludes that there is no ultimate juridical solution to collisions and tensions that can arise between institution and charism. The Church, after all, is not a totalitarian system. Rather, "all must recognize their limitations and treat the others with patience, respect and charity."[45]

Conclusion

This chapter has explored the significance of charisms, particularly how charism and institution are co-essential in the life of the Church. John Paul II and others have presented the dynamic between charism and institution as a way of putting in proper context the phenomenon of movements in the Church today. The last word, perhaps, belongs to one of the great bearers of a charism in the history of the Church — Francis of Assisi. Like other founders of great movements of reform such as Benedict, Ignatius of Loyola, and Teresa of Avila, Francis was a devoted servant of the Church in its institutional or hierarchical-sacramental dimension. Immersed in the heritage of the Church they were able to love, transform and renew it. In his testament of 1226, the year of his death, Francis writes:

---

44. Ibid., 37.
45. Ibid., 38.

Afterwards the Lord gave me, and gives me still, such faith in priests who live according to the rite of the holy Roman Church because of their order that, were they to persecute me, I would still want to have recourse to them. And if I had as much wisdom as Solomon and found impoverished priests of this world, I would not preach in the parishes against their will. I desire to respect, love, and honor them and all others as my lords. And I do not want to consider any sin in them because I discern the Son of God in them and they are my lords. And I act in this way because, in this world, I see nothing corporally of the Most High Son of God except His most holy Body and Blood which they receive and they alone administer to others.[46]

---

46. Francis of Assisi, *The Saint* (Francis of Assisi: Early Documents, vol. 1); edited by Regis J. Armstrong, J. A. Wayne Hellmann, William J. Short (New York: New City Press, 1999), 125.

10

Movements and Apostolic Succession

In his May 1998 address to the World Congress of Ecclesial Movements, Cardinal Joseph Ratzinger suggested that movements be considered an expression of apostolic succession. In many ways this talk remains the "Magna Carta" for a theological and ecclesiological reading of the movements. This chapter offers an exposition of Ratzinger's main points, recognizing that that theme of apostolic succession is much discussed, particularly in the fields of ecumenism and Church ministry.[1]

Unsatisfactory Dialectic Approaches

In the first part of his talk Cardinal Ratzinger acknowledges both the value of and the limitations of different interpretative keys. For instance, although the institution-charism duality might seem the most useful model for thinking through the theological place of movements, it risks setting up a dialectic between institution and charism; such an "antithesis between the two terms gives no satisfactory description of the reality of the Church."[2] Although the Church indeed does contain institutions of primarily human and sociological origin that carry out various roles of administration, organization and co-ordination, its fundamental institutional structure is linked with the sacramental ministry, which is itself a gift of the Spirit. The dialectic breaks down because the service of bishops, priests and deacons itself is charismatic, that is, a gift of the Spirit.

---

1. See William Henn, "The Hermeneutics of Apostolicity: The Lutheran and Roman Catholic Responses to the Faith and Order Document, *Baptism, Eucharist and Ministry*"; and Gerald O'Collins, "Origins of Apostolic Continuity in the New Testament," in F. Chica et al, *Ecclesia Tertii Millennii Advenientis* (Casale Monferrato: Piemme, 1997), 741–754 and 830–841 respectively. See also Francis Sullivan, *From Apostles to Bishops: The Development of the Episcopacy in the Early Church* (New York: The Newman Press, 2001).
2. "The Ecclesial Movements," 28. For a critique of ecclesiologies based on an interpretation of charism and institution as dialectical opposition between the individual and authority, see E. D. O'Connor, "Charisme et Institution," *NRT* 106 (1974): 3–19.

The Church comes into existence first and foremost by God's call, in other words, at the charismatic and pneumatological level through the sacraments. Because the Church comes into being through divine means, it cannot be interpreted through institutional or sociological criteria alone. Indeed, Ratzinger notes that if we attempt to distinguish between institution and charism, the concept of institution "falls to bits in our hands as soon as we try to give it a precise theological connotation."[3] Institution is charism! Ratzinger concludes, moreover, that in order to prevent institutional hardening, sacramental ministry must be charismatically understood and lived. The Church "must not over-institutionalize herself."[4]

He then examines the dialectic between the Christological and pneumatological view of the Church in contemporary theology. Some maintain that sacraments belong to the Christological-incarnational aspect of the Church, supplemented by its pneumatological-charismatic dimension. Here again, however, Ratzinger sees a limit. Understood dialectically, such a distinction again seems to fall to pieces. A distinction does need to be drawn between Christ and the Spirit; nevertheless, "Just as the three persons of the Trinity should be treated not as a communion of three gods, but as the one triune God, so the distinction between Christ and Spirit can be rightly understood only when their diversity helps us better to understand their unity."[5] The Spirit cannot be rightly understood without Christ and Christ cannot be rightly understood without the Spirit. Moreover, examining the inter-relationship between the Spirit and the Risen-crucified Christ as reflected in the Tradition, Ratzinger arrives at the need to reflect on the theme of apostolic succession. He returns to this relationship as a main concept in answering his initial question of how best to understand movements in the Church.

A third model that might interpret and explain the relationship between the sacramental-institutional side of the Church and the ever-new irruptions of the Spirit is hierarchy and prophecy. As Ratzinger puts it, "Building on Luther's interpretation of Scripture in terms of the dialectic of Law and Gospel, there are those who place particular stress on the dialectic between the cultic-sacerdotal aspect on the one hand and

---

3. Ibid., 25.
4. Ibid., 29.
5. Ibid., 30.

the prophetic aspect of salvation history on the other."[6] From such a perspective, movements would be an expression of the prophetic aspect. This interpretation, he feels, has value but "It is extremely imprecise and hence unusable in this form." Again, Ratzinger seems concerned about the dialectic of hierarchy and prophecy. While not going into detail, he remarks there is no Scriptural justification for a dualism between a prophetic class and hierarchical order. Biblical prophets actually defended the Law by vindicating its true meaning. In the Old Covenant, they were never viewed as a class in contrast with a class of priests (see Amos 7:10–17; 1 Kings 22; Jer 37:19). Again, Ratzinger comments that the various functions within the Church should not be viewed dialectically, but organically: "What only remains true is that ... God continually inspires prophetic men and women ... who would not derive the necessary strength in the normal course of the 'institution' to make ... charismatic appeal to the Church."[7]

Opting for a Historical Approach

Cardinal Ratzinger concludes that using a dialectic of principles is unsatisfactory in trying to determine the place of ecclesial movements in the Church. He chooses instead an historical approach. He examines the history of the Church, highlighting the link between apostolic succession and apostolic movements. In doing so he makes significant theological clarifications.

Ratzinger explains that apostolic succession does not mean that the faithful become independent of the Spirit through the continuous chain of succession from one generation to the next. The link between the "once" and the "for always" of the Christ event is made visible in the sacraments. The sacraments transmit the presence in pneumatical form of the Church's historical origin in every age. In other words, the Lord himself, in the power of the Spirit, works through the sacraments to build up his Church. The originating event of Jesus Christ is communicated by the gift of the Holy Spirit who is the Spirit of the Risen Lord: "The Incarnation does not stop with the historical Jesus.... The 'historical Jesus' has eternal significance precisely because his 'flesh' is transformed in the resurrection, so

---

6. Ibid., 31.
7. Ibid., 32.

that he can make himself present in all places and at all times in the power of the Holy Spirit."[8]

Cardinal Ratzinger reflects upon the very origins of the Church. While recognizing the historical difficulties in examining the early Church, he writes that from Pentecost onward the immediate bearers of Christ's mission were the Twelve who soon appeared under the name of "apostles." Their mission was to go out to the whole world and build up the one Church of Christ. They were not bishops of particular local churches but rather "apostles" in the full sense of the term, sent out to the whole world and to the whole Church. The notion of apostle extended beyond "the Twelve" to other travelling evangelists in the early Church. This is presupposed by Paul's description of Andronicus and Junias as apostles in the Letter to the Romans (see 16:7). All of these first apostles had a supra-local or universal ministry. Once established, local churches appointed local leaders. Their task was to guarantee unity of faith with the whole Church while also developing missionary outreach within the local churches. Ratzinger refers to the *Didache*, which describes how early in the second century prophets were clearly understood as fulfilling a missionary supra-local ministry. Eusebius, a fourth century historian, describes the dual ministry that co-existed well into the second century:

> Indeed, most of the disciples of that time, struck in soul by the divine Logos with an ardent love of philosophy, first fulfilled the Savior's command and distributed their goods among the needy, and then, entering upon long journeys, performed the work of evangelists, being eager to preach everywhere to those who had not yet heard the word of faith and to pass on the writings of the divine Gospels. As soon as they had only laid the foundations of the faith in some foreign lands, they appointed others as pastors and entrusted them with the nurture of those who had recently been brought in, but they themselves went on to other lands and peoples with the grace and the co-operation of God.[9]

---

8. Ibid., 31.
9. Eusebius, *Church History*, III, 37, in Philip Schaff and Henry Wace (eds.), *Nicene and Post-Nicene Fathers*, Vol. 1, second series (Peabody, MA: Hendrickson Publishers, 1994).

The early Church on the one hand included the itinerant apostolic ministry and on the other the services of the local church, which gradually took on the fixed form of bishop, priest and deacon. When these universal itinerant missionaries died out, the bishops who presided over the local churches that had been set up by the apostles came to recognize, as the second century bishop and theologian Irenaeus of Lyons states, that they are now the successors of the apostles and the apostolic mission lay on their shoulders. Apostolic succession entailed guaranteeing a sacramental continuity and unity of the faith. It entailed ensuring the continuation of Jesus' mission to make all nations disciples and bring the gospel to the ends of the earth.

Restricting the ministry of apostolic succession to the local bishops, priests and deacons, however, might always run the risk of withering into a purely local ecclesial ministry, dimming the universality of Christ's mission in the local community's mind and heart.

Apostolic Movements in the History of the Church

Ratzinger notes that in the second century, as the supra-local universal ministry was dying out and being absorbed by the local episcopal ministry (not without the risks of stagnation), a new phenomenon emerged — the monastic movement. Following the person often considered the founder of monasticism, Abbot Anthony (c. 251–356) into the desert, the first monks moved beyond the local in "a deliberate abandonment of the firmly established structure of the local Church." Fleeing a Christianity that was progressively adapting itself to the needs of secular life, Anthony's choice actually "gave rise to a new spiritual fatherhood; and this spiritual fatherhood, while it had no directly missionary character, did nonetheless supplement the fatherhood of bishops and priests by the power of a whole pneumatic life."[10] Indeed, "the monastic movement created a new centre of life that did not abolish the local ecclesial structure of the post-apostolic Church, but that did not simply coincide with it either." Monasticism was "active ... as a life-giving force, a kind of reservoir from which the local Church could draw truly spiritual clergy in whom the fusion of institution and charism was constantly renewed."[11]

---

10. Ibid., 37.
11. Ibid., 38–39.

The fourth century founder of communal monasticism, Basil (330–379), recognized that the movement to follow Jesus Christ in an uncompromising fashion could not be merged completely with the local Church. In the second draft of a rule, Basil describes the monastic movement as a "transitional form between a group of committed Christians open to the Church as a whole and a self-organizing and self-institutionalizing monastic order." The monastic community was to serve as leaven, a "small group for the revitalization of the whole."[12] Noting that the emergence of this new dimension of ecclesial life did not coincide with the configuration of the local churches, Ratzinger presents a brief historical overview of the apostolic movements of the Church's journey in fidelity to its apostolic origins and form.[13]

The monasteries, which began as points of spiritual renewal, soon developed into a great missionary movement. Pope Gregory the Great (490–604) realized their missionary potential. This monastic renewal led to evangelization in Germany and many other parts of Western and Eastern Europe.

In the tenth century, a reform movement started within the Benedictine order. Associated with the Abbey of Cluny and carried out primarily by St. Odo (c. 878–942), in this movement individual monasteries affiliated themselves into a single congregation. Because it freed religious life from domination by episcopal feudatories, the Cluniac reform can be linked with the shaping of the idea of Europe. Later, in the eleventh century, it contributed to the emergence of the Gregorian Reform (based on a series of reforms initiated by Pope Gregory VII [1073–85]), "which rescued the papacy from the perils of worldliness and the quagmire of strife among the Roman nobility."[14]

Thirteenth century mendicant orders such as the Franciscans and Dominicans wanted to recall the Church to the whole message of the gospel and proclaim it beyond the frontiers of Christendom to the ends of the earth. At the University of Paris, conflict broke out

---

12. Ibid., 38 citing von Balthasar, *Die Großen Ordensregegln*, 7th ed. (Einsiedeln: Johannes Verlag, 1994), and J. Gribomont, "Les Règles Morales de S. Basile et le Nouveau Testament," in *Studia patristica*, ed. K. Aland, vol. 2 (Berlin: Akademie-Verlag, 1957): 416–426.

13. For a text that develops this line of thought by reflecting on other moments in the history of the Church, see Julian Porteous, *A New Wine and Fresh Skins*, 51–72.

14. Ibid., 41.

between the mendicants and the secular clergy. The secular clergy preferred a type of monasticism separated from the local Church; the new preachers, however, in the light of Jesus' missionary instruction to the apostles in Matthew 10:5–15, worked in the towns and moved between states. "The exponents of a restricted and impoverished idea of the Church, that absolutizes the structure of the local Church, could not tolerate the intrusive new class of preachers. The latter, for their part, necessarily found their support in the holder of a universal ecclesial ministry, in the Pope, as guarantor of the mission and the upbuilding of the one Church. It is no surprise, therefore, that all this gave a great boost to the development of the doctrine of primacy."[15]

The evangelization movements of the sixteenth century embarked on a world-wide mission in America, Africa and Asia. Cardinal Ratzinger mentions the Jesuits who were prominent among these evangelizers, as well as the Dominicans and Franciscans who "thanks to their enduring missionary impulse, did not lag far behind."[16]

The evangelizing dynamic continued in the spate of movements that began in the nineteenth century. Surveying the whole history of the Church, Ratzinger acknowledges the co-responsibility of women in the apostolic life and in its universal mission, particularly in the nineteenth century.

> It [the nineteenth century apostolic movement] was characterized by a strong emphasis on *caritas*, on care for the suffering and for the poor: We know what the new women's communities have meant, and continue to mean, for the hospital apostolate and for the care of the needy. But they also assumed a very important role in the fields of schooling and education. In this way, the whole range of service to the Gospel was made present in the combination of teaching, education and charity.[17]

Drawing his review of apostolic movements in the history of the Church to a close, Ratzinger concludes that the papacy did not create these movements; rather, the popes saw their missionary potential and became their main supporters. This could happen precisely because the pope is not merely the bishop of the local church of Rome.

---

15. Ibid., 43.
16. Ibid., 44.
17. Ibid., 44.

His unique universal ministry leads him to have a special interest in encouraging movements whose apostolic dynamism goes beyond the structure and range of the local Church.

Ratzinger summarizes his review by underlining how, on the one hand, the local Church "necessarily determined by the episcopal ministry is the supporting structure that permanently upholds the edifice of the Church throughout the ages," binding it to the Paschal events of Jesus' life, death and resurrection.[18] On the other hand, the history of the Church also has been "traversed by successive waves of movements that renew the universalistic aspect of her apostolic mission and thus serve to foster the spiritual vitality and truth of the local Churches."[19]

Movements and the Notion of Apostolic Succession

Based on his survey of the main apostolic movements in the history of the Church, Cardinal Ratzinger concludes that the concept of apostolic succession must be broadened and deepened. Certainly, the sacramental structure of the Church forms the core of the notion of apostolic succession: "The sacrament means that the Church lives and is continually recreated by the Lord as 'creature of the Holy Spirit.'"[20] The Church, bound to the unique and unrepeatable Incarnation and the Easter events, has a Christological-incarnational aspect. Simultaneously, it also has a Christological-pneumatological side, that is, "the making present of this event in the power of the Holy Spirit" in each new era of history, which "guarantees at once the newness and the continuity of the living Church."[21]

The notion of apostolic succession, however, cannot be limited only to the sacramental structure of the local Church. This can be seen, for example, in the Petrine ministry. The successor of Peter indeed is the local bishop of Rome, but his mission extends to the whole Church and in the whole Church. In that capacity, he doesn't bear on his own the burden of bringing about the universal dimension of the apostolic succession. Other ministries and missions not tied to the local Church alone serve the universal mission and the preaching of the gospel. The pope relies on them, and they on him.

---

18. Ibid., 39.
19. Ibid., 38.
20. Ibid., 45.
21. Ibid.

Accordingly it is "in the harmonious interaction between the two kinds of mission the symphony of ecclesial life is realized."[22]

For Cardinal Ratzinger, then, apostolic succession includes apostolic movements that appear in ever-new forms throughout history as the Spirit's gift and answer to the ever-changing situation in which the Church lives. A retrospective historical glance indicates that "through all her trials and tribulations, the Church has always succeeded in finding room for all the great new awakenings of the spirit that emerge in her midst."[23] The movements and communities are self-realizations of the Church event itself in and for the one Catholic Church, with practical reference to the local Church. The apostolicity of the Church, guaranteed by its sacramental and ministerial constitution, is constantly re-proposed and enriched by the newness that the Spirit suggests to the churches in each new era of history (see Rev 2:7).

Because the movements have an apostolic nature, the Petrine ministry exercised by the Bishop of Rome is their natural reference point. It approves them but also gives them space to express themselves and engage in evangelization.[24] Admittedly, as Ratzinger recognizes, this can lead to a critique of movements as being linked to a centralizing vision of Church. The connection between movements and the papacy might seem to contradict the ecclesial nature and mission that has emerged in the light of Vatican II's theological rediscovery of the local Church, episcopal collegiality, and the principle of synodality. Ratzinger acknowledges this risk, but affirms that primacy and episcopacy, the local ecclesial system

22. Ibid., 46.
23. Ibid., 47.
24. See also G.K. Chesterton's comment to this effect, "It will be found again and again, in ecclesiastical history, that the new departure, the daring innovation, the progressive party, depended directly on the Pope. It was naturally more or less negatively resisted by the bishops, the canons, the clergy in possession.... Official oligarchies of that sort generally do resist reform and experiment, either rightly or wrongly.... But whenever there appeared, in Catholic history, a new and promising experiment, bolder or broader or more enlightened than existing routine, that movement always came to be identified with the Papacy; because the Papacy alone upheld it.... So ... it was really the Pope who upheld St. Francis and the popular movement of the Friars. So, in the sixteenth century, it was really the Pope who upheld St. Ignatius Loyola and the great educational movement of the Jesuits. The Pope, being the ultimate court of appeal, cannot for shame be a mere expression of any local prejudice; this may easily be strong among local ecclesiastics, without any evil intention; but the remote arbiter at Rome must make some attempt to keep himself clear of it" (*Chaucer CW* 18:186).

and the apostolic movements, need each other. Where any one dimension is weakened, the Church as a whole suffers.[25]

Conclusion

Because movements are part of the apostolic dimension of the Church, those involved in them need to recognize more clearly how they are called to follow Christ radically. Cardinal Ratzinger comments that "the wish to lead the *vita apostolica* must be fundamental for them in every period." This apostolic life creates freedom for service, particularly proclamation of the gospel as the missionary element par excellence, with charity as its inner source.

> All this presupposes — mainly thanks to the power and inspiration of the original charism — a deep, personal encounter with Christ. The becoming a community and the building up of the community, does not exclude the personal dimension, indeed it demands it. Only when the person is struck and penetrated by Christ to the depths of his or her being, can others too be touched in their innermost being; only then can there be reconciliation in the Holy Spirit; only then can true community grow.[26]

A later chapter will return to the advice Ratzinger offers regarding the relationship between movements and the local churches. This chapter, however, concludes with the cardinal's gratitude for movements as a contemporary expression of the Church's apostolic dimension, thankfulness "that the Holy Spirit is quite plainly at work in the Church and is lavishing new gifts on her in our time too, gifts through which she relives the joy of her youth.... Christ lives and he sends the Holy Spirit from the Father — that is the joyful and life-giving experience that is given to us by the meeting with the ecclesial movements in our time."[27]

---

25. Ibid., 51.
26. Ibid., 49.
27. Ibid., 51.

11

Movements and Evangelization

The 2008 Synod on the Word of God in the life and mission of the Church "recognized with gratitude that the ecclesial movements and the new communities are a great force for evangelization in our times and an incentive to the development of new ways of proclaiming the Gospel."[1] Evangelization, which is said to be the very identity of the Church, is seriously challenged both by the new geographical distribution of Catholics and by the drama, especially in the Western world, of the split between faith and culture.[2] Movements have often been interpreted in terms of a providential response to these contemporary challenges. Considering this key for interpreting the significance of movements demands a working definition of evangelization. It has been pointed out that there are at least seventy-nine definitions of what authors mean by evangelism or evangelization![3] Pope Paul VI's words, therefore, provide a valuable synthesis:

> Evangelization ... is a complex process made up of varied elements: the renewal of humanity, witness, explicit proclamation, inner adherence, entry into the community, acceptance of signs, apostolic initiative. These elements ... are complementary and mutually enriching. Each one must always be seen in relationship with the others.[4]

---

1. See Pope Benedict's Apostolic Letter, *Verbum domini* (September 30, 2010), Part 3.
2. See Pope John Paul II's encyclical letter on the permanent validity of the Church's missionary mandate in *Redemptoris missio* (July 12, 1990). For an overview of Louis Dupré's understanding of the foundations of the spiritual predicament of our age, see Peter Casarella, " 'Modern Forms Filled with Traditional Spiritual Content': On Louis Dupré's Contribution to Christian Theology," in Peter J. Casarella and George P. Schner, *Christian Spirituality and the Culture of Modernity* (Grand Rapids, MI: Eerdmans, 1998), 275–310.
3. See David B. Barrett and James W. Reapsome, *Seven Hundred Plans to Evangelize the World: The Rise of a Global Evangelization Movement* (Birmingham: New Hope, 1988), 42–45.
4. Paul VI, Apostolic Exhortation on Evangelization, *Evangelii nuntiandi* (December 8, 1975), n. 24.

Since the early twentieth century, there has been an enormous shift in mission and evangelization. As Vatican II put it, "The human race is involved in a new stage of history. Profound and rapid changes are spreading by degrees around the whole world."[5] In *Transforming Mission: Paradigm Shifts in Theology of Mission*, David Bosch contends that the 1910 Edinburgh missionary conference marked the "all-time highwater mark in Western missionary enthusiasm, the zenith of the optimistic and pragmatist approach to missions."[6] Western Christians saw themselves with a vast mission of renewing the face of the earth, given they had the possibilities to do so. Works and initiatives abounded — mission stations, schools, hospitals and shelters for the poor. John R. Mott, the long-serving leader of the YMCA and the World Student Christian Federation, was convinced that given the rate of the progress of modern science and the opportunities it was offering, the world could be evangelized in his generation, opening door after door to the power of the gospel. Providence and revelation were combining in such a remarkable manner that, "The victory may not be easy, but it is sure."[7]

Europe and America saw themselves at the center of Christianity, with "missions" at the world's periphery. In 1900, 85% of Christians lived in Europe and America. Of the 1200 delegates at the Edinburgh conference in 1910, 1170 were Western (500 British, 500 American and 170 from the rest of Europe). Only 30 delegates attended from India, China and Japan, and none from either Africa or Latin America.[8]

By 2000, however, the percentage of the world's Christians in Europe had fallen to under 40% and by 2050 possibly under 30%. In 1960 over 50% of Catholics lived in North America and Europe; by 2000 that had fallen to 38%. In 2010, over 50% of the world's Catholics lived in South America.

Beyond mere statistics, a deeper reality is operating. Since the early twentieth century, practical atheism has spread throughout the Western world, driving a wedge between the Transcendent and day-

---

5. *Gaudium et spes*, 4.
6. David J. Bosch, *Transforming Mission: Paradigm Shifts in Theology of Mission* (New York: Orbis, 2004), 338.
7. See John R. Mott, *The Evangelization of the World in This Generation* (New York: Student Volunteer Movement for Foreign Missions, 1904).
8. See Kenneth R. Ross, "Edinburgh 1910 — Its Place in History," Manuscript, 5 (http://www.towards2010.org.uk/downloads_int/1910–PlaceHistory.pdf; accessed, December 22, 2010).

to-day cultural expressions of life such as economics, politics, family life and education. These vast issues defy easy categorization.[9] There is something of an irony, then, that in the very year (2010) marking the hundredth anniversary of the Edinburgh Conference, whose Western-centered perspective surveyed the rest of the world in an optimistic drive to bring the gospel everywhere, Benedict XVI established a new Pontifical Council "whose principal task will be to promote a renewed evangelization in the countries where the first proclamation of the faith has already resonated and where Churches with an ancient foundation exist but are experiencing the progressive secularization of society and a sort of 'eclipse of the sense of God,' which pose a challenge to finding appropriate means to propose anew the perennial truth of Christ's Gospel."[10]

Compared to 1910 and its sense of mission, the Christian world is in a very different place. In many ways the mission Christ entrusted to the Church "is still very far from completion"; indeed, "this mission is still only beginning."[11] The West needs a new "leap of faith," both in terms of the act of faith and in the way of expressing and communicating it. At the same time a vast worldwide network of evangelical and charismatic movements has emerged rapidly, especially in the Southern hemisphere, calling for the Catholic Church to find new ways to ensure its members have valid, attractive community experiences.[12]

What a 1963 missionary conference said still rings true — mission today is to be carried out on "six continents ... from everywhere to everywhere."[13] The Second Vatican Council marked a major turning point in the Catholic Church becoming what Karl Rahner called a "world Church," developing among all the baptized a vibrant sense

---

9. For a brief analysis that was considered a milestone in a Church document see *Gaudium et spes*, 19–21. See also Thomas Norris, *A Fractured Relationship: Faith and the Crisis of Culture* (Dublin: Veritas, 2007; New York: New City Press, 2010). See also Brendan Purcell, *"Fides et Ratio*: Charter for the Third Millennium," in James McEvoy (ed.), *The Challenge of Truth: Fides et Ratio* (Dublin: Veritas, 2002), 240–253.

10. See his homily at First Vespers of the Feast of Sts. Peter and Paul, Basilica of Saint Paul Outside the Walls, Sunday, June 28, 2010.

11. Pope John Paul II, Encyclical *Redemptoris missio*, n. 1.

12. Philip Jenkins, *The Next Christendom: The Coming of Global Christianity* (Oxford: Oxford University Press, 2002).

13. See the 1963 CWME Conference in Mexico City, and Michael Nazir-Ali, *From Everywhere to Everywhere: A World View of Christian Mission* (London: Collins, 1990).

of the missionary calling. All people have the right to hear the Good News and all believers are called as a service of love to respectfully proclaim it. The question remains, however — how to evangelize in the present age?

In creating the Council for a New Evangelization, Benedict XVI has taken up a theme, the New Evangelization, that John Paul II had made the central motif of his pontificate.[14] John Paul II, in an often-cited 1983 speech to the Bishops of South America, spoke of it as "one that is new in its ardor, new in its methods, and new in its means of expression."[15] In his Letter to the Catholics of Ireland (n. 12), addressing the issue of the sexual abuse of children by priests and religious, Benedict XVI commented that in "our increasingly secularized society, where even we Christians often find it difficult to speak of the transcendent dimension of our existence, we need to find new ways ... a new vision is needed, to inspire present and future generations."

Mystery, Communion and Mission

As the Church looks out for such "new ways," it must attend to what the Spirit indicated at the great Pentecostal event of the Second Vatican Council. At a 2000 Congress on Catechesis and Evangelization, Cardinal Joseph Ratzinger offered his personal recollection of preparations for the Council. As a young theologian, he had accompanied Cardinal Frings as an adviser. Like many others, in their preparatory deliberations, the German bishops were beginning to focus on the topic of Church as the issue for the Council. Ratzinger recalls Frings telling him, however, that at a certain point during their discussions, the elderly but much-esteemed Bishop Buchberger of the diocese of Regensburg offered his simple advice: "My brothers, at the Council you must above all talk about God. This is what is most important." Ratzinger agreed that "the Second Vatican Council certainly did intend to subordinate what it said about the Church to what it said about God."[16]

---

14. Avery Dulles, "John Paul II and the New Evangelization," *America* 166 (1993/3): 23-29. William J. Levada, *"New Evangelization Requires a New Catechesis,"* in *L'Osservatore Romano* (English edition), January 7, 1998, #11.

15. Pope John Paul II to CELAM meeting in Port-au-Prince, Haiti, on March 9, 1983.

16. "The Ecclesiology of the Constitution, *Lumen Gentium,*" in Joseph Cardinal Ratzinger, *Pilgrim Fellowship of Faith: The Church as Communion* (San Francisco: Ignatius, 2005), 123–152 at 125–126.

less by a general appeal to Christian values. The courageous and integral appeal to principles is essential and indispensable; yet simply proclaiming the message does not penetrate to the depths of people's hearts, it does not touch their freedom, it does not change their lives. What attracts is, above all, the encounter with believing persons who, through their faith, draw others to the grace of Christ by bearing witness to him.[19]

At a time when personal, communitarian, and social witness is central in evangelization, movements provide experiences of a life of communion that others can "come and see" (see Jn 1:46).[20] They are living spaces of encounter with Christ and also provide ways that the journey of faith can be traveled together. Some provide an experience of "pentecostalizing" Catholic liturgy, with the maximum participation of all the faithful and the inclusion of emotional elements, especially popular songs and healing ceremonies. Beyond the liturgy, however, the community element is important. As creative minorities the movements respond to the recognition that to mend "the Christian fabric of society" the Church also needs to "remake the Christian fabric of the ecclesial community itself."[21] Interestingly, José Comblin, a South American writer who had been critical of movements, wondered whether this communitarian experience might have more to offer than first thought:

> The structures of the Catholic Church, and even the structures of the basic ecclesial communities, no longer succeed in trans-mitting or inspiring faith ... they are not equipped to arouse it. Today, by contrast, it is often the charismatic movements that succeed in inspiring faith and in transforming the life of their converts.... In practice they are alone in converting the new generations, whatever their secret is.... Twenty-five years ago the Church laid down a certain model of community life which formed the root of the basic ecclesial communities. Today we know that the possible form of community for the start of the third millennium still remains indefinite — but very different

---

19. Address to the Bishops of Portugal, Fatima, May 13, 2010.
20. See also Cardinal Angela Scola, "Ecclesial Movements and New Communities in the Mission of the Church. Priorities and Perspectives," in Pontifical Council, *The Beauty*, 59–83, at 70.
21. *Christifideles laici* (December 30, 1988) 34: *AAS* 81 (1989), 393–521, particularly 454–57.

Although the Council sought to reflect on the Church, its clarion call became Jesus Christ and the life of Triune God. That life opens up for human beings through encounter with Christ in the world, where the Holy Spirit "in a manner known only to God offers to everyone the possibility of being associated with this paschal mystery."[17] The Church, icon of the Trinity, evangelizes through its unity, which mirrors and participates in the triune unity of God. The ecclesial movements contribute to evangelization in three ways that correspond to the three central motifs of Vatican II — mystery, communion and mission.

The charism at work in an ecclesial movement or community instills in those who are part of it profound conviction and promotes missionary drive. This drive is based on a personal and vibrant encounter with Jesus Christ that transforms individuals' lives, leading them to take as their own Paul's words, "Woe betide me if I do not proclaim the gospel!" (1 Cor 9:16). Such persons want to witness to a new life, a life of communion rooted in the God who has revealed himself eschatologically in Jesus Christ. This return to an original experience of the gospel of the crucified and risen Christ becomes urgent in view of the challenge of post-modernity and globalization. In a 1995 essay Avery Dulles commented that "too many Catholics of our day seem never to have met the Lord. They know a certain amount about him from the teaching of the Church, but they lack direct, personal familiarity."[18] Only a personal experience of the faith can insert the leaven of the Kingdom of God into the human and cultural contexts where the future of the millennium will be determined. Proclaiming principles is important, but not enough. That's why the evangelizers need to be evangelized. And for that something more is needed. Benedict XVI explains:

> In fact, when, in the view of many people, the Catholic faith is no longer the common patrimony of society and, often, seen as threatened and obscured by the "gods" and masters of this world, only with great difficulty can the faith touch the hearts of people by means simple speeches or moral appeals, and even

---

17. *Gaudium et spes*, 22.
18. See Avery Dulles, "John Paul II and the New Evangelization — What Does it Mean?" in Ralph Martin and Peter Williamson (eds.), *Pope John Paul II and the New Evangelization* (San Francisco: Ignatius Press, 1995), 37.

from the expectations that people had twenty-five years ago.... The image of the new historical model will gradually appear ... it will arise from the experiences made.[22]

Finally, at a time when the Church senses the need to "launch into the deep," movements also provide new forms and strategies of witness, dialogue, and proclamation as well as incarnation of the gospel and service of the poor. This is important because evangelization does not come about only through the parish. People spend much of their day in a range of different environments from family to sport, from work to entertainment, from travel to the internet, and with a range of people, both religious and non-religious. As Bishop Porteous comments, "To attempt to catalogue the ways in which this work of evangelization is being realized is impossible. They are legion."[23]

As mentioned earlier, movements engage in a number of social and cultural projects as well as in ecumenical and interreligious dialogue. Charity and justice go together. Andrea Riccardi, of the Community of Sant'Egidio, notes that movements

> look to the whole world, even if they are not present everywhere.... The movements represent a network of universal Christian brotherhood through the participation of people of different national origins. This network transcends ethnic and cultural frontiers.... The experience of the movements ... shows quite clearly that the faith and the ecclesial life turn the Christian into a citizen of the world.... This is why the movements have the experience of sharing the same destiny as various peoples. This is due to the mission that characterizes them, and hence their outreach to everyone.... But it is also because they represent, within themselves, a community of persons of different origins, bound together in a common sense of belonging and shared missionary dynamic. In the life of the movements, in different degrees and perspectives, we may perceive that what is distant, is not alien; indeed it represents a deep challenge. Poverty and suffering in far-off places are an appeal to the Christian that he or she cannot evade.[24]

---

22. "Reino de Deus: utopia profetica de Jesus," in *Vida Pastoral* 38, n. 197 (1997): 6–7, quoted in P. Coda, "The Ecclesial Movements," 99.

23. Julian Porteous, *A New Wine and Fresh Skins*, 107–108.

24. See "Charity and Justice: Challenges for the Movements," in Pontifical Council for the Laity, *Movements in the Church*, 185–192, at 186–187.

Taking into account the importance of missionary communion, the German Jesuit theologian Medhard Kehl writes that the new movements "represent an authentically Christian response to the challenge of the contemporary cultural situation in proportion as they try expressly to live ecclesial 'communio' in conditions of modern individualization." He notes that the spiritual experience provided by movements touches

> the existential core of man in his relation of faith with God and love for his neighbor. The conscious decision to embrace the faith, the experience of its beauty and reciprocal support make such Christians capable of conforming their concrete mode of life to the spirit of the Gospel and thus acting in a missionary sense within our society. It is surprising that, even among the ranks of those "far from the Church," many feel attracted by these communities: here the Church is undoubtedly presented to them in a surprising humanity and immediately.

Kehl concludes that the movements "may be the most authentically and (from a practical point of view) effective Christian response to many religious and quasi-religious needs of people in our society; a response which the highly institutionalized churches are no longer thought capable of giving, and which is therefore being sought in large part among the most varied mystic-natural currents."[25]

Movements and People's Spiritual Needs

In many ways, people today search for an experience of salvation not simply as a distant future reality but as an experience of human fulfillment and realization within history, here and now. At a major conference in Rome during the Jubilee Year 2000, Cardinal Ratzinger spoke in clear terms of the urgent need for such a new evangelization.[26] Describing its heart as demonstrating a path towards happiness and teaching an art of living that many want to learn, he pointed out that the classic means of spreading the gospel such as Mass, the sacraments, preaching, even institutional

---

25. See *Wohin geht di Kirche? Eine Zeitdiagnose* (Freiburg: Herder, 1996), 153–157. See also Kehl, *Die Kirche: Eine katholische Ekklesiologie* (Würzburg: Echter Verlag, 1992).
26. See his address to catechists and teachers of religion during the Jubilee, Sunday, December 10, 2000.

commitment to the causes of justice and peace are essential, but not sufficient. Something more is needed, a new way:

A large part of today's humanity does not find the Gospel in the permanent evangelization of the Church: That is to say, the convincing response to the question: How to live? This is why we are searching for ... a new evangelization, capable of being heard by that world which does not find access to "classic" evangelization.

He then points out that Christians discover that the "art of living" can be communicated only by those who have life — those who personify the gospel. After he had been elected pope he granted Peter Seewald an extended interview, which was published as *Light of the World*. In it, describing the search for ways suited to the times and situations and that correspond with the power of the Holy Spirit, Pope Benedict calls attention to the importance of spiritual communities.[27]

Addressing the Bishops of Ghana during their February 23, 1993 *ad limina* visit, John Paul II also remarked that the attraction of movements sometimes lies in their apparent success in responding to the spiritual needs of the people, the hunger of their hearts for something deeper: "to build up such family-like parish life with small communities, groups, movements and the like where people feel at home, can be also the answer to the often heard argument that people leave the Church because they find themselves at home in the small communities of the sects."

A Gospel "Leaven" in Society

Some who critique movements and their significance for the Church's evangelizing mission sense in them a certain naiveté, or the risk of falling into a regressive and traditional Catholicism. Sometimes movements are seen as emphasizing private interior experience or as promoting a triumphalistic "new Christendom" that contradicts the deepest intentions of Vatican II.

The Council did propose a new vision of the Catholic Church as a presence in the world of culture and society to supplant the notion of *Christendom*, a term that suggests a combined religious and civil power that the Church has left behind. Nor does the Church

---

27. Benedict XVI in conversation with Peter Seewald, *Light of the World: The Pope, the Church and the Signs of the Times* (San Francisco: Ignatius Press, 2010), 66.

want to present itself as a "perfect society" *(societas perfecta)*, an alternative, self-sufficient order that parallels or stands in opposition to cultures that organize themselves according to non-Christian principles.[28] In rejecting the desire for privilege or hegemony, at Vatican II the Church took up instead the difficult and risky logic of seeing itself as a gospel "leaven" in an increasingly pluralistic society searching for common points of convergence.

In their finest expression, movements have emerged to respond to just such needs. They have been born from the impulse to maintain the original baptismal source experience as a living historical presence of Christianity in the world. They want to serve the Church, which sees itself as casting the seed of the Word of God widely in culture; not closing in on itself in self-defense, but voyaging into the deep with courage and prudence (always in communion with the bishops), sowing the Word of God in the vast field of history.

Movements must realize the two directions in which they can move forward.[29] On the one hand, they can be practical expressions of the Christian mission to be "salt" or "leaven" (see Mt 5:13; Lk 13:20–21), without which human history loses direction and meaning. This is the course proposed by *Gaudium et spes* and the decree on the laity, *Apostolicam actuositatem*, which affirms the positive meaning of temporal realities, as formulated in *Dignitatis humanae*'s principle of religious freedom. In following this course, drawing upon the Christian conception of human nature and society, they offer a response to the needs around them while remaining open to dialogue at all levels. On the other hand, movements must remain vigilant against the temptation to work, consciously or otherwise, to "regain" the hegemonic position of Catholicism under the guise of serving the gospel.

The movements can be a true leaven in society by promoting a full humanism that finds its measure in the person of Jesus Christ. The life of communion and co-responsibility that movements live can permeate civil society, providing a creative and critical resource for the participative praxis of democracy. And that too can be evangelization.[30]

---

28. See *Gaudium et spes*, 76.
29. See Piero Coda, "Movimenti ecclesiali e nuove comunità nella missione della Chiesa: collocazione teologica, prospettive pastorali e missionarie," in *Nuova Umanità* XXXI (2009), 213–228.
30. See Amelia J. Uelmen, "Reconciling Evangelization and Dialogue through Love of Neighbor" in *Villanova Law Review* 52 (2007): 303–329.

12

The Ecclesial Movements and the Marian Principle

During preparations for the Great Jubilee of 2000, John Paul II commented, "At the dawn of the new millennium, we notice with joy the emergence of the 'Marian profile' of the Church that summarizes the deepest concerns of the conciliar renewal."[1] The new ecclesial movements were among the signs he referred to as that profile's manifestation. This "Marian profile" is a fifth key to reading the phenomenon of movements in our time.[2]

This line of reflection includes several strands. First, many movements draw inspiration from Mary, the first disciple of Jesus. Sometimes stories of their origins are even linked to Marian feast days or shrines. For instance, the Schoenstatt movement began on October 18, 1914, when Joseph Kentenich (1885–1968) and a few others sealed their "covenant of love" with Mary. After several years in the concentration camp in Dachau and other difficult periods where he had to prove his love for the Church despite rejection and anxiety, he died on the feast of Mary's Assumption, September 15, 1968. The Teams of Our Lady movement began at the end of the 1930s when a number of married couples, under the guidance of Fr. Henri Caffarel, began to meet every month in each other's houses. It was formally established on the feast day of the Immaculate Conception, December 8, 1947 with the promulgation of the Équipes Notre-Dame Charter. The Emmanuel Community is named after the passage of Scripture, "Behold, a young woman shall conceive and bear a son, and shall call his name Emmanuel" (Is 7:14; see Mt 1:23).

Many movements, to a greater or lesser degree, draw inspiration in their story or spirituality from some aspect of Mary's life or doctrine about her. As mentioned in earlier chapters, the Legion of Mary movement drew its inspiration from Louis de

---

1. John Paul II, Weekly Catechesis, "Spirit Leads Church on Path to Renewal," November 25, 1998.
2. See my work on the theme of the Marian profile in the ecclesiology of Hans Urs von Balthasar, *The Marian Profile* (New York: New City Press, 2000).

Montfort. The Focolare Movement is also officially known as the "Work of Mary." Many Charismatic Renewal communities highlight Mary as their model.

Von Balthasar

Swiss theologian Hans Urs von Balthasar, a man keenly sensitive to what has flowered in the Church's garden, reflected on this Marian principle and its connection to the movements.[3] These sources of renewal and hope have come about, he explains, not from the hierarchy of the Church or out of necessity or utility. Rather, they express what he calls the subjective, Marian principle of the Church.[4] His encouraging and clarifying reflection on this phenomenon is important. For instance Libero Gerosa, a canonist, claims that theologians and the magisterium itself owe much to von Balthasar, especially his complex and organic thought about the two poles of ecclesiology, the two central dimensions – the Marian and the Petrine — around which all discussion of the Church revolves.[5]

A brief outline of von Balthasar's personalist ecclesiology illustrates what Gerosa means. For von Balthasar, the Church revolves around archetypal or model faith experiences. Starting from the gospel, he indicates how "the risen Lord who wills to be present in his Church all days to the end of time, cannot be isolated from the 'constellation' of his historical life."[6] He notes, "The history recounted in the New Testament is both spiritual and theological."[7] The constellation around Jesus of Mary, John the Baptist, the twelve apostles, and the sisters of Bethany is not limited to the Church's origins. Through the Holy Spirit, Peter and the other apostles "have founding missions and, in their own way,

---

3. See Paul Cordes, *Charisms and the New Evangelisation*, 163–171.
4. See Hans Urs von Balthasar, "Lay Movements in the Church," in *The Laity and the Life of the Counsels*, 252–282, at 254.
5. See Libero Gerosa, "Secular Institutes, Lay Associations, and Ecclesial Movements in the Theology of Hans Urs von Balthasar," in *Communio* 17 (1990): 343–361, at 346. David Schindler has also drawn on von Balthasar's writings regarding the movements. See Schindler's "Institution and Charism," in Pontifical Council for the Laity, *Movements in the Church* (Vatican, 1999), 53–76.
6. *Der antirömische Affekt* (Freiburg im Breisgau, 1974), 115–187, here, 136.
7. Ibid., 125.

have no less a continuing life and representation in the Church."[8] In other words, through the work of the Spirit, these archetypal faith-experiences flow into the Church as constitutive dimensions or profiles or principles.

In particular, von Balthasar reflects on two co-essential principles that form the epicenter of the Church as a dynamic sphere of mutual love: the Petrine point of unity (the Pope but also the hierarchical-sacramental structure of the Church, in terms of the hierarchy's role in community building through apostolic preaching and sacraments); and the Marian point of unity in terms of a living actualization of the gospel in holiness, witness and transformation of the world. In an address to the Roman Curia, taking up von Balthasar's line of thought, John Paul II spoke of the Marian profile as equally fundamental and characteristic of the Church to the Petrine, if not more so.[9] Benedict XVI has also elaborated upon this theme.[10]

Mary and the Spirit

By concluding its constitution on the Church, *Lumen gentium*, with a chapter on Mary, the Second Vatican Council directed attention to the woman who is an "integral part of the economy of the communication of the Trinity to the human race."[11] Mary stands at the place where the drama of divine freedom and human freedom — and history — intersect in Jesus Christ. She represents a co-operating response (see 1 Cor 3:9) to grace, to the divine invitation to enter the rhythm of "trinitization" of humankind: "... that they may all be one. As you, Father, are in me and I am in you, may they also be in us, so that the world may believe that you have sent me.... I in them and you in me, that they may become completely one, so that the world may know that you have sent me and have loved them even as you have loved me" (Jn 17:21–23).[12]

---

8. Ibid., 133.

9. Address to the Cardinal and Prelates of the Roman Curia on December 22, 1987, printed in *L'Osservatore Romano*, December 23 (Italian edition), 1987; See *Insegnamenti di Giovanni* Paolo II 5, 3 (1987): 1671–1683.

10. See his homily on the occasion of the Eucharistic Concelebration with new cardinals, March 27, 2006.

11. See John Paul II, "Mary in Trinitarian perspective," *L'Osservatore Romano*, January 1996.

12. See the Second Vatican Council's definition of the Church as the "sacrament of unity": *Lumen gentium*, 1 and 4.

More and more, Mary's link with the Holy Spirit has been explored. This first disciple of Jesus worked together with the Holy Spirit to allow the event of Jesus' life, death and resurrection take place in history. The gospels present Mary on three occasions in particular: the "yes" of the Annunciation (Lk 1:38), the second "yes" at the foot of the Cross (Jn 19:25–27) and her presence in the midst of the community awaiting Pentecost (Acts 1:14). In Luke's Gospel, when Mary says: "Behold I am the servant of the Lord, let what you have said be done unto me" (1:38), she lets the Word become flesh in her. It becomes history through her. Representative of humanity, she lets the Word live her. That first "yes" in a sense contains all future "yeses." It's a "yes" every person can repeat. It's the total readiness to let God's action become history through us, with us and in us.

Saying "yes" to God is never simply a private or individual matter. The iconic moment presented in the Fourth Gospel, that of Mary at the foot of the Cross, reveals that. For himself, Jesus substitutes the beloved disciple (see Jn 19:25–27). Mary "loses," as it were, "her" God and, in the place of Jesus, welcomes one of his disciples. In doing so she opens without reserve to others, to every person, to the whole of humanity, building up the new "Christified" transformed humanity. She and the beloved disciple form the first cell of mutual love at the heart of the Church.

Objective-Subjective Holiness

Von Balthasar reflects on Mary's link with the Spirit in terms of objective and subjective holiness. The Spirit, he says, gifts the Church with both forms of holiness. Objectively, from the very beginnings of the Church, in the power of the Holy Spirit, the Crucified-Risen Christ works through the Word of God proclaimed, the sacraments administered and ministerial guidance.[13] These three foundations of ecclesial life — Word, sacraments and ministry — constitute the sure objective basis of the Church as a people gathered in communion and called to communicate the life of communion. As such these pillars form the "rock" that upholds the whole edifice. In this sense, through his personalist ecclesiology, von Balthasar links

---

13. See this theme developed also in the 1982 Faith and Order Lima text, *Baptism, Eucharist, Ministry.*

them with the "Petrine" (from Peter, rock) principle. Ultimately, this "rock" is Christ himself present in the midst of the community, the Risen Crucified Christ who speaks and works in the Word, the sacraments, and his ministers.

Through the "objective" gifts (Word, sacrament and order/ministry), the Spirit "objectively" guarantees the gathering presence of the Crucified-Risen Christ who continues to generate the Church, his other self, the people of God, journeying through history. But the Spirit also pours out charismatic gifts that open up the "subjectivity" of all the baptized — ordained and lay — to be able to receive, respond and render fully effective the objective gift that the Church has received. In other words, the objective gift is not enough; or rather, it is the means towards a goal — the transformation of human life, indeed of humanity. The effect of the objective sacramental means must become visible and tangible in history.

Mary, who von Balthasar calls "the supreme, normative subjectivity" of the Church, is the particular model and interior form of the receiving and actualizing, the making history of the life in the Church that comes through objective sacramental-hierarchical means.

The history of the Church is the time between the Christ event and humankind's letting it happen, their response, one that will be complete only when all the Church and humanity become totally open to God and his gifts, inhabited by the Word, gathered in Christ and so permeated by the Spirit of the Risen Christ, Christified and "Trinitized." The Church's pilgrim journey revolves around the inter-action of the objective-institutional and subjective-charismatic polarities of holiness that shape its members being "in Christ."

Throughout this perspective, von Balthasar is drawing on the ecclesiology of the Letter to the Ephesians. That letter brings together many motifs. One of the most significant is the theme of how the communion of love lived in God among the three divine Persons is imaged in creation through the man-woman relationship, in this new creation becoming the language to express something of the Christ-Church, Bridegroom-Bride relationship.[14]

---

14. See John Paul II's Apostolic Letter on the Dignity and Vocation of Women, *Mulieris dignitatem* (August 15, 1998), 7.

Charisms and Movements

According to von Balthasar, within this objective-subjective polarity of the Church's holiness the charisms of founders of orders, communities, and movements work in synergy with the apostolic ministry. In doing so, they reflect the Marian dimension of the Church. On the journey towards the fullness of truth,[15] the Holy Spirit underlines, highlights, and renders operative a particular aspect of the infinite mystery of Christ that responds to a particular need or feature of an era. Each of the charisms, von Balthasar affirms, is like a bolt of lightning, destined to illuminate a new or original point of God's will for the Church in a given era. Each charism shows a new way to follow Christ, a new illustration of how to live the gospel, a new interpretation of revelation.[16] The movements that charisms generate are expressions of the life of communion, communicated sacramentally, taking on ever new forms along the Church's journey.

Accordingly, the presence of new movements that have come to life through charisms — involving all the vocations of the Church — is a sign of the emergence of the Church's Marian profile, a profile that needs to be rediscovered. Along this way, the movements' focus on spirituality, their mainly lay profile, their strong ecclesial sense and evangelizing dynamism provide a stimulus for the Church to recognize its full identity.

Von Balthasar's own invitation to understand the nature of the Church in its deepest profile by looking to Mary provides a fitting conclusion to this chapter:

> Perhaps it is precisely our time that especially needs to see Mary. To see her as she shows herself, not as we would like to imagine her. To see her, if at all, in order not to forget her essential role in the work of salvation and in the Church. In reality, she shows herself and defines herself as the archetypal Church, whose form we have to take as our pattern. We. That means every single Christ, and yet it may mean even more: our image of what Church is. We are busily refashioning and

---

15. See *Dei verbum*, 8.
16. See Hans Urs von Balthasar, *Two Sisters in the Spirit: Thérèse of Lisieux and Elizabeth of the Trinity* (San Francisco: Ignatius Press, 1992), 25.

improving this Church according to the needs of the times, the criticisms of our opponents, and our own models. But do we not lose sight in all this of the only perfect criterion, that is, of the archetype? Should we not keep our eyes fixed on Mary in all of our reforms — not in order to multiply Marian feasts, devotions, or even definitions in the Church, but simply in order to remain aware of what Church, ecclesial spirit, ecclesial conduct really are?[17]

---

17. See "Mary in the Church's Doctrine and Devotion," in Hans Urs von Balthasar and Joseph Cardinal Ratzinger, *Mary: The Church at the Source* (San Francisco: Ignatius Press, 2005), 99–124 at 123–124.

Part 3
Considerations and Perspectives

This third part explores specific aspects not yet examined but that merit attention. To begin, some points of criticism regarding movements need be acknowledged and put in perspective. Second, the topic of the relationship between movements and parishes is addressed. Third, since many priests are members of movements, their position in them will be examined. Fourth, the engagement of many movements in ecumenical and interreligious dialogue will be discussed. Fifth, some aspects of movements will be examined from the perspective of canon law. Finally, one crucially important topic that needs to be considered is the relationship between movements and the spirituality of communion, which has been acknowledged as a priority for the Church's future progress.

13

Always in Reform

Any study of ecclesial movements should acknowledge criticism of their external and internal workings. For instance, some claim that they form a "church within a church," with the risk that they constitute a closed society which considers their specific charism the one way for everyone. They can be highly independent and as isolated as any traditional monastic community.[1] Some fear their power.[2] Others are troubled at the notion that the movements can become conservative and reactionary forces.[3]

The internal workings of movements are sometimes criticized. Although "the ideal and vision may be beautiful, holy and inspired ... the concrete realities are relative to circumstances and to people as they are with their beauty, inner fears, blockages and brokenness."[4] As do all human organizations, movements can contain elements of pride, excess, fear and insecurity. Sometimes, power can be employed in a dominative and manipulative way.[5] The more extreme critics accuse movements of being like sects that manipulate their members through brainwashing, isolation and alienation from the world, estrangement from family members, or over-dependence on charismatic leaders and personalities.[6]

This book does not attempt to answer each single criticism. Some accusations are based on individual bad experiences. Others may reflect institutional issues that need to be addressed.[7] It would be useful, however, to provide various perspectives from which to consider the issues. Such perspectives depend upon a point noted

---

1. Walsh, "That New-time Religion," 503–504.
2. See Gordon Urquhart's criticism of the Neocatechumenal Way, Communion and Liberation, and the Focolare Movement in *The Pope's Armada*.
3. See Tony Hanna's reference to Raniero Cantalamessa in this regard, in *New Ecclesial Movements*, 254.
4. Ibid., 256.
5. See Rahner on this in "Aspects of the Episcopal Office," in *Theological Investigations*, Vol. 14. Trans. David Bourke (New York: Seabury, 1976), 188–189.
6. For a treatment of accusations that some movements are sects, see Christoph Schönborn, "Are there Sects in the Catholic Church?" in *L'Osservatore Romano* (English Edition), 13/20 (August 1997): 3.
7. On criticism of movements, see Julian Porteous, *A New Wine and Fresh Skins*, 42–49.

elsewhere in this book: each movement has its own specific profile arising from its originating charism, history and formative processes. Each movement therefore needs to evaluate itself and be evaluated on the basis of its distinct physiognomy and particular contribution to the life of the Church. Not everything presented in these pages applies to every movement or every aspect of their communities! Von Balthasar's remark is relevant in this context:

> Not everything that is blossoming today need remain valid for centuries; there exist fainter charisms, more superficial groups, which answer a transient purpose, quickly shoot up, and then die. Others may have to struggle perhaps for decades with difficulties that may be imposed on them by God as their starting capital. This is why one should not be hasty in passing judgment on others in mutual encounters.[8]

In a Church That Is "Always Reforming"

First, it is important to note that, as expressions of the Church, movements are called to the constant reform underlined by the Second Vatican Council:

> Christ summons the Church to continual reformation.... The Church is always in need of this, insofar as she is an institution of men and women here on earth. Thus if, in various times and circumstances, there have been deficiencies in moral conduct or in church discipline, or even in the way that church teaching has been formulated — to be carefully distinguished from the deposit of faith itself — these can and should be set right at the opportune moment.[9]

What the Church says of itself is clearly relevant to movements within it.

One striking feature of the post-Vatican II era is the recognition that the Church journeys within history. Christians are a pilgrim people. That in itself means reform is an essential dimension of the Church's very nature. The Church is not a static, lifeless reality; it is dynamic, developing in an organic fashion and interacting with the events and

---

8. Von Balthasar, "Lay Movements in the Church," 281.
9. See *Unitatis redintegratio*, 6.

circumstances of history. Like the mustard seed mentioned in the gospel, the Church is cast into the furrows of history to grow, develop and become a large tree.

Referring to the gospel image of fishermen, Guy Bedouelle comments on how the Church does not cast its nets as if it existed outside of an Incarnation, but acts within history, facing challenges as well as experiencing temptations within itself since it is a holy Church made up of sinners.[10] Benedict XVI himself has recognized that "the greatest persecution of the Church comes not from her enemies without, but arises from sin within the Church."[11] Bedouelle adds that in addition to sin there are interior challenges — "not necessarily faults, but often ... lesser, secondary values, or simply values which are inadequate in view of the Church's mission to proclaim the salvation come from on high."[12]

The Church will become the perfect divine community of the kingdom of God only after the proving and sifting time of history and the final judgment. It is the seed and beginning of the kingdom; but it is important to remember the Kingdom is only partially realized.[13] The theologian Marie-Joseph le Guillou writes that "the benefits of the Kingdom (the inheritance) which are the fruits of the Spirit, knowledge and glory, are possessed by the Church individually and collectively, in an imperfect manner" (1 Cor 13:2).[14] This "midway situation," standing between what has come and what is yet to come, "has a profound effect on the whole nature of the Church and explains a great number of its characteristics, in particular its crucified state."[15]

The Church has undergone and is undergoing a purification of memory in recognizing the wrongs done by those who have borne or still bear the name of Christian. In view of this, as the International Theological Commission reiterates, in any assessment of the Church (and by implication any specific expression of the Church) two things must be avoided: an apologetics that seeks to justify everything in

---

10. Guy Bedouelle, *The History of the Church* (London: Continuum, 2003), 32.
11. Interview with journalists during the flight to Portugal, May 11, 2010.
12. Bedouelle, 32.
13. See *Lumen gentium*, 3, 5, 9.
14. Marie-Joseph le Guillou, "Ecclesiology," in Karl Rahner (ed.), *Encyclopedia of Theology: A Concise Sacramentum Mundi* (London: Burns & Oates, 2004), 209–221, at 216.
15. Ibid.

the past history of the Church, as well as the unwarranted laying of blame, based on historically untenable attributions of responsibility. The Church is "not afraid of the truth that emerges from history and is ready to acknowledge mistakes wherever they have been identified, especially when they involve the respect that is owed to individuals and communities."[16] The Church, as Vatican II recognizes, truly is "at the same time holy and always in need of being purified"; therefore, it always needs to follow "the way of penance and renewal."[17]

What the Church says about the need to focus constantly on renewal applies, obviously, to movements and communities that are an expression of the Church. Movements, born from charisms within the Church and at the service of the Church, cannot claim to be exempt from limitations and sin. Though vehicles of renewal, they too must always heed the need for reform, renewal and purification. The words of the First Letter of St. John resonate here: "If we say we have not sinned, we make him a liar, and his word is not in us" (1 Jn 1:10). Ambrose of Milan reiterates John's statement: "Let us beware then that our fall not become a wound of the Church."[18] Apart from sinfulness, movements always risk simply falling away from their original inspiring spark. In particular, the requisite institutional aspect of each movement must not slide into institutionalism. That is, it must not so focus on the formal structural elements that it neglects primacy of the life of the Gospel and the charism. What the Second Vatican Council taught regarding the need for renewal of religious life applies to the movements. It established as normative "the continual return ... to the original inspiration of the institutes" and fidelity to the "spirit of the founders."[19]

Historical Perspectives

Tensions regarding movements and their relationships with others can arise for any number of reasons. As Cardinal Ratzinger put it, given the strength of the original spiritual awakening that gives rise to a movement "it is almost inevitable ... that the vitality and totality

---

16. See International Theological Commission, *Memory and Reconciliation: The Church and the Faults of the Past* (December 1999), section 4.2.

17. *Lumen gentium,* 8.

18. St. Ambrose, *De virginitate* 8, 48; *PL* 16, 278D. *Lumen gentium* 11 also mentions the wound inflicted on the Church by the sins of her children.

19. *Perfectae caritatis,* 2.

of the original charismatic experience should time and again give rise to conflicts with the local community, a conflict in which both sides may be at fault, and both may be spiritually challenged."[20]

It has always been the case that new ecclesial communities can cause discomfort or suspicion. Any organic reality, including the life of the Church, has growing pains. New communities and movements can unsettle the more stable, pre-existing institutional aspects of the Church's life. Moreover, the new movements' tendency, especially at the beginning, to focus solely on their specific charism can be unsettling.

History contains some dramatic episodes of the tensions that arise when new movements appear. Pope Gregory the Great (540–604) describes the strain that grew between St. Benedict and Florentius, a priest who bitterly envied his good reputation and ability to attract many followers. The envy reached such a point that the priest tried to poison Benedict's bread! When that failed, Florentius tried to test him and defame him.

During the thirteenth century, the evangelical poverty and widespread preaching of the Franciscans and Dominicans generated an inevitable conflict between these new mendicant orders and the local institutional church, particularly with the secular clergy at the University of Paris. Faced with the local church's self-enclosed resistance to the new spiritual impulse, Thomas Aquinas defended this move toward evangelization, pointing out that religious life extends beyond living poverty, chastity, and obedience in isolated monasteries; it includes the universal proclamation of the gospel. Interestingly, Ratzinger notes that the papacy of that time, with its universal ecclesial ministry, supported such new movements of the Spirit and "all this gave a great boost to the development of the doctrine of primacy," allowing the Petrine office to be "understood anew in the light of its apostolic roots."[21]

At their beginnings the Jesuits also faced opposition because its priests were not tied to a monastic cloister nor did they live as simple friars. They resembled the secular clergy in their loose structure, in their private celebration of the divine office, and in their not being

---

20. Ratzinger, "The Ecclesial Movements," 49. On the tensions that arose throughout history in new attempts at ecclesial renewal, see Cordes, *Charisms*, 65–93.
21. Ratzinger, "The Ecclesial Movements," 43.

committed to community life. This new form of religious life suited the time, but faced resistance.

The opposition that movements faced did not come only from institutional officeholders. The French theologian Louis Bouyer discredits the notion that Church authorities always block new movements as a caricature that can be traced to the eighteenth century pietistic preacher and teacher, Gottfried Arnold. In his review of history, Bouyer notes that Church authorities generally tried to avoid condemning movements, instead integrating them into the life of the Church for the benefit of the whole Christian body.[22] Occasionally movements or charismatic groups have demonstrated a certain arrogance by presenting themselves as the perfect Church. Such an attitude reveals a Messianic complex that forgets the reality that God the Father's house has many rooms, many ways of living the same faith. Such was clearly the case with the Montanists in the first millennium or the Cathars in the second.

Insertion into the Local Church

Inserting ecclesial movements into the local diocesan communities often causes controversy. Given their international identity and their status as pontifical associations, the movements in a certain sense transcend diocesan structures. To what extent should movements tailor their activities to fit diocesan programs? How do movements relate to other diocesan bodies, groups, orders and associations?

The question is linked to an ecclesiological issue much discussed in recent years — the relationship between the universal and local churches. A 1992 letter to bishops from the Congregation for the Doctrine of the Faith states:

> From the Church, which in its origins and its first manifestation is universal, have arisen the different local Churches, as particular expressions of the one unique Church of Jesus Christ. Arising *within* and *out of* the universal Church, they have their ecclesiality in it and from it. Hence the formula of the Second Vatican Council: *The Church in and formed out of the Churches*

---

22. See Louis Bouyer, "Some Charismatic Movements in the History of the Church," in Edward D. O'Connor, *Perspectives on Charismatic Renewal* (1975), 114.

... is inseparable from this other formula: *The Churches in and formed out of the Church.* Clearly the relationship between the universal Church and the particular Churches is a mystery, and cannot be compared to that which exists between the whole and the parts in a purely human group or society.[23]

Each Christian is baptized into the Church in this twofold dynamic. Movements, in their universal extension, reflect the Church's universal as well as its particular dimensions. New associations or movements are not alternatives to already existing institutions, but a gift of the Spirit to help the overall renewal of the Church in every era, particularly in the one following Vatican II.

Old and new must discover together how to live in a spirit of communion so that the Church may appear before the world with its many forms of holiness and service, as "a kind of instrument or sign of intimate union with God, and of the unity of humankind" (*Lumen gentium*, 1). Newer movements need to value the reservoir of wisdom and experience that older institutes have gained through their courageous acceptance down the centuries of the severest of hardships. Old institutes can be enriched through dialogue and an exchange of gifts with the foundations appearing in recent history.[24]

A later chapter on the movements and parishes will consider this topic from another perspective. For now it is enough to recall Cardinal Ratzinger's advice quoted earlier (see p. 63), that it is not possible simply to give a recipe for how this is to happen. Each bishop, as head of the Church in his own diocese, is the final arbiter. Certainly "some rules are necessary but then a great deal depends on the persons involved. That is my experience. If the persons — the parish priest, the groups and also the bishops — are amenable, solutions will be found."[25]

Maturity and Leadership

Tensions due to the internal workings of movements sometimes arise because of a simple lack of maturity early in their growth. Children cannot run before they begin to walk. Something similar

---

23. See the Congregation for the Doctrine of the Faith's Letter to the Bishops of the Catholic Church, *Some Aspects of the Church Understood as Communion*, May 28, 1992.
24. See Ellen Leonard, "Ecclesial Religious Communities Old and New," in *The Way Supplement* 201 (2001): 119–128.
25. *Pastoral Concern of the Bishops*, 232.

is true of new communities in the life of the Church. They may have to learn more than they anticipated. For instance, some might feel tempted to hold on to ways of doing things not essential to the charism, or indeed that block its evolution in the Spirit of God. In their desire to be vehicles of change, others might not heed the words of Ecclesiastes 3 that there is a time for everything, resorting instead to contentious polemics. It is also true that not all founders succeed equally in passing on their original vision.

Strong leadership is good, but not at the cost of diversity and creativity. Individuals have their own psychological and sociological experience that marks their unique spiritual journey. Leaders need to be attentive to help them grow and develop in maturity. Members do find great support in the communitarian experience of a movement, but it must help each one discover the unique plan God has for him or her. As von Balthasar remarks, "the leadership of the community must seek from the outset to develop the personality of the members in such a way that they can fulfill their task in the world autonomously."[26] In this regard he also advocates that

> a capacity for dialogue ought to be a concern for all the leaders of such movements, whether this means ecumenical dialogue with non-Catholic Christians or dialogue with those of other faiths.... One will not learn this art of dialogue without some training; if such training is lacking, they, the lay movement, will end up contradicting its proper essence by closing in upon itself. This is why each one ought to acquire an appropriate knowledge of other world views and learn to discern which points in them are compatible with one's own world view, where the differences lie, and what can lead to damaging developments for human culture. It may be that conversations among members, where some are more versed in the culture of dialogue than others, can accomplish more here than all-too-theoretical courses.[27]

Concerning members who veer towards doctrinaire traditionalism, von Balthasar comments that "they fail to see that the letter without the spirit is fatal, that tradition is above all something living, that it

---

26. Ibid.
27. Von Balthasar, "Lay Movements in the Church," 278.

is a forwards impulse, a continuous immersion in the living Word, in prayer and contemplation."[28]

Renewal through Contact with Others

The founder of the L'Arche community, Jean Vanier, has noted two distinctive differences that become evident as communities or movements grow, deepen their spirituality, and are recognized by the Church. First, what becomes increasingly significant is the need that the movement or community be there for each person, to foster growth into freedom and a deepening personal consciousness. Second, the movement must not remain closed in upon itself. As they grow to maturity, community members must be encouraged to maintain contact with other Christians, movements, spiritual leaders and theologians in the Church.[29] Indeed, Vanier believes that contact with other initiatives within the body of the Church contributes to a constant renewal of movements.

The work of the Spirit is manifest when a movement, acknowledging its own limits, weaknesses, and insularity, realizes it has committed errors: "We all need to be pruned and purified in order to be faithful to the Holy Spirit. Only then can we remain grounded in our identity, charism and spirituality, while at the same time being open to evolving in accordance with the needs of the times."[30] Although commenting on wider ecclesial realities, John Paul II's words hold true for the movements as well: "Acknowledging the weaknesses of the past is an act of honesty and courage which helps us to strengthen our faith, which alerts us to face today's temptations and challenges, and prepares us to meet them."[31]

Sinfulness can strike at any level within the life of a movement. Indeed, Thomas Aquinas' teaching that charisms are gifts endowed for the benefit of others suggests how, because of sin, a charism that does good for others may not necessarily sanctify the one who has received it, be that person a founder or member of a movement. In other words, the grace of the charism can work though someone,

28. See von Balthasar, "Integralismus heute," *Diakonia* 19 (1988): 226ff. Cited in Angelo Scola, "The Reality of Movements in the Universal Church and in the Local Church," in *Movements in the Church*, 105–129 at 116, n. 29.

29. Vanier, "Know Them by Their Fruits," in *The Tablet* (March 15, 1997): 346–347, at 346.

30. See Vanier, "Know Them by Their Fruits," 347.

31. *Tertio millennio adveniente*, 33.

but that particular person might not personally respond to the grace. Albert Vonhoye comments, "It is possible that a grace *gratis data* is in no way useful to the one who has received it, but only to other people. However, this does not correspond to God's intentions; it happens on account of the sin of the individual."[32]

In addressing movements' need for renewal from within, Jean Vanier proposes that outside help is necessary:

> Movements and communities will normally need help from outside in order to face their shadow side, to perceive and evaluate how authority has been exercised, how power is used and abused. They will also need to listen and accept criticism, to have the courage to question themselves, the honesty to admit shortcomings and the energy to change.... The presence of the poor and the weak keeps a movement humble and prevents it from closing in upon itself.[33]

Of course, the principal "outside" help is the authoritative role of the Church's magisterium. The continuing development of movements depends upon their statutes or rules of life being approved by the Church authorities. These statutes or regulations form an objective reference point to assist reform. The canonist Gianfranco Ghirlanda describes how a collective charism becomes a canonical institute when the Church recognizes its usefulness for a specific mission and approves the statute or regulation governing it. These statutes or constitutions, given by a founder, express "in an immediate manner the charism and the specific way for living it according to its own immanent demands."[34] A movement based on a charism bears within

---

32. See Albert Vonhoye, "Charism" in René Latourelle and Rino Fisichella, *Dictionary of Fundamental Theology*, 103–108, at 105. The case of Father Marcial Maciel Degollado, founder of the Legionaries of Christ and the Regnum Christi movements, illustrates this point. Discovering and coming to know the truth about the founder has caused the members of these movements shock, bewilderment, and deep pain. A communiqué released on May 1, 2010 by the Holy See, regarding meetings held with the visitors who it had sent to the Legion of Christ, notes how the pope urges them not to lose sight of the fact that their vocation, which originates in Christ's call and is driven by the ideal of being witnesses of his love to the world, is a genuine gift from God, a treasure for the Church, and the indestructible foundation on which each of them can build their own future and that of the Legion, http://www.zenit.org/article-29109?l=english (accessed December 4, 2010).

33. Vanier, "Know Them by Their Fruits," 347.

34. See Ghirlanda, "Istituzione," in Gianfranco Calabrese, Philip Goyret, Orazio Francesco Piazza, eds., *Dizionario di Ecclesiologia* (Rome: Città Nuova, 2010), 770–784, at 783.

itself, in other words, an immanent structure that shapes the way in which it can and must be exercised in the Church. Movements, therefore, need to exercise their own capacity for self-criticism in the Spirit, both in terms of their own approved structures and also through engagement with issues arising from the wider Church body.

Above all, by keeping holiness — the perfection of charity — as a goal and the gospel as a code of life, a movement will always desire for itself as a whole — and so for its members — fidelity to truth, love and justice. By being "re-evangelized," movements remain faithful to their founding vision. No evangelization can take place without prior constant re-evangelization. *Verbum domini*, which specifies the place of the Word of God in the life and mission of the Church, notes that Christian communities, parishes, associations, and movements always have to be "examining the ordinary activities … to see if they are truly concerned with fostering a personal encounter with Christ, who gives himself to us in his word."

The gospel provides proof that the Spirit is at work: the tree is known by its fruits (see Mt 7:16). History provides the surest way of verifying the gifts of God. [35]

---

35. See Vanier, "Know Them by Their Fruits," 346–347.

14

The Parish and Movements

The parish has been defined as the "most immediate and visible expression" of the Church, the place where the Church is seen locally, "living in the midst of the homes of her sons and daughters."[1] The place of movements in the life of a parish needs to be explored.

The identity of the parish has been and still is passing through substantial changes. In the past the parish had served, especially in rural areas, as a center of social and religious life. Rapidly changing cultural and social circumstances, however, have rendered it more a "service station" for religious functions. Although those who continue to practice their faith still view it as an indispensable structure, the profound cultural and social changes since Vatican II have made it clear that the parish needs to be renewed.

Surprisingly, however, the final redaction of the documents of the Second Vatican Council does not include a direct, systematic treatment of parishes. The preparatory texts did address the topic, but as the final documents were formulated it disappeared.[2] This change in focus suggests that the renewal of the parish is to be understood against the broader canvas of the renewal of the whole Church, a renewal that the Council promoted in terms of mystery, communion and mission. The documents of Vatican II present the unity of the Church in terms of the People of God, Body of Christ and Temple of the Holy Spirit. In its ecclesiology of communion, the many bonds of communion are emphasized, not least of which is the communion of bishops around the pope, expressing the communion of many local churches in the one universal Church of Christ. The parish expresses the same dynamic of communion within the diocesan church, gathered around the bishop as the visible point of unity.

Paraphrasing Paul VI regarding the Church as a whole, theologian Federica Rosy Romersa writes, "Just as the Church so too the parish can be asked: 'Parish who are you? What do you do? Where are you

---

1. See John Paul II, *Christifideles laici*, 26.
2. See F. Coccopalmerio, "Il concetto di parrocchia nel Vaticano II," in *La Scuola Cattolica* 56 (1978): 123–142.

going?' " The answer comes from the whole Council, which John XXIII purposefully intended to be primarily pastoral.[3]

The Council documents do not provide a full definition of parish, but their various references to the parish, its nature and tasks offer many valuable perspectives and horizons.[4] *Sacrosanctum concilium*, n. 42, for instance, presents a description of the parish subsequently used in the Code of Canon Law (c. 515, 1): the parish is a community of the faithful (*communitas christifidelium*), organized locally and under the guidance of a pastor who takes the place of the bishop. Such a definition is not intended, however, as a juridical outline. *Sacrosanctum concilium* expands on that definition, proposing that the parish is not merely a portion of Church, but is the Church itself in a particular place: "the parishes ... represent the visible Church constituted throughout the world." *Lumen gentium*, n. 26, also affirms this idea. While strictly speaking it refers to dioceses, it can be read also in reference to parish communities: "This Church of Christ is truly present in all legitimate local congregations of the faithful which, united with their pastors, are themselves called churches in the New Testament. For in their locality these are the new People called by God, in the Holy Spirit and in much fullness." The parish is, as it were, a "sacrament" of the universal Church that in it is really present.

Clearly, Vatican II envisions the diocese as the unit that can be called "church" in the full sense, and the parish in a subordinated manner. The parish is Church to the extent it is inserted into the context of its own local Church and united through its pastors with the bishop. In that sense, the parish is, as another Vatican II document puts it, "a kind of cell" of the diocese.[5] Because the parish is called

---

3. See Federica Rosy Romersa, *Il rinnovamento della parrocchia nella Chiesa Italiana dal Concilio ad oggi* (Rome: Mursia, 1999), 63.

4. See *Sacrosanctum concilium*, 42 (on strengthening the liturgical life of the parish); *Lumen gentium*, 26 (presence of the Church in all the legitimate local assemblies), *Christus dominus*, 30 (the parishes and their functions); *Actuositatem apostolicam*, 10 (the apostolate of the laity in the context of the communities of the Church), *AA*, 26 (councils for the collaboration between priests, religious and laity at parish level); *Ad gentes*, 15 (the formation process of the Christian communities); *AG*, 37 (missionary duty of the Christian communities); *Presbyterorum ordinis*, 6 (formation and life of authentic Christian communities).

5. *Actuositatem apostolicam*, 10. This was a point emphasized by the pastoral theologian D. Grasso just before the Council began in "Osservazioni sulla teologia della parrocchia," in *Gregorianum* 40 (1959), 297–314, at 305–307.

to be Church, it must be open to the whole Church. In terms of mystery, each part contains the whole and all that has to do with the whole concerns each particular parish community. In other words, the parish is itself only if it is beyond itself.

This explains the Council's invitation to broaden outreach and mission. Speaking of the apostolate of the lay faithful it says:

> They should not limit their cooperation to the parochial or diocesan boundaries but strive to extend it to interparochial, interdiocesan, national, and international fields. This is constantly becoming all the more necessary because the daily increase in mobility of populations, reciprocal relationships, and means of communication no longer allow any sector of society to remain closed in upon itself. Thus they should be concerned about the needs of the people of God dispersed throughout the world.[6]

Bishops are called to exercise their functions so that "pastors and their assistants should so fulfill their duty ... that the faithful and the parish communities will truly realize that they are members both of the diocese and of the universal Church."[7]

Renewal of the parish must be guided by the conviction that pervades the Council: it is not individual Christians who first and foremost make the Church; rather the Risen Christ generates the Church in the Spirit. The community, as it were, "receives" itself from him. The Council highlights three living principles that build up the local assemblies: the proclamation of the Word, the celebration of the Eucharist (which presupposes hierarchical communion) and unity in charity.[8]

The parish community exists inasmuch as it "receives" itself from Christ, but Vatican II also clarifies that the parish is not itself unless it is giving of itself. The parish community must be missionary: "The grace of renewal cannot grow in communities unless each of these extends the range of its charity to the ends of the earth, and devotes the same care to those afar off as it does to those who are its own members."[9] Again the Council underlines how the very life of

---

6. *Actuositatem apostolicam*, 10.
7. *Christus dominus*, 30.
8. *Lumen gentium*, 26.
9. *Ad gentes*, 37.

the parish *community* itself must be missionary: "The parish offers an obvious example of the apostolate on the community level inasmuch as it brings together the many human differences within its boundaries and merges them into the universality of the Church."[10] The parish "is not principally a structure, a territory, or a building but the 'family of God,' a fellowship afire with a unifying spirit.... Plainly and simply the parish is founded on a theological reality, because it is a Eucharistic community."[11]

Pastoral Renewal

The Council provides parameters for pastoral renewal. The Code of Canon Law translates those parameters into the definition of the parish as "a definite community of the Christian faithful established on a stable basis within a particular church" (c. 515.1). Following the Council, through reflection on parish identity and pastoral renewal, experts have sought to formulate the vocational identity of parishes.[12] In recent times there is more participation and responsible collaboration among ordained ministers and laity. Yet, while Canon Law may have translated the Council's vision into the notion of the parish as a community of the faithful,[13] the actual lived experience is one of massive transition from a monologue parish to a dialogue parish, from a clerical parish to a ministerial parish, from a Sunday parish to a daily parish, from an "introverted" parish to an "extrovert parish."[14] Parishes are undergoing a great transformation into a living community rooted in the Word of God, animated by a spirit of true communion and so being "a family home, fraternal and warmly receptive."[15] Such transformation requires a change of mindset:

---

10. *Actuositatem apostolicam*, 10.

11. *Christifideles laici*, 26.

12. See for instance, Sabbas Kilian, *Theological Models for the Parish* (Staten Island, NY: Alba House, 1977); Barbara Anne Cusack and Teresa Sullivan, *Pastoral Care in Parishes Without Pastors* (Washington: Canon Law Society of America, 1995); James A. Coriden, *The Parish in Catholic Tradition: History, Theology, and Canon Law* (New York and Mahwah, NJ: Paulist Press, 1997); Carole Ganin, *Shaping Catholic Parishes: Pastoral Leaders in the Twenty-first Century* (Chicago: Loyola Press, 2008).

13. See canons 515–552.

14. See Adolfo Raggio (ed.), *The Parish Community: A Path to Community* (New York: New City Press, 2000), 45.

15. John Paul II, Apostolic Letter on Catechesis in our Time, *Catechesi tradendae* (October 16, 1979), 67.

It is necessary to improve pastoral structures in such a way
that the co-responsibility of all the members of the People of
God in their entirety is gradually promoted, with respect for
vocations and for the respective roles of the consecrated and
of lay people. This demands a change in mindset, particularly
concerning lay people. They must no longer be viewed as "col-
laborators" of the clergy but truly recognized as "co-responsible" for the Church's being and action, thereby fostering the
consolidation of a mature and committed laity.[16]

As well as a new mindset, pastoral renewal requires new ways
of acting. Lay ministries have developed greatly in the past fifty
years.[17] One ecclesiological theme that has emerged more and more
since the Council is that of synodality (from the Greek words *syn* [to-
gether] and *hodos* [a way]). The notion of *synod* involves a dynamic
sense of journeying along the same road, going together, being a
group of people on a journey. The Second Vatican Council, among
its many contributions, highlighted how from the very beginning
of the Church synodality has characterized the Christian ecclesial
experience. It has taken undeniably hard work to put synodality into
practice. Doing so means learning how to make all occasions when
the community gathers "synodal," moments to prepare to welcome
the presence of the risen Christ and his Spirit working among
them.[18] Romersa identifies synodality as the hermeneutical key to
the profound innovations of the Code in how it views the parish as
the community of faithful. Once, while attending a Sunday liturgy in
a Roman parish, Pope Paul VI commented on the need of this sense
of journeying together with Christ amidst the community:

Are the faithful united here in love, in the charity of Christ? Then
certainly this is a living parish. The true Church is here since the

16. Pope Benedict to the Convention of the Diocese of Rome on the theme: "Church Mem-
    bership and Pastoral Co-Responsibility" (May 26, 2009). See also, *Lumen gentium*, 32.
17. See Zeni Fox, *New Ecclesial Ministry: Lay Professionals Serving the Church* (Chi-
    cago: Sheed & Ward, 2002). See also James D. Davidson and Suzanne C. Fournier,
    "Recent Research on Catholic Parishes: A Research Note," in *Review of Religious
    Research* 48 (2006/1): 72–81.
18. See Piero Coda and Brendan Leahy (eds.), *Preti in una Chiesa che cambia* (Rome:
    Città Nuova, 2010), and Brendan Leahy, "People, Synod and Upper Room: Vatican
    II's Ecclesiology of Communion," in Dermot A. Lane and Brendan Leahy (eds.),
    Vatican II: Facing the 21st Century: Historical and Theological Perspectives
    (Dublin: Veritas, 2006), 49–80.

divine-human phenomenon that perpetuates the presence of Christ among us is blossoming here. Are the faithful gathered together merely because they are registered on the local area register or the baptismal register? Are they gathered together simply because they're here on Sunday to hear Mass without knowing each other even though they stand shoulder to shoulder? If that's how it is, the Church is not connected together; the cement that is to form everyone into a real, organic unity is not yet working.... Remember Christ's words. They will know you are my disciples if you love one another; if there's this warmth of affection and sentiments; if there's this love vibrating (in the parish) ... with that greatness of heart and the capacity of generating Christ among us.[19]

The Movements and the Parish

Ecclesial movements illustrate how the Holy Spirit is offering new ways. Their sense of belonging, their spiritual and doctrinal formation, and their missionary vigor demonstrate important dimensions of Church life. Parishes could benefit from the positive attributes that movements offer, although the connection between the two has not yet been developed. Making that connection is complicated because parishes vary greatly. On the one hand, contemporary parishes often operate in clusters or parish units; many no longer have resident priests. On the other hand, movements themselves vary in their approach to parish life. Some maintain only minimal contact; some are highly involved, even holding their own liturgies or para-liturgical services in the parish.

The Council noted how lay associations "sustain their members, form them for the apostolate, and rightly organize and regulate their apostolic work so that much better results can be expected than if each member were to act on his or her own." Group apostolate "happily corresponds to a human and Christian need and at the same time signifies the communion and unity of the Church in Christ, who said, 'Where two or three are gathered together in my name, there am I in the midst of them' (Mt 18:20)." In short, Vatican II commends the "united effort" that associations manifest.[20]

---

19. *Insegnamenti di Paolo VI*, II (Vatican City, 1964), 1072–1073.
20. *Actuositatem apostolicam*, 18.

John Paul II, taking up the Council's encouraging attitude, advocated that parishes offer movements recognition, esteem, and support.[21] Acknowledging that movements need to integrate their activities with the pastoral guidelines of the bishop of a diocese, he envisioned how they could contribute to developing the spiritual life of the parish, forming young people, and reaching out to the needy.[22] His encyclical on mission, *Redemptoris missio* elaborates the connection between the two:

> I call to mind, as a new development occurring in many churches in recent times, the rapid growth of "ecclesial movements" filled with missionary dynamism. When these movements humbly seek to become part of the life of local churches and are welcomed by bishops and priests within diocesan and parish structures, they represent a true gift of God both for new evangelization and for missionary activity properly so-called. I therefore recommend that they be spread, and that they be used to give fresh energy, especially among young people, to the Christian life and to evangelization, within a pluralistic view of the ways in which Christians can associate and express themselves. (N. 72)

Benedict XVI also has encouraged communion between parish structures and movements. He sees that movements can contribute to building up small Christian communities, offer a sense of belonging, and generate new ideas for missionary outreach.

The Need for Dialogue

The Australian Bishop Julian Porteous summarizes the possible tensions that can arise between parishes and movements:

> Tensions exist when a pastor senses that the movements draw people away from a fundamental allegiance to the parish. They can feel that the movements demand a total adherence to their life and activities and so limit the availability of their members to assist in the life of the parish. A particularly

---

21. See his Address to the Bishops of Lombardia on their *ad limina* visit, December 18, 1986.
22. See his address to the bishops of the apostolic region of southwest France, February 25, 1977, in *La Traccia*, 18 (February 1, 1997), 71–72.

thorny issue is the question of a movement wishing to have its own celebration of the Sunday Eucharist.... Parishioners can also feel second rate in the level of their life and services when they see what a movement is capable of doing. They sometimes feel that members of movements consider themselves above ordinary parishioners. Movements can also give the impression of being separatist, with their own spirituality and practices.[23]

Parishes and movements need to maintain a balanced interaction. On the one hand, in their desire for simplicity and authentic gospel life movements must avoid considering themselves the only way of being Church and so detach themselves from valid institutional structures. On the other hand, the parish must avoid a self-perception that it offers the only valid ecclesial structure for carrying out apostolate, thus constraining every activity within the straightjacket of a narrowly focused parish pastoral plan.

Movements can find their place in the parish if everyone involved — pastors, members of movements, agents of parish programs — work out their relationship through open, attentive dialogue. By doing so, it can be discerned how movements can contribute to diocesan programs while remaining faithful to their specific charism, and movements can discern how, in cooperation with other diocesan entities and other movements, they can be co-responsible within a diocese. Hans Urs von Balthasar offers a roadmap for such dialogue:

> The existence of movements with and alongside one another in one limited area of the Church places high Christian demands on the various groups: first, they must accept the validity of other programs, priorities, and charisms, to the extent that the Christian discernment of spirits makes this at all possible; then, in circumstances where this is possible and feasible, a mutual promotion for the greater good of the larger whole (the small parish or the large diocese) of which both are a part. Corresponding demands are made of the parish priest and the bishop: they must remain objective as they test the values that belong to the different movements, not allowing themselves

---

23. Julian Porteous, *A New Wine and Fresh Skins*, 150–151.

to be biased by personal preferences and prejudices and being concerned as much as possible to enable the peaceful collaboration of the movements.[24]

Movements are not merely pious groups on the margins of parish life. Rather, group endeavors, movements, and communities express within the parish a "co-essential" charismatic dimension of the Church. Anthony Oelrich, quoting Pope Benedict's remark that being a Christian is not "the result of an ethical choice or a lofty idea, but the encounter with an event, a person, which gives life a new horizon and a decisive direction," goes on to say "the parish is that concrete place where Christianity takes on its nature as event, as encounter."[25] According to William A. Clark, "The Church is made present and becomes 'event' in the communion of persons tangibly experienced in a particular location."[26] If this is so, then within the parish movements can be particular points where people can experience the nature of the Church as "event."

The hierarchical charism of ordained ministers is essential in making visible the universal Church in the local community. The Code of Canon Law states that "The pastoral care of the parish is entrusted to a pastor as its own shepherd under the authority of the diocesan bishop" (c. 515.1). In a parish, priests take the place of the bishop. That role includes teaching, sanctifying, and building up the community in the name of Christ "so that the new commandment of charity may be fulfilled by all."[27] Since Vatican II, however, ordained ministers are summoned to a new way. It is not enough that they follow Jesus in response to a personal conversion through the action of the Spirit. They also need a ministerial conversion, a new attentiveness to the plurality of the presence and action of the Spirit in the Church and in the world. No one has a monopoly on the Holy Spirit — neither the hierarchy, nor a consolidated tradition, nor this or that new organization. The Spirit, who "blows where it chooses" (Jn 3:8), requires learning anew how hierarchy and charism discern together the direction they are being led.

24. "Lay Movements in the Church," 276.
25. See Anthony Oelrich, "Trinity and the Parish: Some Insights from the Theology of Yves Congar, OP," in *Chicago Studies* 46 (2007/2): 176–189, at 183.
26. William A. Clark, *A Voice of Their Own: The Authority of the Local Parish* (Collegeville, MN: Liturgical Press, 2005), xix.
27. *Lumen gentium*, 32.

The parish must be understood via what might be called a "Trinitarian logic." The three Divine Persons are One, yet distinct, totally-for-one-another. This is the model of parish that the Council suggests. Inter-relating by "living the life of the Trinity" is the challenge.[28] The Council envisaged a network of councils that would assist the interaction among all in the parish.[29] Such a network might help to discern the place of movements in a parish. Parishes and movements alike have to develop their awareness of what and how movements can contribute to and be more integrated into parish life. Renée M. La Reau's comment regarding ecclesial movements in America sums up that status of movements throughout the Church: "Though the new ecclesial movements have a ways to go before they work their way into the mainstream U.S. church, they're an important phenomenon worth paying attention to."[30]

---

28. See John Paul II, *Novo millennio ineunte*, 29. See also Anthony Oelrich's "Trinity and the Parish," and Daniel Barnett's "Trinity and the Parish: A Response to Fr. Anthony Oelrich," *Chicago Studies* 46 (2007/2), 190–208.

29. *Actuositatem apostolicam*, 26. See Brendan Leahy, "Pastoral Councils: Making Communion Visible," *Doctrine and Life* 55 (2005/4), 11–21.

30. See Renée M. LaReau, "Super Catholics? Sizing up the New Lay Movements," *U. S. Catholic*, February 2006, 12–17, at 17. She has also written *Getting a Life: How to Find Your True Vocation* (New York: Orbis, 2003).

15

Priests and Ecclesial Movements

More and more priests belong to ecclesial movements, where they find an experience that enriches their life and ministry. Such participation, however, raises certain questions. How can priests join movements? Isn't the priesthood meant to serve everyone? Don't priests have their own spirituality? This chapter reflects on such issues, particularly in the light of the invitation Benedict XVI offered in his letter proclaiming 2009–2010 a Year for Priests: "I would like to invite all priests ... to welcome the new springtime which the Spirit is now bringing about in the Church, not least through the ecclesial movements and the new communities."[1] According to the pope, the gifts of the Spirit give rise to movements and awaken in many people a desire for a deeper spiritual life which "can benefit not only the lay faithful but the clergy as well."

What Are Priests Saying about Their Experience in the Movements?

Describing his involvement in the Legion of Mary, the late Father Tom O'Flynn, C.M., former spiritual director in Clonliffe College, Dublin, notes "the happiness we receive ... from reports not only from the home country but from abroad and from the most distant parts of the world. Through this salutary sharing of apostolic experience we, like the early Christians, are one in thought ... and in affection with our brothers and sisters throughout the world. We are encouraged by news of their enterprise and ... share our experiences ... with them."[2] The well-known spiritual writer and pastoral theologian, Henri Nouwen spoke of discovering the L'Arche community as a "home." In 1986 he accepted the position of pastor for a L'Arche community near Toronto, Canada called "Daybreak." The German bishop and theologian, Klaus Hemmerle, described his encounter as a young priest with the Focolare Movement as an

---

1. See Letter to Priests, proclaiming a year for priests on the 150th anniversary of the birthday of the Curé of Ars, June 16, 2009.
2. Taken from the Legion of Mary review, *Maria Legionis,* September 1996.

opportunity to enter into a new experience of the closeness of God. His theological studies had made him understand that God wants to become the center of each person's life. They didn't explain, however, what people must do for that to happen. He couldn't seem to find room for such closeness in his daily life. There was a gap between what he wanted and what he was living: "I needed a link. In the first Mariapolis [the Focolare's annual gathering] I attended, this emptiness was completely filled. God was simply there. He permeated our mutual relationships. I felt irresistibly drawn to this new life."[3]

The Community of Sant'Egidio is founded on the three pillars of prayer, friendship and poverty. Commenting on what it meant to him to be involved from his youth in that community, the Italian bishop Vincenzo Paglia writes, "Our meeting with the Gospel saved us from the great risk of ideologies.... One of the strengths of the Sant'Egidio community was putting the Word of God at the center of its life. This meeting with the Word more and more became a listening to the Word and prayer. We gradually came to understand that in the Church it is more important to be disciples than activists or protagonists."[4]

Understanding Vocations Together

Reflection on priests' involvement in movements can profit from what John Paul II said in *Christifideles laici*. Summarizing Vatican II, he points out that all vocations in the Church must be understood together. What is distinctive to any specific calling can only be worked out in terms of the inter-relationship of vocations within a commonly shared baptismal calling:

> In Church Communion the states of life by being ordered one to the other are thus bound together among themselves. They all share in a deeply basic meaning: that of being *the manner of living out the commonly shared Christian dignity and the universal call to holiness in the perfection of love.* They are *different yet complementary,* in the sense that each of them has a basic and unmistakable character which sets each apart, while at the same time each of them is seen in relation to the other and placed at each other's service.[5]

3. Klaus Hemmerle, "Tell Me about Your God," *Being One* 5 (1996), 13–20 at 13–14.
4. "The Community of St. Egidio," *Being One* 10 (2001), 109–117 at 111–112.
5. *Christifideles laici*, 55.

The distinction of vocations is at the service of the one mission of the whole Church:

> Thus the *lay* state of life has its distinctive feature in its secular character. It fulfills an ecclesial service in bearing witness and, in its own way recalling for priests, women and men religious, the significance of the earthly and temporal realities in the salvific plan of God. In turn, the *ministerial priesthood* represents in different times and places, the permanent guarantee of the sacramental presence of Christ, the Redeemer. The *religious state* bears witness to the eschatological character of the Church, that is, the straining towards the Kingdom of God that is prefigured and in some way anticipated and experienced even now through the vows of chastity, poverty and obedience. All the states of life, whether taken collectively or individually in relation to the others, are at the service of the Church's growth. While different in expression they are deeply united in the Church's "mystery of communion" and are dynamically coordinated in its unique mission.[6]

Priests are called first and foremost to witness to the presence of God in history, Jesus himself living and working among two or more united in his name, in the mystery of communion (Mt 18:20). All priests find the basis of their spirituality by living out the common ecclesial spirituality which the whole people of God is called to live and manifest, that is, baptismal spirituality, the living out of baptismal priesthood. According to scripture scholar Albert Vanhoye,

> Baptismal priesthood and ministerial priesthood must go together. When we exercise our ministry, we must offer ourselves too, in union with Christ's offering. At a personal level, the baptismal priesthood is more important than the ministerial priesthood. The ministerial priesthood is a gift of Christ to the Church, a wonderful gift. It is not something that belongs to us personally, it is not something that increases our personal value. The most important thing for us personally is the way in which we offer ourselves, just as every believer is called to offer him or herself. We must add that this exercise of baptismal priesthood has, for us, a specific form: pastoral charity. Baptismal priesthood is always an exercising of charity, but the specific aspect of this

---

6. Ibid.

for us is pastoral charity. Baptismal priesthood and ministerial priesthood must be united in our lives.[7]

Through the sacrament of ordination, priests are ordained in the service of the whole Christian community, in unity with the bishop and in fraternal collaboration with the presbyterate as a whole. They stand "before" the Church, sacramentally representing Christ, head of the body, spouse of the bride, the Church.[8] In particular, the Spirit is calling priests to focus on the life of communion among the People of God, a life in which they also share. This understanding of ordination, one of the principal reforms of Vatican II, is vitally important for priests at a time when their social identity is undergoing profound transformation. Through baptism all are called to share in the communitarian holiness of the People of God. *Pastores dabo vobis*, n. 17, states:

> The ministerial priesthood conferred by the sacrament of holy orders and the common or "royal" priesthood of the faithful, which differ essentially and not only in degree, are ordered one to the other — for each in its own way derives from the one priesthood of Christ. Indeed, the ministerial priesthood does not of itself signify a greater degree of holiness with regard to the common priesthood of the faithful; through it Christ gives to priests, in the Spirit, a particular gift so that they can help the People of God to exercise faithfully and fully the common priesthood which it has received.[9]

Experiencing Communion — Learning the "Co-essentiality" of Hierarchy and Charism

In their role of building community in the parish or other ministries, priests can find themselves isolated or "above" the community. This can happen no matter how much they work "for" the community in hope of collaborating "with" others. Subtle, historically-rooted clerical isolation or separation often lingers among those with and for whom priests minister. This sense can be compounded if priests exercise

---

7. Albert Vanhoye, *Accogliamo Cristo nostro Sommo Sacerdote* (Vatican City, 2008), 175–176.

8. See the Apostolic Exhortation on the Formation of Priests in the Circumstances of the Present Day, *Pastores dabo vobis* (March 25, 1992), 16–18.

9. Ibid.

their role of testing and discerning, recognizing and fostering the gifts of the laity, in a way that leaves them, perhaps unwittingly, aloof.[10] An Oxford theologian, Ian Ker writes, "The sacrament of holy orders does set apart in the sense that the one who receives it shares in the ministerial priesthood — but it does not set apart the priest in the sense that somehow he no longer shares in, because he has risen above, the common priesthood of the baptized."[11]

Priests need a home, a place where they can experience the light and warmth of fraternal communion that helps them to mature in their own Christian journey as brothers among all their brothers and sisters. Movements which have a charism that draws people together can offer a particular experience of such communion. These pockets of communion arising from charisms of the Spirit "always create affinities, destined to be for each person a support for their object task in the Church."[12] So for a priest, belonging to a movement is not first and foremost a pastoral tool, but rather a chance to grow in his own personal life and ministry.

John Paul II tells how, "'touched' and 'attracted' by the same charism, sharing in the same story, inserted into the same group, priests and lay people share an interesting experience of co-fraternity among the 'faithful' that build each other up mutually without confusion."[13] A priest of the Neocatechumenal Way describes his experience: "For me one of the most important things is that I find myself part of a community of brothers and sisters, not under them or above them, but with them, and I too began to live the fullness of my baptism. Once you have had this experience in the community it changes you. You realize that priesthood is only one charism among many and you want to see all the other charisms develop too."[14]

---

10. See *Presbyterorum ordinis*, 7.
11. Ian Ker, "The Priesthood and the New Ecclesial Movements," *Louvain Studies* 30 (2005): 124–136, at 134.
12. See John Paul II's address to priests connected with the *Communion and Liberation* movement (September 12, 1985), *AAS* 78 (1986), 256. Canon 278 provides for the right of clergy to associate with groups "for the achievement of purposes befitting the clerical state."
13. John Paul II; Letter to Cardinal James Francis Stafford, President of the Pontifical Council for the Laity on the occasion of a pastoral meeting organized by the Focolare Movement at Castelgandolfo, "Ecclesial Movements for the New Evangelization," June 21, 2001. In *Origins* 31 (10) (August 2, 2001): 187–188. See *also Pastores dabo vobis*, 31.
14. See Alan Fudge, "The Neocatechumenal Way," *New City* 30 (2000/Aug-Sept), 4–5 at 4.

Reinforced by this experience of communion, which itself is missionary, priests gain zeal to carry out with missionary drive their many and varied ministerial tasks. Paradoxically, by engaging in a strong experience of baptismal communion they strengthen their own specific ministry. This is important also because priests, who continually encounter the sacred, run the risk of becoming professionals of the sacred and unwittingly let their pastoral service and sacramental life become a mere habit, failing to "perceive the great, new and surprising fact that (Jesus) himself is present, speaks to us, gives himself to us."[15] For many priests, every time they live a moment of deep spiritual communion with their lay brothers and sisters in an ecclesial community or movement, they come away with a new conviction of the reality of God, Jesus, and the Church. Again to quote John Paul II, "The priest must find in the movement the light and warmth that will enable him to be faithful to his bishop, ready to fulfill his institutional duties, and attentive to ecclesiastical discipline: in this way his faith will resonate to greater effect and his fidelity be more fruitful."[16]

Involvement in a movement offers priests an opportunity to appreciate in their own personal life and ministry the "co-essentiality" of the hierarchical and charismatic dimensions of the Church. What happens in their own lives and those of others teaches them how the Spirit uses charisms to guide the Church. Because they are part of the sacramental line of apostolic succession, particularly in their power to celebrate the Eucharist, priests have a unique role in and link with the hierarchical dimension of the Church. Such a position does not make them more "important" than others who are endowed with other charisms. St. Benedict and St. Francis were not priests, nor was Mother Teresa.

In many ways, movements help priests discover that priesthood itself is charismatic! Ministerial priesthood is not simply an office, a function, or a job. As ordained ministers, anointed by the Holy Spirit, the charism that priests bear makes them share in the responsibility for the Church's openness to the action of the Holy Spirit. Priests, in turn, can assist by facilitating the movements' own "ecclesial maturity."

---

15. See Pope Benedict's remarks at the Chrism Mass, March 20, 2008.
16. John Paul II, "To the Priests of Communion and Liberation," 256.

Priests and Spirituality

Although ordained ministers are called to live out as priests the same baptismal calling they share with all their brothers and sisters, they do have a spirituality particularly theirs. Indeed, they are required to strive towards the perfection of love in the very woof and warp of their daily activities, even those that are humdrum. Vatican II states, "Priests who perform their duties sincerely and indefatigably in the Spirit of Christ arrive at holiness by this very fact."[17] Their spiritual life grows through the relationships that day by day they establish in performing their duties. According to St. Gregory the Great, the deeper the root, the higher the plant grows. The priest's everyday "outside" relationships with others and his everyday "inside" union with God nourish each other.

The particular features of priests' spirituality are shaped by the relationships and actions that flow from Holy Orders, which configures them to Christ the head, spouse and shepherd of the Church. Through this sacrament are constituted their special link with the bishop and the presbyterate, their celebration of the sacraments, especially the Eucharist, and the relationships and actions that flow from their life of pastoral charity.

The specific diocese to which they belong — its geographical location as well as its demographic and social make-up — also colors the spirituality of priests and contributes to their identity. Each diocese has its own unique history, experience, witnesses, traditions and events. *Pastores dabo vobis*, n. 31, explains the relationship between priesthood and the local church:

> The priest needs to be aware that his "being in a particular Church" constitutes by its very nature a significant element in his living a Christian spirituality. In this sense, the priest finds precisely in his belonging to and dedication to the particular Church a wealth of meaning, criteria for discernment and action which shape both his pastoral mission and his spiritual life.

To sum up, priests are called to live out the spirituality of communion together with all the baptized. In addition, ministry itself shapes their spiritual life.

---

17. *Presbyterorum ordinis*, 13.

There is, however, a question that must be asked: How is spirituality nourished or formed? Is spirituality one's own creation? In other words, must diocesan priests work out for themselves their own spiritual life? Of course, everyone must personally carve out his or her spiritual journey in accordance with the grace of God. In practice, however, how, over the centuries, have priests been nourished in their spiritual life?

Throughout the history of the Church, they have drawn on the spiritual pathways that have emerged around key charismatic figures. Augustine's Rule, for example, had a great influence on diocesan priests; Benedict inspired Gregory the Great's *Pastoral Rule* that shaped so many priests' lives and ministry, as have the spiritualities of Francis of Assisi (the Franciscans), Ignatius of Loyola (the Jesuits), and Vincent de Paul (the Vincentians) on countless generations of seminarians and priests. Great charisms have always opened windows onto the gospel, enlightening, enriching, and animating diocesan priests. In the present era, as in those past, new movements and communities offer priests life-transforming spiritual pathways.

Living Priestly Fraternity

Movements also afford occasions for the priesthood to be lived out in companionship among fellow priests. The sacrament of Holy Orders sets up a vital sacramental communion between priests and their bishop and among priests themselves, made manifest especially in Eucharistic concelebration. But this fraternal communion needs to be translated into various concrete expressions of an effective and affective community of priests. *Pastores dabo vobis*, n. 68, offers this encouragement: "The fact that ... diocesan priests take part in particular spiritualities or ecclesial groupings is indeed, in itself, a factor which helps growth and priestly fraternity."

Such companionship is vital to living fully the gift of celibacy. While Jesus called his disciples personally, he did not intend them to live as isolated individuals. Within movements and communities priests can experience fraternal communion not only with lay people but also among their fellow priests. Within the charism of a movement they too can find a light that clarifies their being with one another in deep communion, sharing, and prayer. Cardinal Kasper points out that:

Through priestly ordination ... we are inserted in one single presbytery. We call ourselves brothers. Priests should therefore meet together, visit one another, share their good and bad pastoral experiences, console and support one another and help one another in solidarity. There ought to be true friendships among priests. The entry of modern bourgeois individualism into the priesthood has not been a good thing. Priestly communities in the style of "Jesus-Caritas" of the community of Charles de Foucauld, Schoenstatt priests, or priest Focolarini can be very helpful and enriching.[18]

Vatican II emphasizes strongly the theme of priestly fraternity and the role of associations in building up a "common life" to avoid the "dangers of loneliness." It recommends a common life among priests, which could "take many forms, according to different personal or pastoral needs, such as living together where this is possible, or having a common table, or at least by frequent and periodic meetings."[19] The issue of fraternity is particularly relevant in allowing priests to be recognized as complete human beings who live in relationship with others, as well as in fostering their own well-being.

It is important to demonstrate that a calling from God that requires a man to leave everything — father, mother, brothers, sisters, family — does not place him in a pitiable lonely existence, but offers him a new "family," a life of communion among his fellow priests. Jesus certainly asked his friends to leave everything and follow him, but at the same time offered and guaranteed them a life together as a body, a new family that practiced a communion of goods as well as communion with him and with one another.

Without mutual Christian love experienced and lived in priestly fraternity, sooner or later an existential emptiness enters a priest's life and everything loses value. Even the vocation itself weakens, becoming a mere sterile professionalism that attracts no one. Priests living a true fraternal life inspire others to consider a vocation to the priesthood. Speaking in 2005 to priests of the diocese of Aosta, Benedict XVI encouraged them to build up a real communion of life

---

18. Walter Cardinal Kasper, *Servitori della gioia. Esistenza sacerdotale — Servizio sacerdotale* (Brescia Queriniana, 2007), 85–86, as quoted in Brendan Leahy and Michael Mulvey (eds.), *Priests Today* (New York: New City Press, 2010), 54–55.
19. See *Presbyterorum ordinis*, 8.

that shows young people, "Yes, this can be a future for me too, it is possible to live like this."[20]

Helping Seminarians

Movements and communities can make an important contribution to the formation of priests, both before and after ordination. This topic was discussed during the 1990 Synod of Bishops. *Pastores dabo vobis,* that synod's final document, presupposing that seminarians will be well integrated into the rule of life established in the seminary, affirms that "associations and youth movements ... can and should contribute also to the formation of candidates for the priesthood."[21] Indeed it goes so far as to say,

> Young people who have received their basic formation in such groups and look to them for their experience of the Church should not feel they are being asked to uproot themselves from their past or to break their links with the environment which has contributed to their decision to respond to their vocation, nor should they erase the characteristic traits of the spirituality which they have learned and lived there in all that they contain that is good, edifying and rich. For them too, this environment from which they come continues to be a source of help and support on the path of formation toward the priesthood.[22]

Through various movements and spiritualities the Spirit offers seminarians different ways of living the gospel message. The Church provides the criteria for discerning the ecclesial identity of movements.[23] If a movement is authentic then a seminarian can "find within [it] the light and warmth which make him capable of fidelity to his bishop and which make him ready for the duties of the institution and mindful of ecclesiastical discipline, thus making the reality of his faith more fertile and his faithfulness more joyful."[24]

---

20. Benedict XVI, Meeting with the Diocesan Clergy of Aosta, Parish Church at Introd (Aosta Valley), Italy, July 25, 2005.
21. *Pastores dabo vobis,* n. 68.
22. Ibid.
23. See the "Criteria of Ecclesiality" outlined above in Chapter 5.
24. See John Paul II's address to priests of Communion and Liberation (September 12, 1985), *AAS* 78 (1986), 256.

Being involved in a movement during their training can help
seminarians learn to respect other spiritual paths, live an experience
of communion and grow in missionary spirit and cooperation, all of
which are important in formation towards their future pastoral life.

Conclusion

According to Ian Ker, before Vatican II the priesthood followed
a model produced by the Council of Trent, but was also deeply
influenced by the many spiritualities that came to life after Trent,
especially that of the Jesuits. The charismatic and educational,
communitarian and missionary drive of movements in the wake of
Vatican II are a providential gift of the Spirit to the Church. As the
Church strives to live out Vatican II's ecclesiology of communion
and embark on a new evangelization, the priesthood of the future
is being shaped also by new charisms that characterize the Church
of the new millennium.[25] In addition to the spiritual pathways that
movements provide, priests also find in them an expression of the
communion within the heart of Church "before" the distinctions
of roles and offices. In this sense, ecclesial communities are not
simply programs to be used in a parish, but new gifts of the Spirit,
experiences that every individual — lay, religious, and priest alike
— can receive and live.

---

25. Kerr, "The Priesthood," 126. For reflections on the priesthood, see Gearóid Dullea,
    On Shepherding: Reflections on the Priesthood (Dublin: Columba Press, 2010).

16

Ecumenical and Interreligious Developments

Many ecclesial movements and communities have committed themselves to ecumenical and interreligious dialogues. This, of course, is to be expected since the Catholic Church has been particularly active in ecumenical and interreligious dialogues since Vatican II.[1] The vast topic of ecumenism and interreligious dialogue would require much greater treatment than is possible here. This chapter, then, can review only some of the elements that movements contribute in those dialogues.

Ecumenical Dialogue

On several occasions in recent years the Catholic Church has affirmed that with the Second Vatican Council it has taken an irrevocable step into the ecumenical movement. Its commitment to ecumenism is steadfast.[2] At a conference marking the fortieth anniversary of the Second Vatican Council's Decree on Ecumenism, *Unitatis redintegratio,* Cardinal Kasper commented, "The Council was able to embrace the ecumenical movement because it understood the Church as a whole as movement, namely as the people of God on the move."[3] In that same talk, he linked the ecumenical movement with the charismatic side of the Church that the Council rediscovered:

> So ecumenism is a new beginning, set in motion by the Holy Spirit.... The Holy Spirit as it were, the soul of the Church, grants unity as well as the multiplicity of gifts and services.

1. See Frederick Bliss, *Catholic and Ecumenical: History and Hope* (Franklin, WI: Sheed & Ward, 1999); Jeffrey Gros, Eamon McManus and Ann Riggs, *Introduction to Ecumenism* (Mahwah, NJ: Paulist Press, 1998); Fitzgerald, Michael, and Borelli, John, *Interfaith Dialogue. A Catholic View* (New York: Orbis Books, 2006); Eugene F. Gorski, *Theology of Religions: A Sourcebook for Interreligious Study* (New York/Mahwah: Paulist Press, 2008).

2. It is beyond the scope of this book to examine the current state of ecumenical dialogue, but for a useful review see the proceedings of a conference near Rome in 2004 marking the fortieth anniversary of the Decree on Ecumenism of the Second Vatican Council, *Unitatis redintegratio,* John Paul II, Cardinal Walter Kasper et al, *Searching for Christian Unity* (New York: New City Press, 2007).

3. See "The Decree on Ecumenism — Read Anew after Forty Years," in John Paul II et al, *Searching for Christian Unity,* 18–35, at 20.

Thus the Council was able to say that spiritual ecumenism is the heart of ecumenism.... As a spiritual movement the ecumenical movement does not annul tradition, rather it grants a new and more profound insight into what has been handed down once and for all; it blazes the trail for the renewed Pentecost which Pope John XXIII predicted in his opening address to the Second Vatican Council; it paves the way for the new historical form of the Church, not a new Church but indeed a spiritually renewed and spiritually enriched church.[4]

The aim of ecumenism is not amalgamation, but full communion. That does not mean uniformity, but unity in diversity and diversity in unity. It does not mean reciprocal absorption or fusion. Nor does it mean false irenics. Spiritual ecumenism is central to the Catholic Church's vision of its engagement in the ecumenical movement. Indeed, in recent times it has promoted a spirituality of communion that can be shared and lived out at many levels by Christians of different denominations. Particularly at this level, movements can contribute to ecumenism.

Focusing on what unites while still respecting the legitimate differences of expression and of life within the same apostolic faith, movements can serve theological dialogue by providing points of encounter within a dialogue of life. In his concluding observations at the 2004 conference, Cardinal Kasper remarked, "We are above all grateful for ecumenical prayer groups and spiritual networks among monasteries, convents, communities and movements. With God's help, spiritual ecumenism is growing. There is no question of an ecumenical 'ice age.'"[5]

Movements provide meeting points of community life around aspects of the gospel. Such encounters become the basis of a common dialogue of life within which Christians of different churches can meet and anticipate something of the unity they long for. On this basis too, movements offer forums for prayer united in the name of Jesus. One of the great doctors of the Church, John Chrysostom

---

4. Ibid., 23. See also Nancy Gower, "The Place of Ecumenical Monasticism in the Ecumenical Movement," in *One in Christ* 41 (2006): 42–76. On movements in ecumenism see, Timothy Watson, "Life Precedes Law: The Story So Far of the Chemin Neuf Community," in *One in Christ* 43 (2009), and Brendan Leahy, "New Paths for Dialogue: Chiara Lubich's Ecumenical Legacy," in *One in Christ* 42 (2008): 246–269.

5. *Searching for Christian Unity*, 212.

(c. 349–407), highlighted the importance of prayer "in agreement, which God holds in the highest consideration and by which he is moved and pleased. 'For where two or three are gathered together in my name' says Jesus, 'there am I in the midst of them' " (Mt 18:20).[6] The Encyclical Letter on Ecumenism, *Ut unum sint*, describes such moments as experiences that anticipate the unity for which Christians yearn: "We gather together in the name of Christ who is One. He is our unity."[7]

A major issue in ecumenism is the official reception of ecumenical dialogue.[8] In this regard, those prepared through involvement in spiritual movements can be instrumental in advancing the acceptance of the fruits of ecumenical dialogue. Clearly, as the Directory for the Application of Principles and Norms on Ecumenism affirms, "Those involved in such groups, movements and associations should be imbued with a solid ecumenical spirit, in living their baptismal commitment in the world, whether by seeking Catholic unity through dialogue and communion with similar movements and associations — or the wider communion with other churches and ecclesial communities and with the movements and groups inspired by them."[9]

In his booklet offering practical suggestions on spiritual ecumenism, Cardinal Kasper notes how movements share a common characteristic of "invit[ing] their members to live their baptismal commitment in the midst of society, through their daily activity in family, social and professional life, and that they seek to develop new and creative means of evangelization. Many of these communities give a privileged place to the poor or marginal in society, to those who are wounded or living with a handicap. Each in its own way can give new expression to a shared discipleship in Jesus Christ." He then describes how movements:

> develop forms of shared ecumenical commitment in social, political and cultural life, by virtue of their lay character and the locus of their activity;

---

6. John Chrysostom, *Epist. II ad Thess. Hom.* 4.4. in PG 62, 491.

7. John Paul II, Encyclical Letter on Ecumenism, *Ut unum sint*, 23.

8. See Walter Kasper, *Harvesting the Fruits: Aspects of Christian Faith in Ecumenical Dialogue* (London: Continuum, 2009); William G. Rausch, *Ecumenical Reception: Its Challenge and Opportunity* (Grand Rapids, MI: Eerdmans, 2007).

9. Pontifical Council for the Promotion of Christian Unity, *Directory for the Application of Principles and Norms in Ecumenism* (Vatican, 1993).

seek appropriate avenues of jointly proclaiming and preaching the Gospel of Jesus Christ in various contexts;

create opportunities for laity and clergy of different traditions to gather, pray and work together in an ecumenical spirit;

organize ecumenical formation programs, weekends of spiritual recollection, seminars on Christian life;

offer to Christians of different traditions a means of giving authentic expression to their real though imperfect unity in Christ, while respecting and even strengthening their rootedness in their own Christian communities.[10]

The "Together For ..." Project

One recent initiative demonstrates how ecclesial movements and communities from different churches can work together in a living dialogue that builds up and bears witness to communion. The project "Together For ..." emerged from the collaboration among leaders of Evangelical Lutheran, Free Church, and Catholic movements and communities. Since 1969, members of German Evangelical Lutheran and Free Church communities have been holding day-long "Leaders' Meetings." On Reformation Day — October 31, 1999 — just after the Joint Declaration on the Doctrine of Justification had been signed, Chiara Lubich and Andrea Riccardi, two founders of Catholic movements, encountered these leaders at the Ottmaring Meeting Center in Germany. New pathways of fellowship opened up.

Catholic and Lutheran movements began an ongoing collaboration. On December 8, 2001, in Munich's Evangelical Lutheran Church of St. Matthew, 800 leaders responsible for more than forty-five movements in various Churches made a "covenant," a heartfelt pact of mutual love and respect. They agreed to bring about as much unity as possible, striving together to be one soul as a present expression of what is to come. Later, some 5,000 members of movements joined them at the Cathedral of Munich.

At that event, the Evangelical Lutheran bishop of Bavaria, Ulrich Wilckens, remarked that if division between the churches had

---

10. See Walter Kasper, *A Handbook of Spiritual Ecumenism* (New York: New City Press, 2007), 83–84.

produced secularization, atheism, and a loss of values, then could not the opposite also be true — that through unity in love among Christians, faith could be strengthened again?[11]

Subsequently, this fellowship spread to include movements of the Orthodox Church. The collaboration among all of them — Catholic, Protestant, and Orthodox — generated a project called "Together for Europe." Their first major event, organized by Catholic groups such as Schoenstatt, Cursillo, the Focolare and Sant'Egidio, as well as representatives of German Evangelical organizations such as the YMCA, and various covenant communities took place in Stuttgart, Germany on May 8, 2004. They wanted to demonstrate that the movements and ecclesial communities can work like spiritual networks spread by God throughout Europe. By growing in communion with one another they could give glory to God (see Mt 5:16) and promote, alongside a political and economic Europe, a "Europe of the spirit." The gathering of members from 189 movements, communities, groups, and associations, together with bishops and church leaders — 9,000 in all — was transmitted simultaneously by satellite to 163 other locations throughout Europe. The president of the European Commission at that time, Romano Prodi, affirmed that momentum toward true European political cooperation could be sustained only through spiritual unity — a "powerful soul" — nurtured by the movements.

Cardinal Kasper, president of the Pontifical Council for Promoting Christian Unity, described the event as a milestone that would provide new energy for the ecumenical movement.

> I see communities and movements as a gift of the Holy Spirit after Vatican II for our churches. These communities and movements certainly need the church. But the church also needs them.... I am sure that with this spirit ecumenism will go ahead. I am happy that you have created a tight network of friendship over and beyond the individual churches, with free churches, with the Orthodox Church.... I believe that through this friendship ecumenism will go ahead. I invite you to continue to build up and extend this network among your communities. I have always dreamt of a network without limits. My dream is that the communities will work together. What we need is a new Pentecost in which, just as happened in the first

11. See Chiara Lubich, *Essential Writings*, 323.

Pentecost, some women and men with Mary met together in the Upper Room and prayed for the coming of the Holy Spirit. We cannot "make" the unity of the Church. We cannot "organize" it. But we must pray that it will come about.[12]

Gerhard Pross, a leader of YMCA in Germany, and Coordinator of the Council of Responsibles of Evangelical Lutheran and Free Church communities, explained how fellowship is sustained among these leaders and communities and movements:

> What is the secret of this communion? When we meet as Leaders, what is most important is that for the sake of unity we put aside our own identity. It is important to consider things with the eyes of the others. It isn't always straightforward. But in this unity we do not lose our identity, neither as individuals nor as movements. Rather we find it in a more well-defined way. Seeking to have this attitude always, we also reach the point of having a shared vision. For us, it is the will of Jesus (Jn 17:21) when he prays to the Father for the unity of Christians so that the world may believe. But this "vision" is already a reality.[13]

The Stuttgart meeting addressed issues such as dialogue with European Islam, the relationship between Europe and Africa, marriage and family, solidarity and development, work and economy, the poor and disadvantaged, peace and justice. John Paul II sent a message emphasizing the role of movements in the new evangelization. Cardinal Kasper comments:

> Today, the Spirit of God has inspired a great variety of spiritual movements, with communities of lay persons or families, groups devoted to evangelization, and charismatic communities.... Pope John Paul II is surely right to say that these movements and communities are a response by the Holy Spirit to the "signs of the times." Many of them are involved in ecumenical work, developing new forms of ecumenical work, developing new forms of ecumenical living in common that point the way ahead for the church, and they have formed ecumenical networks.... [E]cumenism began, before the council, in groups of friends; today, it will receive a fresh impetus above all in

---

12. See *Together for Europe* (Rome, 2004), 30–31.
13. Ibid., 34.

groups of friends, communities, and places where people share their lives with one another.... I place a very high value on this spiritual ecumenism in so many spiritual communities.[14]

Through the Stuttgart event, many new links were forged. In 2007, participants representing 240 movements and communities met in Rome for another large ecumenical convocation. On behalf of the steering committee, Emma Barnes of Alpha International welcomed them, saying, "In 2004, we forged many friendships and we reaped the rewards in many tangible ways. Today more than 200 movements, communities and different groups are represented here.... And it is clear that what unites us is greater than what divides us."[15] Speaking of that same meeting, Gerhard Pross, quoting Revelations 5:9, described the togetherness in diversity and unity that had grown among the leaders and communities: "They sang a new hymn."

At the 2007 gathering Cardinal Kasper elaborated on the significance of this new way of sharing spirituality:

> God does not want a new Church, but he wants a new way of being Church. We don't need a new program. The Gospel is valid for once and for all. The Gospel gives hope and enthusiasm.... Pope John Paul II in his testament spoke of a "spirituality of communion," not one of individualism and solitude.... You, movements and communities, have new possibilities of creating this togetherness, and your spending time in churches and communities, is a sign of this and a new way of sharing spirituality. A spirituality of solidarity: this solidarity is already an element, a guarantee of peace, and a guarantee for a regime of peace not only here in Europe but also beyond.[16]

Pastor Ingold Ellssel commented, "It is not a question of uniting different institutions from different churches, but it is primarily a question of gathering together in the name of Jesus Christ who is the only way to reach God. So we have to gather together. Our Lord Jesus Christ has promised that when we love one another, we are able to change and that by loving one another, the world will

---

14. Walter Cardinal Kasper, *Sacrament of Unity: The Eucharist and the Church* (New York: Crossroad, 2004), 75–78 passim.

15. *Together for Europe* (Rome, 2007), 5.

16. Ibid., 9–10.

recognize that he was sent by the Father. This is what we have to learn, and hence the importance of meeting each other."[17]

At the 2007 gathering, Nicky Gumbel, president of Alpha International, shared the experience of the Alpha course, which started in 1977 and is now proceeding worldwide in 33,000 churches of many denominations (Catholic, Orthodox, Lutheran, Baptist, Methodist, and Anglican). Of those who attend Alpha courses, seventy percent are aged between eighteen and thirty-five. The course centers on what unites people as Christians — the person of Jesus Christ. Gumbel gave the example of Paul Cowley, of Manchester, who had led a difficult life, marked by broken relationships and time in prison. He had not seen his son for twelve years. Then, during an Alpha course held in his church, he came to faith in Jesus Christ. His life changed totally. Cowley took the Alpha course into prisons, where it runs now in eighty percent of those in the UK, as well as in penal institutions across Europe and throughout the world. His faith also led him to establish an organization that is now offering care and support to thousands of ex-offenders. The gospel changed Paul Cowley's life; through him the experience of a relationship with Jesus Christ has transformed the lives of many others.[18]

Sharing such experiences constitutes the "Together For..." project. The communion or fellowship among communities and movements that it promotes is an expression of a living dialogue that furthers spiritual ecumenism. Unity and fellowship among communities, of course, is not built up by human effort alone. It must pass through love of the Crucified and Risen Christ. Participants recognize him in their own limits, difficulties and needs; as a consequence, movements and communities grow in spiritual communion. On this basis, dialogue is possible among people united in mutual love, prayer, action, ideas and initiatives.

Through this dialogue, these movements can help shape the future of ecumenism. Bishop Wolfgang Huber, President of the German Evangelical Churches, explains the value of the unity generated by these conferences: "The meeting with movements which believe, which manage to put faith and life together, witness and social commitment, has become much more important for me. I say this with gratitude. These movements have a future; they represent not just

17. Ibid., 11.
18. See Nicky Gumbel, "I Am Not Ashamed of the Gospel," in *Together for Europe*, 14–15.

the past but they are important companions for our shared journey towards the future."[19]

Interreligious Dialogue

Beginning from the Second Vatican Council's Declaration on Interreligious Dialogue, *Nostra aetate*, the Catholic Church has embarked on a new level of dialogue with world religions, entering "with prudence and charity into discussion and collaboration with members of other religions."[20] Even before the Council, pioneers such as Louis Massignon (1883–1962), Jules Monchanin (1895–1957), Henri Le Saux (1910–1973) and Thomas Merton (1915–1968) had devoted their lives to such dialogue. After the Council, however, this spirit spread throughout the Catholic Church. The 1986 Assisi gathering of religious leaders constituted a powerful icon of this development.

Issues relating to interreligious dialogue are among the most salient concerns in theology today.[21] A summary statement in the Pontifical Council for Inter-Religious Dialogue's document, *Dialogue and Proclamation* (1991), clarifies the forms of interreligious dialogue. It refers to four dialogues: life, actions, theological exchange, and religious experience.[22] Naturally, where they are a minority Christians enter interreligious dialogue in their daily experience. Because of increasing mobility and migrancy, however, Christians everywhere encounter members of other religions. In its official interreligious dialogue, the Church co-operates with international bodies and institutions such as Religions for Peace and the International Council of Christians and Jews. It sends greetings to leaders of religious communities on significant feast days and promotes international meetings and conferences. Although interreligious dialogue has become more and more common, many issues remain concerning how to accomplish it and how to understand it.

---

19. *Together for Europe* (2007), 40.

20. Declaration on Interreligious Dialogue, *Nostra aetate*, 2.

21. See the Congregation for the Doctrine of the Faith's Declaration on the Unicity and Salvific Universality of Jesus Christ and the Church, *Dominus Iesus* (June 16, 2000). See also "An Interview with Cardinal Francis Arinze," *Building Bridges: Interreligious Dialogue on the Path to World Peace* (New York: New City Press, 2004).

22. See Marcello Zago's article that distinguishes dialogue of life, co-operation, religious experience, theological dialogue and dialogue among religious authorities. See "Mission and Interreligious Dialogue," in *International Bulletin of Missionary Research* 22 (1998/3): 98–101.

Since the 1970s the value of monasticism in interreligious dialogue has come to the fore.[23] The reasons are obvious. In many places the Church is recognized more for its organized response to humanitarian needs than for its contemplative dimension. Nevertheless, in some places, for instance in Asia, the contemplative aspect is vital in making contact with other religions. Monasteries can use their ascetic and mystical experiences and traditions to build bridges, offering forums where the dialogue of religious experience can be nurtured. *Dialogue and Proclamation* explains the particular relevance of monasticism in interreligious dialogue: "[Such] dialogue does not merely aim at mutual understanding and friendly relations. It reaches a much deeper level, that of the spirit, where exchange and sharing consist in a mutual witness to one's beliefs and a common exploration of one's respective religious convictions" (n. 40). The Benedictine tradition in particular has established inter-monastic exchanges and dialogues with both Buddhists and Hindus. This has resulted in the 1996, 2003 and 2008 Gethsemani Encounters between Christian and Buddhist monastic leaders.[24]

Movements' spirituality, lay membership, projects, and initiatives allow them to provide bridges of dialogue with members and movements of other religions. Since the 1970s, especially since the 1986 Assisi Meeting of World Religions Together for Prayer, new movements such as Communion and Liberation, Catholic Charismatic Renewal, the Focolare Movement, L'Arche, Sant'Egidio, and the Communauté Chemin Neuf have engaged more and more frequently in interreligious dialogue.

At the end of the 1986 Assisi meeting, John Paul II encouraged all the participants: "Let's keep spreading the message of peace and living the spirit of Assisi." In response to the pope's invitation, the Sant'Egidio community began holding interreligious meetings in various cities, primarily in Europe (although one was held in Washington, D.C., in 2006). They aimed to promote mutual understanding and dialogue among religions as part of a general attempt to create a culture of peace. The Communion and Liberation movement fosters ecumenism and interreligious dialogue as part of its

---

23. See Anthony O'Mahony and Peter Bowe, *Catholics in Interreligious Dialogue: Monasticism, Theology and Spirituality* (Leominster: Gracewing, 2006).
24. See Donald Mitchell and William Skudlarek, *Green Monasticism (Gethsemani Encounters)* (Brooklyn: Lantern Books, 2010).

program of promoting the universal religious sense and its quest for meaning. Its August 2010 *Meeting* in Rimini, Italy focused not only on the religious sense but also exploring interreligious dialogue from the point of view of culture. This *Meeting* featured a panel that included Cardinal Jean-Louis Tauran, president of the Pontifical Council for Interreligious Dialogue, an imam, and a Buddhist monk. At the end of October 2010 Communion and Liberation sponsored another such *Meeting* in Cairo.

Since the 1960s, but especially since 1977 when its founder, Chiara Lubich, was awarded the Templeton Prize for Progress in Religion, the Focolare Movement has engaged in interreligious dialogue at many levels. On Lubich's first visit to Tokyo in 1981, at a large Buddhist gathering organized by Rissho Kosei-kai, the Focolare was presented as "a new Christian movement that, as part of the big family of God, aims at bringing about his Kingdom, a community based on love."[25] The Focolare Movement is involved in active dialogue with, among others, Jews, Muslims, Hindus, Buddhists and Sikhs. Of particular note is the friendship between Lubich and Imam W. D. Mohammed, leader of a group of African-American Muslims.[26]

Movements within many different religions contribute to promoting dialogue. In the twentieth century, various movements of spiritual renewal have come to life and grown, including the Rissho Kosei-kai, the Japanese Mahayana Buddhist movement, and the Ghandian Hindu movement. Robert Catalano comments, "It seems that the birth and development of renewal movements within the various religions has offered fertile terrain for interreligious dialogue also through some common characteristics that seem to facilitate greatly interreligious contact."[27] These renewal movements, all born in the twentieth century, try to respond to contemporary social problems and issues such as politics, mass-media, education, economics, and art. They are often founded and directed by lay people with a certain charismatic authority.

Movements are particularly attentive to the communitarian aspect of religion, often providing forums where faith can be explained,

---

25. See Chiara Lubich, *Incontri con l'Oriente* (Rome: Città Nuova, 1987), 192.
26. On the Focolare's dialogue with Muslims, see "Mysticism and God-relatedness," in *Islamochristiana* 34 (2008): 79–86.
27. See Roberto Catalano, *Spiritualità di comunione e dialogo interreligioso: L'esperienza di Chiara Lubich e del Movimento dei Focolari* (Rome: Città Nuova, 2010), 149 (my translation).

lived, and shared. Ecclesial movements, along with other religious orders and congregations, can enrich the Church's dialogue as they engage in interreligious dialogue in conformity with their spirituality and apostolic goals.[28] They express what Paul VI affirmed in his first encyclical, *Ecclesiam suam*, n. 65: "The Church must enter into dialogue with the world in which it lives. It has something to say, a message to give, a communication to make." The movements, expressions of the Church's charismatic dimension, are called to express its interreligious dialogue, paying attention to the working of the Holy Spirit in the religious traditions of the world, always remaining mindful of the need to communicate their discovery of Jesus Christ. John Paul II elaborates on the careful discernment that this requires:

> Whatever the Spirit brings about in human hearts and in the history of peoples, in cultures and religions serves as a preparation for the Gospel.... Moreover, the universal activity of the Spirit is not to be separated from his particular activity within the body of Christ, which is the Church. Indeed, it is always the Spirit who is at work, both when he gives life to the Church and impels her to proclaim Christ, and when he implants and develops his gifts in all individuals and peoples, guiding the Church to discover these gifts, to foster them and to receive them through dialogue. Every form of the Spirit's presence is to be welcomed with respect and gratitude, but the discernment of this presence is the responsibility of the Church, to which Christ gave his Spirit in order to guide her into all the truth (see Jn 16:13).[29]

---

28. See M. Zago's comment to this effect in his preface to Lubich, *Incontri con l'Oriente*, 6.
29. See John Paul II, *Redemptoris missio*, n. 29.

17

Issues in Canon Law

Although legal documents may not interest most people, they are important because law supports and facilitates fraternal relations among people in their everyday interactions. For instance, in promulgating the 1983 Code of Canon Law, John Paul II pointed out that the Code "is to create such an order in the ecclesial society that, while assigning the primacy to love, grace, and charisms, it at the same time renders their organic development easier in the life of the ecclesial community and the individual persons who belong to it."[1] The juridical structure helps protect the spiritual order, provide clarity, and build up communion.

For similar reasons, movements have been encouraged to present their statutes to the Holy See. The statutes of 122 movements already have been recognized. Bishop Porteous explains the value of such recognition.

> Canon law can be a useful instrument at the service of the movements, because it provides ... the opportunity to clearly identify the nature of their charism and thus provide a lasting written testament describing it. This can help the movement retain its identity as time elapses and founding members die. It provides means for new members, who do not know the first days of the movement, to have a clear exposition (composed by the first members) of the character of the charism.[2]

Several canons are relevant for ecclesial movements and communities. Most adopt a legal structure called "Associations of the Faithful." Canon 215, taking up Vatican II's acknowledgement of the right of the faithful, laity, and clergy to form associations (indeed, the Council warmly recommended that such associations be established), states that "Christ's faithful may freely establish and direct associations which serve charitable or pious purposes or which foster the Christian vocation in the world, and they may hold meetings to pursue these purposes by common effort." Canon 214 recognizes the right of the

---

1. See Apostolic Constitution, *Sacrae disciplinae leges* (1983).
2. Julian Porteous, *A New Wine and Fresh Skins*, 139–140.

faithful "to follow their own form of spiritual life provided it is in accord with Church teaching." In doing so, canon 209.1 affirms that "Christ's faithful are bound to preserve their communion with the Church at all times, even in their external actions."

The main juridical framework for considering, recognizing, and approving ecclesial movements and communities is to be found in canons 298–326, which deal with associations of the faithful. For instance, canon 298 states:

> In the Church there are associations which are distinct from institutes of consecrated life and societies of apostolic life. In these associations, Christ's faithful, whether clerics or laity, or clerics and laity together, strive with a common effort to foster a more perfect life, or to promote public worship or Christian teaching. They may also devote themselves to other works of the apostolate, such as initiatives for evangelization, works of piety or charity, and those which animate the temporal order with the Christian spirit.

In other places, canon law deals with the various types of associations, how such associations are established, the role of competent ecclesiastical authority — either the local bishop or authorities in Rome — in discerning the authenticity of movements, and other legal details concerning how associations are run.

Msgr. Miguel Delgado of the Pontifical Council for the Laity has produced a guide to assist movements in compiling their statutes. The statutes should include the following elements:[3]

1. A premise to the statute which includes a brief history of the association.
2. A brief description of the juridical nature of the association, of the charism, of the spirituality of the association, the goals to be reached by the association, and its legal address.
3. The various categories of membership and the requisites to become part of the association. The formation of the various members, the duties and rights of members, and norms regarding resignation or dismissal.
4. The structure and organization of the association and the government bodies at the international, national and diocesan level.

---

3. See Porteous, 154.

5. The nomination process for the various mandates and their requisites.
6. Instructions regarding the administration of material goods.
7. Norms regarding the procedure for the modification of the statute, the dissolution of the association and the destination of the material goods.

Problematic Issues

Although the framework provided by the Code of Canon Law has facilitated the approval of the movements, its structure has not proved sufficient for containing various complex aspects of the new movements.[4] The phenomenon of such movements differs in many ways from associations of the faithful that were established in the past. The Jesuit professor of canon law, Gianfranco Ghirlanda, notes that the structure which canons 298–329 provides for the associations of the faithful "is sufficiently flexible to permit the ecclesial movements to remain within this general category," but is "insufficient to regulate what is specific about them."[5] Another renowned canonist who was involved in the drafting of the final revision of the new Code of Canon Law has noted that the juridical figure of "association" cannot adequately contain new ecclesial movements which originate from a charism given to a founder.[6]

Not Easily Defined

These new associations, movements, groups and communities often do not share the same characteristics. They differ in many ways.[7] The sheer range of situations, formation methods, and history defies easy definition and distinction.[8] Some movements, for instance, do not have a specific mission. Instead, they "set before

---

4. See Gianfranco Ghirlanda's preface to Christoph Hegge, *Il Vaticano II e i Movimenti Ecclesiali: una recezione carismatica.*
5. See Gianfranco Ghirlanda, "Charism and Juridical Status of the Ecclesial Movements," in *Movements in the Church,* 131–148, at 134.
6. See Eugenio Corecco, "Profili istituzionali di Movimenti nella Chiesa," in M. Camisasca and M. Vitali (eds.), *I Movimenti nella Chiesa* (Milan, 1982), 203–234.
7. See C. I. Heredia, *La naturaleza de los movimientos eclesiales en el derecho de la Iglesia. Excerpta ex Dissertatione ad Doctoratum in Facultate Iuris Canonici Pontificae Universitatis Gregorianae,* Buenos Aires, 1994, 79–83.
8. See J. Beyer, *Istituti secolari e movimenti ecclesiali,* 181–183.

themselves the broad apostolic purpose of the Church."[9] Although most members are laypeople, the movements also include priests, religious, and bishops. In some movements, lay members live a consecrated life by taking vows or promises to live the evangelical counsels.[10] Likewise, the issue of members of other churches and religions belonging to movements raises canonical issues.

Porteous identifies three general approaches to formation. In some movements a person is invited to take part in the life of the movement and, by association, is formed in its spirit through texts of the founder. A second approach focuses on teaching programs so that a member goes through a graduated system of formation. Some take a third approach, providing a manual that expounds their way of life.[11]

The Incardination of Priests

A particularly thorny question arises when some consecrated laymen, encouraged by the movements to which they belong, seek ordination. Canon law does provide for priests to associate with movements, but it does not envisage incardination in movements. The issue does not arise for diocesan priests who become involved in movements, but it does for laymen already in movements who want to be ordained while remaining in some direct way at the service of the movement and its mission.

To resolve this issue, some movements have established their own internal Society of Apostolic Life, such as the Communion and Liberation movement's Priestly Fraternity of the Missionaries of St. Charles Borromeo. In other movements, priests become incardinated in a diocese with the agreement that they will be released to work for the movement. The Directory on the Life and Ministry of Priests states, "The priests, then, incardinated in a diocese, who are serving an ecclesial movement ... are aware of being members of the presbyterate of their diocese....The Bishop of incardination, on his part, must respect the way of life required by the membership to a

---

9. See *Actuositatem apostolicam*, 19, 1.

10. Ghirlanda points out that the tendency of many members of associations and movements to seek the perfection of charity through evangelical counsels and at the same time their desire to live fully and deeply the lay vocation in the Church "is in conformity with can. 298.1 that provides for associations that strive, through common action, to the increase of a more perfect life." See G. Ghirlanda, *Il diritto nella chiesa mistero di comunione. Compendio di diritto ecclesiale* (Rome: PUG, 1990), 239. See also See J. Beyer, "I movimenti nuovi nella Chiesa," in *Vita Consacrata* 27 (1991), 61–77, at 64. Also, see *Vita Consecrata*, 62.

11. Julian Porteous, *A New Wine and Fresh Skins*, 87–94.

movement, and it may be fitting ... to permit the priest, to lend his services to other churches, if this forms part of the charism of the movement itself."[12]

Some movements have established their own seminaries in accordance with the provision in Canon Law (canon 237) that allows a bishop to set up a "missionary seminary" in his diocese. Although the bishop appoints a formation team that may consist of individuals suggested by the movement, the seminary is clearly still bound by his directives.

Various Attempts

Because some canonical issues that arise are so complex, the new ecclesial movements and communities sometimes find themselves trying to adapt themselves to canonical structures that don't always reflect their actual life. In some cases, the provisions for the institutes of consecrated life and societies of apostolic life (canons 573–746) can be helpful. Sometimes, however, a movement has to seek separate approval for its various branches — male, female, clerical, lay, contemplative, apostolic — and then attempt to form some kind of federation among them. A movement can end up with an institute of apostolic life or fraternity of priests, while the non-clerical members become a lay association. Personal prelatures are exclusively clerical structures (see canon 294) in which the laity cooperate with the work from outside, so they do not offer a useful solution to canonical regulation of movements. All in all, then, the current canonical situation is not totally satisfactory because the solutions proposed to give canonical shape to movements risk jeopardizing the unity of each movement. As Ghirlanda points out, history shows that institutes that derive from the same founder and charism, if approved in autonomous and separate forms, after the founder's death often end up going their separate ways.[13] That runs counter to the ecclesial movements' very newness, as Ghirlanda notes: "It would be contrary to the Spirit to try and force them, at the time of their approval, into the straightjacket of already existing juridical forms."[14]

---

12. Congregation for the Clergy, *Directory of the Life and Ministry of Priests* (January 31, 1991), 26.
13. Ghirlanda, 134.
14. See "Charism and Juridical Status of the Ecclesial Movements," in *Movements in the Church*, 131–148, at 134.

The Vatican itself sometimes has difficulty determining where to "house" the movements. At present they come under the Pontifical Council for the Laity. Nevertheless, since they include bishops, priests, and religious as well as laity, the Council has to consult with other offices of the Roman Curia on matters that involve joint responsibility.

How Life Evolves

Acknowledging the difficulties in providing canonical arrangements for movements is not simply a negative observation. Difficulties can be providential in prompting canonists and others to examine things more deeply. Cardinal Ratzinger's sound advice holds true here too: "It is better to see how life evolves, without rushing to tackle the organizational questions."[15] It is the Holy Spirit who is bringing things forward, and canon law too is an instrument that serves the law of the Spirit. Shortly after the Second Vatican Council, Paul VI wrote that "alongside the Christology and ecclesiology of the Council, there must also be a new study and a renewed worship of the Holy Spirit, as an indispensable complement to the teaching of the Council.... We would like to invite canonists too to share in this effort.... (The law of the Church must) express and favor the life of the Spirit, produce fruits of the Spirit, be an instrument of grace and bond of unity."[16] Although the revised Code of Canon Law makes many references to the Holy Spirit, in its final draft the term "charism" was unexpectedly eliminated (it had appeared seven times in the *Preparatory Scheme* of 1982). Now, however, the reality and experience of the new ecclesial movements is prompting renewed reflection on charism as a fundamental element of the Constitution of the Church.[17]

---

15. *Pastoral Concern of the Bishops*, 230.
16. Paul VI, Address on September 17, 1973.
17. See E. Correco, "Institution and Charism with Reference to Associative Structures," in Graziano Borgonovo and Arturo Cattaneo, *Canon Law and Communio: Writings on the Constitutional Law of the Church* (Vatican, 1999), 316–340.

A New Juridical Form for Ecclesial Movements and Communities?

One way forward would be to establish a new juridical form specifically for ecclesial movements and communities. Most movements today are approved as public or private associations. The distinction between the two can be helpful, but the difference is not always so clear-cut.[18] Broadly speaking, a private association exists by private agreement among its members. It is recognized by the Church after the movement's statutes have been reviewed by the competent authority. This is a very light form of juridical status. It lacks, however, the security and opportunities for recognition accorded public associations.

A public association is constituted by a competent authority and pursues, *in the name of the Church*, the ends of the association. Jean Beyer, former professor of canon law at the Gregorian University, contends that the public juridical status should be conferred on all ecclesial associations. He maintains that all associations, including those that are private, to the degree they are "ecclesial" share in some way in the *potestas* that derives from the hierarchical *potestas* of the twelve apostles and their successors, and that finds expression in the formation of statutes of association.[19] An association of the faithful is not founded simply upon the free will of association for an action or apostolate, but upon the call of God through an originating charism lived in a collective and communitarian way. By virtue of the charisms recognized by the competent authority, all ecclesial movements carry out a public function. Christoph Hegge, a canon lawyer and auxiliary bishop, agrees that ecclesial movements could be considered public associations in accordance with canon 301.2. Such status means they can teach "in the name of the Church" (canon 301.1). Indeed, he agrees that through their charisms, movements contribute much in the service of Church proclamation. He also suggests that movements' public character would be advanced if those approved as

18. See E. M. de Beukelaer, *Willem Onclin et la distinction des associations de fidale en publiques et privées. Arbeit zur Erlangung des Grades eines Lizentianten im Kanonischen Recht der Katholisch-Theologischen Fakultät der Westfälischen Wilhelms-Universität Münster* (pro manuscript), 1994, 69–71

19. Beyer, *Dal Concilio al Codice*, 80.

public association of pontifical right (canon 312.1.1), as is done through canon 579 of the 1983 Code and 357.1 of the 1990 Code of the Eastern Churches, were allowed to incardinate priests through a special concession by the Apostolic See (although he believes the possibility of incardinating priests in a public association would overload the canonical notion of association).[20]

Hegge also points out, however, that there are disadvantages in simply recognizing movements under the juridical form of public associations. The movements are a new form of association that has no real analogy to the actual juridical forms of association.[21] In particular, he highlights how the notion of charism is essential to movements in a way that is not true for other older forms of association. Charism, he believes, is a central defining feature that distinguishes ecclesial movements and communities from other working forms of association.[22]

Ecclesial movements are associations on the basis of charisms and prophetic vocations, not simply on the basis of apostolic goals or their own free decision.[23] The charism itself joins together various orders and categories of people of all ages: priests, deacons, seminarians, lay men and women, married, single and widows, young and older people, consecrated, contemplatives, religious and bishops. The life of the community that emerges from a charism corresponds to the charism's specific focus. Following a charism involves the whole person, so people in movements often share goods, live a fraternal missionary communion, and share an experience of communion in obedience to one another and the leaders of their community, while also dedicating themselves to the apostolic works of the movement. Some movements include ecumenical and interreligious outreach. Movements are called "ecclesial" precisely because in and through their charisms they want to present the Church's own life as an organic communion of many vocations.

---

20. Hegge points out that such a possibility was first proposed by canon 691 in the 1980 draft of the Commission of the Revision of the Code for public associations and clerical societies of pontifical right, but it was not included in the final version of the 1983 Code. See G. Ghirlanda, "Questioni irrisolte sulle associazioni di fedeli," 91–96.

21. See also G. Ghirlanda, "I movimenti nella comunione ecclesiale e la loro giusta autonomia," 57.

22. See A. Favale, "Le aggregazioni laicali nella Chiesa: varietà e vivacità carica di promesse," 80. See also K. Lehmann, "I nuovi movimenti ecclesiali; motivazioni e finalità," in *Il Regno-Documenti* 32 (1987): 27–31, at 27.

23. L. Gerosa, *Charisma und Recht*, 254ff.

Hegge's point is that the category of public association as articulated in the 1983 Code does not address adequately the charismatic origin and character of ecclesial movements. To do so, the competent ecclesiastical authority that oversees public associations (canons 312.1, 315) would need to establish a relationship with the ecclesial movements which fall under its purview that acknowledges the autonomy of their charisms and recognizes the aspects of the movements which their charisms require (i.e., their own structure, mission, apostolic mission and formation). Hegge maintains that ministry (i.e., the ecclesiastical authority) and charism (i.e., the movements themselves) have distinct origins and their own essential qualities (although the hierarchical ministry does exist in its own right, independent of the movements, and does not depend on them for its existence). The section of Canon Law that governs public associations does not reflect this relationship. As public associations, movements operate on the basis of a concession bestowed on them by competent ecclesiastical authority. And yet the teaching within ecclesial movements is based also on the authority of the charism that lies at the origin of that movement.

While suggesting that the canon law covering public associations might be revised along these lines, Hegge proposes another route — establishing a new juridical form for ecclesial movements that is different from public and private associations and traditional forms of institutes of consecrated life. He bases his suggestion on John Paul II's apostolic exhortation, *Vita Consecrata* (1996) n. 62, which indicates criteria for future juridical forms for new movements and foundations. *Vita Consecrata* points to the need for a discernment of charisms. Hegge also refers to Beyer's proposal that canon 605 offers the basis for juridical sanction of ecclesial movements directly through the Holy See (see canons 331; 333.1–2 and 337.1), as is done for the institutes of consecrated life (canons 579, 589, 593) as "new forms of consecrated life," because "the new realities must be approved as new and their statutes must be elaborated in faithful recognition of their charism that is a gift of the Holy Spirit."[24] Hegge believes canon 605 suggests the possibility of such new structures:

---

24. J. Beyer, "I movimenti ecclesiali," 146. See also "Il nuovo diritto dei religiosi e la vita associativa della Chiesa," in *Vita Consacrata* 24 (1988): 344–358; 827–839.

The approval of new forms of consecrated life is reserved to the Apostolic See. Diocesan bishops, however, are to endeavor to discern new gifts of consecrated life which the Holy Spirit entrusts to the Church. They are also to assist promoters to express their purposes in the best possible way, and to protect these purposes with suitable statutes, especially by the application of the general norms contained in this part of the Code.

This canon highlights how the newness of the Spirit and the new forms of life that come to life through the Spirit's action provide the basis for a corresponding canonical structure that safeguards the original charism and helps it develop fully. An autonomous and unitary juridical form for "ecclesial movements" could be developed.

Some movements have ended up with a juridical structure that splits them into different sectors. These correspond to the routes by which various Vatican dicasteries approved them under different names, some as religious institutes or societies of apostolic common life, others as associations of faithful or secular institutes of consecrated life. Hegge maintains that it would be better to approve them in one juridical form with a common structure for the whole movement and under the direction of a president, guaranteeing the unity of the whole community by nominating or electing representatives. There could be two degrees of leadership: general leadership for the whole movement, and specific responsibilities for each category of persons and sector. Such an approach might allow for incardination of priests within a particular branch of the movement under the direction of a priest, without having to set up a separate fraternity or association within the movement. Hegge suggests that the Holy See could establish a commission or council for movements that, in consultation with other dicasteries, would have the competency to examine, approve, and recommend new movements and communities.

18

Conclusion: Learning a Spirituality of Communion Together

This book has examined the phenomenon of ecclesial movements against the background of the Second Vatican Council, which prepared the Church for a new "launch into the deep" in terms of its own renewal and outreach. That "launch" involves a new leap in faith.[1] More precisely, not just a new leap *in* faith, but a new leap *of* faith, that is, a new leap into the new things that God is doing in the world and the new ways he is setting before the Church in a new moment of history. In many ways the Church is being invited to focus on solidarity, purification, and dialogue because it needs to be seen for what it is — the event of communion, mutual love, and unity that has opened up in Jesus Christ, offering life, healing and meaning.

The Church's credibility and its own contemporary evangelization depend on the readiness among all who are part of the Body of Christ to let this event happen. Jesus himself had said as much: "By this everyone will know that you are my disciples, if you have love for one another" (Jn 13:35) and "that they may all be one ... so that the world may believe" (Jn 17:21). Bonaventure, the great medieval Franciscan theologian, underlined this in his eloquent summary definition: the Church is mutual love.[2] More recently, quoting Augustine, Benedict XVI reminded the faithful that God shows himself to the world as love: "If you see charity, you see the Trinity."[3]

Putting mutual love at the core of communion in all levels of Church life requires a change in mindset. Benedict XVI has described this as the co-responsibility of all members of the Church.[4] Certainly, ordained ministers are entrusted with the authoritative proclamation and celebration of the sacraments, but giving life to the Church as an

---

1. See John Paul II, *Novo millennio ineunte*, 38.
2. St. Bonaventure, *Esamerone* I, 4. According to Klaus Hemmerle, it is "the most daring definition of the Church" that he has heard. See *Partire dall'unità, La Trinità come stile di vita e forma di pensiero* (Rome: Città Nuova, 1998), 45.
3. Benedict XVI, Encyclical Letter on Christian Love, *Deus caritas est*, 19. See also *De Trinitate*, VIII, 8, 12: CCL 50, 287.
4. Benedict XVI to the Convention of the Diocese of Rome on the Theme: "Church Membership and Pastoral Co-Responsibility," May 26, 2009.

event of communion and of unity, and making it recognized as such in contemporary history is a particular task for its lay members.[5]

Yves Congar, the renowned French theologian and significant contributor to the Second Vatican Council, noted that people must rediscover the Church "from below, through little Church cells wherein the mystery is lived directly and with great simplicity ... patterned by give-and-take and a pooling of resources."[6] Movements have been the creative minorities that have enabled many to rediscover the gospel and the Church. Involvement in movements has helped them be evangelized together with others. They have experienced the Church's missionary mandate to show Christ present in the midst of two or more gathered in his name (see Mt 18:20).

The Church as a whole can be considered a movement — the People of God on the move. Together, all the baptized — lay faithful and bishops, religious and priests, deacons and lay ministers, young and old, in movements or not — all are called to be the Church in movement. Since the Council, the Spirit has called attention in many ways to this missionary togetherness. Everyone in the Church has the same general task, which John Paul II stated clearly: "To make the Church *the home and the school of communion.*" In *Novo millennio ineunte*, his apostolic letter that caught people by surprise when he issued it at the conclusion of the 2000 Jubilee Year, he called such communion the "great challenge facing the Church."

Needing to Promote a Spirituality of Communion

The life of communion can never be presumed. Although it is communicated by the sacraments, it needs to be worked at and extended day by day and at every level of the Church's life — in relations among bishops, priests, and deacons; between priests and laity; between clergy and religious; between associations and ecclesial movements. The life of communion demands a change of mindset, but that alone is not enough. It demands conversion through a *spirituality* of communion.

The theme of spirituality is attracting increasing interest. Every person has his or her own spiritual journey, colored by the bits and pieces of life. Thomas O'Meara describes spirituality in this sense:

---

5. See *Lumen gentium*, 12, 32–33; *Presbyterorum ordinis*, 9.
6. Congar, *Lay People in the Church*, 339–340.

A spirituality is a way of life and a way of seeing life; a spirituality is doctrine in praxis. A spirituality is a tradition and a school, a cluster of beliefs about God and self. Where does a spirituality come from? A person living in a cultural era selects and emphasizes out of his or her faith ways of encountering the realm of the holy and of the revealed. That arrangement of gospel truths into a pattern is stimulated by a particular person and time. Life's and love's preferences lead one to select, to arrange, to emphasize a coherent gathering of teachings and images. That cluster, very much one's own, is a spirituality.[7]

A personal spirituality, however, needs to grow and mature through living the spirituality of communion that flows from baptismal identity. It is tempting to construe building up the Church primarily in terms of each person's individual personal spirituality, or in terms of a desire for progress that consists in taking action or setting up programs. Instead, however, the spirituality of communion can be the guiding principle to be shared wherever priests, lay ministers, pastoral workers, families, movements, and communities relate to one another.

Unpacking the concept of a spirituality of communion, the Irish theologian, Thomas Norris, quoting the Spanish Carmelite Jesus Castellano, proposes that it means moving from an individual-centered spirituality to one of communion:

> In the history of Christian spirituality, it was said: "Christ is in me, he lives in me," and that is the perspective of individual spirituality, life in Christ. When it also was said: "Christ is present in my brothers," this develops the perspective of works of charity, but it falls short of saying that "if Christ is in me and Christ is in you, then Christ in me loves Christ in you and vice versa."[8]

It is not only that I do good works for my neighbor in a one-way street of Christian love, but rather that my neighbor is constitutive of my journey to God in the mutuality of our relationship. He or she

---

7. Thomas O'Meara, *Theology of Ministry* (New York: Paulist Press, 1999), 232.

8. Thomas J. Norris, *The Trinity: Life of God, Hope for Humanity* (New York: New City Press, 2009), 13. See also, Gerard Rossé, *A Community of Believers: A New Look at Christian Life in the Writings of Saint John* (New York: New City Press, 2009).

gives me the opportunity to create a living cell of the mystical body of Christ, and so experience the presence of the Risen Christ who wants to journey among us through our mutual love (see Jn 13:17).

Karl Rahner foresaw the need for a conscious turn towards living a communitarian spirituality: "I suspect that the element of a fraternal, spiritual fellowship, of a communally lived spirituality, can play a greater part and will be slowly but courageously acquired and developed."[9] For Rahner, continuing in an individual I-God shaped spirituality dressed up in community guise is insufficient. Recalling the first Pentecost, he notes that it was "a communal experience of the Spirit, clearly conceived, desired and experienced in a general way," not "an accidental local gathering of a number of individual mystics, but an experience of the Spirit on the part of a community as such."[10]

A spirituality of communion is much more than good pastoral or spiritual practice. It is more than supporting one another as side by side we move along through life. A spirituality of communion contributes to a more active sense that the Spirit of the Risen Christ is working among the faithful. The theologian Valentino Maraldi explains:

> The Holy Spirit is given and "gives himself," as the effective power of renewal and unity: where the Spirit is present, there communion arises, there humanity is gathered in the unity of the Father, Son and Holy Spirit, and there the Church is present: *ubi Spiritus Dei, illic Ecclesia.* On the other hand, he is present in the Church as fruit. Where the ecclesial praxis is operated *en agape*, there he becomes (in some sense) something that previously was not there: the source of ecclesial communion in the midst of the community, the space of the shared and hence unifying action.... Where believers live in communion, there he becomes shared Spirit, there he is transmitted by ecclesial *communio* itself: *ubi Ecclesia, ibi est Spiritus Dei.*[11]

---

9. Karl Rahner, "Spirituality of the Future," in *The Practice of Faith* (London: SCM, 1985), 18–26.

10. Ibid.

11. See V. Maraldi, *Lo Spirito e la Sposa: Il ruolo ecclesiale dello Spirito Santo dal Vaticano I alla* Lumen gentium *del Vaticano II* (Casale Monferrato: Piemme, 1992), 342. Quoted in P. Coda, "The Ecclesial Movements," 82.

Describing Dimensions of the Communitarian Spirituality

John Paul II's description of communion in terms of love among brothers and sisters elaborates the key features of the communitarian spirituality from which all vocations in the Church spring.[12]

First, it involves "the heart's contemplation of the mystery of the Trinity dwelling in us, and whose light we must also be able to see shining on the face of the brothers and sisters around us." This means entering into a reciprocal pact or covenant whereby each person shares that one glance of the heart on the mystery of the Trinity that dwells within and in which, through grace, is already in some way shared in mutual relations with one another: "No one has greater love than this, to lay down one's life for one's friends" (Jn 15:13).

A spirituality of communion also means "an ability to think of our brothers and sisters in faith within the profound unity of the Mystical Body, and therefore as 'those who are a part of me.'" Here the pope underlines a new "thinking" and "feeling" in terms of sharing with others "their joys and sufferings ... their desires and ... their needs." This means offering deep and genuine friendship.

Based on the theological dimension of charity, a spirituality of communion implies also "the ability to see what is positive in others, to welcome it and prize it as a gift from God: not only as a gift for the brother or sister who has received it directly, but also as a 'gift for me.'"

Finally, the pope points to another "asceticism" connected with communion that people need if they are to be regenerated through renewed relationships in every expression of life and activity of the Church. They must know how to "make room" for their brothers and sisters, bearing each other's burdens (Gal 6:2) and resisting the unavoidable selfish temptations that provoke competition, careerism, distrust, and jealousy.

The spirituality of communion would be a utopia were it not based on what John Paul II calls the "mystery within the mystery" — Jesus Crucified and Forsaken.[13] Building up communion comes by emulating in every relationship the "emptying" shown in Christ's paschal mystery. Paul explained to the Philippians how to pattern their relationships on the "mind" of Jesus Christ:

---

12. *Novo millennio ineunte*, 43.
13. See *Novo millennio ineunte*, n. 22. See also Hubertus Blaumeiser and Helmut Sievers (eds.), *Chiesa-Comunione* (Rome: Città Nuova, 2002).

Be of the same mind, having the same love, being in full accord and of one mind.... Let each of you look not to your own
interests, but to the interests of others. Let the same mind be in
you that was in Christ Jesus, who, though he was in the form
of God, did not regard equality with God as something to be
exploited, but emptied himself, taking the form of a slave, being born in human likeness. And being found in human form,
he humbled himself and became obedient to the point of death
— even death on a cross. (Phil 2:5–8)

Movements, Missionary Communion, and Holiness

Having described the spirituality of communion, John Paul II con-
firms its importance when he comments: "Let us have no illusions:
unless we follow this spiritual path, external structures of communion
will serve very little purpose. They would become mechanisms without a soul, 'masks' of communion rather than its means of expression
and growth."[14] True Christian communion must never be confused for
its counterfeits.

Genuine communion is also missionary. The preparatory document
(*Instrumentum laboris*) for the 2001 ...Synod of Bishops states that
"communion and mission enrich each other. The force of communion
makes the Church grow in extension and depth. At the same time,
mission makes communion grow, extending it outwards in concentric
circles, until it reaches everyone. Indeed, the Church spreads into
various cultures and introduces them to the Kingdom, so that what
comes from God can return to him. For this reason, it has been said:
'Communion leads to mission, and mission itself to communion.' "[15]

Ecclesial movements are shaped by communion and mission,
each in its own way and both together. They are called to bring their
contribution to the wider life of the Church precisely in terms of
communion and mission. But in underlining these key elements,
the movements also highlight the call to holiness. Movements are

---

14. Ibid.
15. *Instrumentum laboris* of the 2001 Synod of Bishops, *The Bishop: Servant of the Gospel
of Jesus Christ for the Hope of the World*, n. 62, http://www.vatican.va/roman_curia/
synod/documents/rc_synod_doc_20010601_instrumentum-laboris_en.html (accessed
January 6, 2011).

"a form of charism lived communally,"[16] providing an environment where holiness as the perfection of love can be nurtured in communion with others and in view of mission. Through living missionary communion, movements — while they themselves are always called to renewal — can be places of formation in the collective holiness for which the People of God strives.

"Prophecies will cease ... The greatest of these is love" (1 Cor 13)

It has been suggested that charisms that give rise to movements are like "incarnations" of particular aspects of Jesus' life, teaching and identity. The Franciscan movement proclaims poverty (Mt 5:3), the Dominicans embody the aspect of Light and Truth, various missionary movements carry out the command to go make disciples of all nations (Mt 28:19), those following the way of Therese of Lisieux exemplify spiritual childhood (Mt 18:3). Chiara Lubich has spoken of the Church as "Christ unfolding through the centuries" with the history of charisms and spiritual movements viewed as a progressive flowering of all the words of God that have been spoken in the Word made flesh, Jesus Christ.[17]

Though there is a great variety among movements, they can lead members to holiness because in different ways each movement emphasizes the fundamental vocation of the Church, the "super-vocation," and that is, to love: "poverty, obedience, chastity, works of mercy of all kinds, preaching, studies or any other activity ... while directed to the good, find their full fruitfulness only in love.... Spiritual movements were founded by their fathers and mothers with this meaning.[18]

It is fitting, therefore, to conclude this study of movements with the testimony of a young person, Chiara Luce Badano, a member of one of the new movements. She died of cancer on October 7, 1990, and was beatified on September 25, 2010. At age 9, when she came into contact with the movement, she was struck by the life she found there. She discovered a new way of living and

---

16. See E. Corecco, 'Profili istituzionali dei Movimenti nella Chiesa," in M. Camisasca and M. Vitali, *I Movimenti nella Chiesa*, 220.

17. See further, Fabio Ciardi, *Carismi: Vangelo che si fa storia* (Rome: Città Nuova, 2011).

18. See "Lo Spirito Santo e i carismi," in Nuova Umanità VI, n. 32 (1984): 3–6, at 6. See also Marc Oullet, *La sfida dell'unità. I carismi e la Trinità* (Rome: Città Nuova, 2011).

thinking that satisfied her thirst for God. After attending a meeting for young people she wrote, "I have discovered the Gospel in a new light. I realized that I haven't been a true Christian because I haven't been living it fully. Now I want to make this magnificent book the only aim in my life."

Through her involvement in the community life of the movement her sense of the Church as well as her joyful outreach to young people and other neighbors around her grew. Sharing a spiritual journey with others forged in her a love of God and neighbor. Being a member of a movement brought her to discover the gospel, to encounter Jesus Christ Crucified and Risen, to missionary zeal and personal formation. Moreover, it brought her the happiness for which every person longs. It helped her reach a point that at the end of her life she was able to bid her mother farewell with these words: "Bye, Mom. Be happy, because I am."[19]

---

19. See Pope Benedict XVI's reference to Chiara Luce Badano in his address to young people and families of Sicily, Palermo, October 3, 2010.

Bibliography

Bouyer, Louis. "Some Charismatic Movements in the History of the Church." In *The Pentecostal Movement in the Catholic Church*, edited by Edward D. O'Connor, 113–131. Notre Dame, IN: Ave Maria Press, 1971.

Coda, Piero. "I movimenti ecclesiali: Una lettura ecclesiologica." *Lateranum* 57 (1991): 55–70.

Ciardi, Fabio, *Carismi: Vangelo che si fa storia.* Rome: Città Nuova, 2011.

―――. "Movimenti ecclesiali e nuove comunità nella missione della Chiesa: collocazione teologica, prospettive pastorali e missionarie." *Nuova Umanità* 31 (2009): 213–228.

―――. "The Ecclesial Movements, Gift of the Spirit." In Pontifical Council for the Laity, *Movements in the Church*, 77–104. Vatican City: Libreria Editrice Vaticana, 1999.

Congar, Yves. *Lay People in the Church: A Study for a Theology of Laity*. Trans. Donald Attwater. London: Bloomsbury, 1957.

Cordes, Paul. *Charisms and New Evangelization*. Maynooth: St. Paul Publications, 1992.

Correco, Eugenio. "Institution and Charism with Reference to Associative Structures." In Graziano Borgonovo and Arturo Cattaneo, *Canon Law and Communio: Writings on the Constitutional Law of the Church*, 316–140. Vatican City: Libreria Editrice Vaticana, 1999.

Cunningham, Lawrence. "New Ecclesial Movements." *Commonweal* 133 (Nov. 3, 2006): 19–29.

Dulles, Avery. *A Church to Believe In: Discipleship and the Dynamics of Freedom*. New York: Crossroad, 1985.

Faggioli, Massimo. *Breve Storia dei Movimenti Cattolici*. Rome: Carrocci, 2008.

Favale, Agostino. *Segni di Vitalità nella Chiesa: Movimenti e Nuove Comunità*. Rome: LAS, 2009.

Fernández, Fidel Gonzáles. "Charisms and Movements in the History of the Church." In Pontifical Council for the Laity, *The Ecclesial Movements in the Pastoral Concern of the Bishops*, 71–103. Vatican City: Libreria Editrice Vaticana, 2000.

Gerosa, Libero. "Secular Institutes, Lay Associations, and Ecclesial Movements in the Theology of Hans Urs von Balthasar." *Communio* 17 (1990): 343–361.

Ghirlanda, Gianfranco. "Charism and Juridical Status of the Ecclesial Movements." In Pontifical Council for the Laity, *Movements in the Church*, 131–148. Vatican City: Libreria Editrice Vaticana, 1999.

Giuseppe Rambaldi. "Carismi e laicato nella Chiesa. Teologia dei carismi, comunione e corresponsabilità dei laici nella Chiesa." *Gregorianum* 68 (1987): 57–101.

Gragnani, Vincent. "The Surprising Growth of Contemporary Lay Movements." *America* 195 (August 14–21, 2006): 17–20.

Hanna Tony. "New Church Movements: Friends or Foes?" *The Furrow* 56 (2005): 83–93.

_____. *New Ecclesial Movements*. New York: Alba House, 2006.

Hayes, Michael A., ed. *New Religious Movements in the Catholic Church*. New York and London: Burns & Oates, 2005.

Healey, Joseph G. and Jeanne Hinton, eds. *Small Christian Communities Today: Capturing the New Moment*. Maryknoll, NY: Orbis, 2006.

Hegge, Christoph. *Rezeption und Charisma: Der theologische und rechtliche Beitrag Kirchlicher Bewegungen zur Rezeption des Zweiten Vatikanischen Konzils*. Würzburg: Echter, 1999.

Hocken, Peter. *Church Forward: Reflections on the Renewal of the Church*. Stoke on Trent: Alive, 2007.

Jenkins, Philip. *The Next Christendom: The Coming of Global Christianity*. New York: Oxford, 2002.

John Paul II, Cardinal Walter Kasper, et al. *Searching for Christian Unity*. New York: New City Press, 2007.

John Paul II. "The Participation of Priests in Ecclesial Movements." *Origins* 31 (2001): 187–188.

_____. *Novo Millennio Ineunte*: Apostolic Letter at the Beginning of the New Millennium. January 6, 2001.

_____. Homily at the First International Meeting of the Movements, September 27, 1981. *Insegnamenti di Giovanni Paolo II* 4, 2 (1981): 305.

_____. Homily on the Occasion of the Meeting with the Ecclesial Movements and the New Communities, May 30, 1998. In Pontifical Council for the Laity, *Movements in the Church*, 219–224. Vatican City: Libreria Editrice Vaticana, 1999.

_____. Message to the World Congress of the Ecclesial Movements, Rome, May 27–29, 1998. In Pontifical Council for the Laity, *Movements in the Church*, 15–19. Vatican City: Libreria Editrice Vaticana, 1999.

_____. *Christifideles Laici:* Post-Synodal Apostolic Exhortation on the Vocation and Mission of the Lay Faithful, December 30, 1988.

Kasper, Walter. *Sacrament of Unity: The Eucharist and the Church*. New York: Crossroad, 2004.

Ker, Ian. "New Movements and Communities." *Louvain Studies* 27 (2002): 69–95.

_____. "The Priesthood and the New Ecclesial Movements." *Louvain Studies* 30 (2005): 124–136.

_____. "The Radicalism of the Papacy: John Paul II and the New Ecclesial Movements." In William Oddie, ed. *John Paul the Great: Makers of the Post-Conciliar Church*, 49–68. London: CTS, 2003.

Küng, Hans. "The Charismatic Structure of the Church." *Concilium* 4 (1965): 23–33

LaReau, Renée M. "Super Catholics? Sizing up the New Lay Movements." *U.S. Catholic*, February, 2006: 12–17.

Leahy, Brendan. " 'Hiding behind the works': The Holy Spirit in the Trinitarian Rhythm of Human Fulfilment in the Theology of Irenaeus." In Vincent Twomey and Janet E. Rutherford, *The Holy Spirit in the Fathers of the Church: The Proceedings of the Seventh International Patristic Conference, Maynooth, 2008*, 11–31. Dublin: Four Courts Press, 2010.

_____. " 'Christ Existing as Community': Dietrich Bonhoeffer's Notion of Church." *Irish Theological Quarterly* 73 (2008): 32–59.

_____. "Charism and Institution." *The Furrow* 50 (1999): 278–285.

_____. "New Paths for Dialogue: Chiara Lubich's Ecumenical Legacy." *One in Christ* 42 (2008): 246–269.

_____. "People, Synod and Upper Rome: Vatican II's Ecclesiology of Communion." In *Vatican II: Facing the 21st Century: Historical and Theological Perspectives*, edited by Dermot A. Lane and Brendan Leahy, 49–80. Dublin: Veritas, 2006.

_____. "St. Paul and the Spirituality of Communion." *The Pastoral Review* 5 (2009/4):16–21.

_____. "The Triune God's Reply to Europe's Contemporary Cry." In *According to Your Word*, edited by Liam Bergin, 47–60. Dublin: Four Courts Press, 2007.

_____. *The Marian Profile in the Ecclesiology of Hans Urs von Balthasar.* New York: New City Press, 2000.

Legion of Mary. *The New Evangelisation: Priests and Laity — The Great Challenge of the New Millennium.* Dublin: Legion of Mary, 2008.

Leonard, Ellen. "Ecclesial Religious Communities Old and New." *The Way Supplement* 201 (2001): 119–128.

Lubich, Chiara. *Essential Writings: Spirituality, Dialogue, Culture.* New York and London: New City Press, 2007.

MacEoin, Gary. "Lay Movements in the United States before Vatican II." *America* 1165 (August 3–10, 1991): 61–65.

Melloni Albert, ed. " 'Movimenti' in the Church." *Concilium* 2003/3.

Norris, Thomas. *The Trinity: Life of God, Hope for Humanity.* New York: New City Press, 2009.

O'Byrne, Maire, *Model of Incarnate Love: Mary Desolate in the Experience and Thought of Chiara Lubich.* New York: New City Press, 2011.

O'Donnell, Christopher. "Movements, Ecclesial." In *Ecclesia: A Theological Encyclopedia of the Church*, 313–315. Collegeville, MN: Liturgical Press, 1996.

_____. "Charism." In *Ecclesia: A Theological Encyclopedia of the Church*, 87–91. Collegeville, MN: Liturgical Press, 1996.

Oullet, Marc, *La sfida dell'unità. I carismi e la Trinità* (Rome: Città Nuova, 2011).

Pontifical Council for the Laity. *International Associations of the Faithful: Directory.* Vatican City: Libreria Editrice Vaticana, 2006.

_____. *La Parrocchia Ritrovata: Percorsi di Rinnovamento.* Vatican City: Libreria Editrice Vaticana, 2007.

_____. *Movements in the Church.* Vatican City: Libreria Editrice Vaticana, 1999.

_____. *The Beauty of Being a Christian: Movements in the Church.* Vatican City: Libreria Editrice Vaticana, 2007.

_____. *The Ecclesial Movements in the Pastoral Concern of the Bishops.* Vatican City: Libreria Editrice Vaticana, 2000.

Porteous, Julian. *A New Wine and Fresh Skins.* Ballan, VIC: Modotti Press, 2010.

Pottmeyer, Hermann J. "A New Phase in the Reception of Vatican II: Twenty Years of Interpretation of the Council." In *The Reception of Vatican II,* edited by Giuseppe Alberigo, Jean-Pierre Jossua and Joseph A. Komonchak; translated by Matthew J. O'Connell, 27–43. Washington, DC: The Catholic University of America Press, 1987.

Rahner, Karl. *The Dynamic Element in the Church.* Freiburg: Herder; London: Burns & Oates, 1964.

_____. *The Shape of the Church to Come.* New York: Seabury, 1974.

_____. "Spirituality of the Future." In *The Practice of Faith,* 18–26. London: SCM, 1985.

Ratzinger Joseph. "The Ecclesial Movements: A Theological Reflection on Their Place in the Church." In Pontifical Council for the Laity, *Movements in the Church,* 23–51. Vatican City: Libreria Editrice Vaticana, 1999. This article was also reproduced as "The Theological Locus of Ecclesial Movements," in *Communio* 25 (Fall 1998): 480–504.

_____. *New Outpourings of the Spirit: Movements in the Church.* San Francisco: Ignatius Press, 2007.

Rausch, Thomas P. "New Ecclesial Movements: The Twelfth Cardinal Bernardin Conference." *Chicago Studies* 47 (2008): 358–365.

Sartori, Luigi. "Carismi." In *Nuovo Dizionario di Teologia,* edited by Giuseppe Barbaglio and Severino Dianich, 79–98. Milan: Paoline, 1988.

Schindler, David. "Institution and Charism," In Pontifical Council for the Laity, *Movements in the Church,* 53–76. Vatican City: Libreria Editrice Vaticana, 1999.

Schönborn, Christoph. "Are there Sects in the Catholic Church?" *L'Osservatore Romano* (English Edition), 13/20 (August 1997): 3.

Scola Cardinal Angelo. "Ecclesial Movements and New Communities in the Mission of the Church. Priorities and Perspectives." In Pontifical Council for the Laity, *The Beauty of Being a Christian: Movements in the Church,* 59–83. Vatican City: Libreria Editrice Vaticana, 2007.

Secondin, Bruno. *Segni di profezia nella Chiesa. Comunità gruppi movimenti.* Milan: Paoline, 1987.

_____. *I nuovi protagonisti. Movimenti, associazioni, gruppi nella Chiesa.* Cinisello Balsamo: San Paolo, 1991.

Sgariglia, Alba. "At the Origin of Everything, the Discovery that 'God is Love.'" In Pontifical Council for the Laity, *The Beauty of Being a Christian: Movements in the Church,* 91–98. Vatican City: Libreria Editrice Vaticana, 2007.

Sicari, Antonio Maria. "Ecclesial Movements: A New Framework for Ancient Charisms." *Communio* 29 (2002): 286–308.

Sullivan, Francis A. *Charisms and Charismatic Renewal.* Dublin: Gill and Macmillan, 1982.

Vanhoye, Albert. "The Biblical Question of 'Charisms' after Vatican II." In René Latourelle, *Vatican II: Assessment and Perspectives: Twenty-Five Years After* (1962–1987), Vol. 1, 439–488. Mahwah, NJ: Paulist Press, 1988.

Vanier, Jean. "Know Them by Their Fruits." *The Tablet* (March 15, 1997): 346–347.

Von Balthasar, Hans Urs. "Lay Movements in the Church." In Hans Urs von Balthasar, *The Laity and the Life of the Counsels: The Church's Mission in the World,* 252–282. San Francisco: Ignatius Press, 2003.

Watson, Timothy. "Life Precedes Law: The Story So Far of the Chemin Neuf Community." *One in Christ* 43 (2009): 27–51.

Index of Names

Acknowledgments

I would like to acknowledge with gratitude the great work of all at New City Press, in particular Gary Brandl for his constant encouragement along the way, Tom Masters for his very careful editing work and Julie James for her diligence in marketing. There are many others, family and friends, colleagues, students of St. Patrick's College, Maynooth, as well as members of movements who have influenced my thinking behind this work. In particular, members of the Focolare Movement. I am indebted to them all. While all errors are mine, I am grateful to those who read initial drafts and provided valuable comments, especially Maire O'Byrne, David Hickey and Michael Mullaney.